THE
WOMAN'S
RETREAT BOOK

The Pregnant Woman's Comfort Book
The Couple's Comfort Book
The Woman's Comfort Book
Comfort Secrets for Busy Women

THE WOMAN'S RETREAT BOOK

A Guide to Restoring, Rediscovering,
and Reawakening Your True Self—in a
Moment, an Hour, a Day, or a Weekend

JENNIFER LOUDEN

HarperSanFrancisco
A Division of HarperCollinsPublishers

To Michele, my sister

HarperCollins books may be purchased for educational, business, or sales promotional use. For information please write: Special Markets Department, HarperCollins Publishers, Inc., 10 East 53rd Street, New York, NY 10022.

HarperCollins Web site: http://www.harpercollins.com

HarperCollins®, ▦ ®, and HarperSanFrancisco™ are trademarks of HarperCollins Publishers, Inc.

Library of Congress Cataloging-in-Publication Data
Louden, Jennifer.
The woman's retreat book : a guide to restoring, rediscovering, and reawakening your true self—in a moment, an hour, a day, or a weekend / Jennifer Louden. — 1st ed.
ISBN 0–06–077673–0
1. Women—Psychology.   2. Self-help techniques.   3. Self-care, Health.   4. Retreats.   I. Title.
HQ1206.L69 1997
646.7'0082—dc21   97–4954

05 06 07 08 09 RRD(H) 10 9 8 7 6 5 4 3 2 1

Contents

Foreword

Retreats. The word has an almost mystical power for me, a feeling of coming home to my deepest truth. Rabbi David Cooper in *Silence, Simplicity and Solitude* writes "All of us have a deep reservoir of mystical experience that sustains the part of what some call the soul. The soul yearns to be nourished, and if the reservoir begins to run low, we feel ourselves becoming dull, empty, brittle, and arid. If it sinks lower, we enter into states of angst, despair, and depression."

In a word, retreats are essential—to our minds, bodies, spirits. Yet retreats don't have to be long or in exotic locales to be effective. Yes, it is often highly valuable to get out of your home, your routine, away from your responsibilities but sometimes, the insights and renewal come from retreating in the midst of your life, just as it is, right this moment. Pixie Campbell discovered just that: "I needed a getaway vacation and wasn't able to arrange one because of running my small business. So early in this first year of running my company, I committed to taking a series of ten minute retreats during the span of each day. I told myself, "Look, ten minutes of forgetting everything will not take anything away from my productivity." So upon finishing a press release, I sat cross-legged on the wood floor in the sunshine, with paperwork all around me, and I closed my eyes and envisioned myself in a sweat lodge. I stayed like this until the timer went off, then got up, stretched a little, and went back to work. This became my new habit, and I felt renewed and energized each time. The best thing about it was being able to completely let go, knowing that in one-sixth of an hour I would be back to work as usual, not missing a beat. It transformed me from worker bee to queen bee. Ten minutes of grateful, mindful, soul nourishing can feel like a much needed vacation!"

It is not that I discourage you from taking longer retreats. There are times when a pilgrimage is exactly what we need – along with the courage to upset the status quo, to risk the comfort of the known (and the good job) to walk to the edge of what's next. Nicky who journeyed from New Zealand with her two sisters to retreat at the Omega Center with myself and twenty-five other women, had this to say, "Because of that retreat, my life totally turned around. Giving myself permission to do something so huge, well I had to ask, what *else* could I do? I left my job to start work on a masters in business administration and became involved in setting up a conference on Spirit at Work in New Zealand. I'm living the life I want now, a rich and juicy life that I deserve!"

Sarah Flick's career burnout as a doctor working in the public health field lead to her retreat. "I was struggling with working in the public health system that was suffering funding reductions. I felt I was living in a culture that was less and less committed to human service and more and more concerned with wealth and power and tax shelters. I wanted to flee and yet, because of family commitments, I needed to stay. I felt trapped. I was exhausted. As I pulled into the retreat center parking lot, I kept seeing the faces of my husband and my child and my ever-growing "to-do" list. I walked into the woods with my journal and this book. I stayed there all afternoon, reading and writing. Over the next two days, I returned again and again to this spot in an oak grove. I felt my body stretch and relax. Insights treaded softly in, insights like the only way to find peace within the forest of the past and the future is to be present right now. On retreat, I found a way to reframe my commitments. I made a covenant with myself and God to spend the summer in interior trust and waiting. Over the summer I was offered an opportunity for a new job. I was tempted but I needed the flexibility of my current job. Because of my retreat, I was able to hold the tension of this choice. Out of my decision to stay in my current position (for now) came a new level of commitment to my current work and the energy to develop the material for a class, which is now evolving into a much bigger project. I hope I'll remember to retreat again and again."

A former coaching client of mine, Shelley, created a six-month retreat for herself near a beach in Florida. "I was outsourced from my job, a job I wanted to leave anyway. I used my retreat to guide me to the next phase of my life. Those six months fundamentally shifted how I am in the world. I made time for the deep rest I so badly needed, and allowed myself to live by my instincts. From drawing labyrinths to writing my fears, anxieties, worries in the sand and watching the waves wash them away, I found myself."

Barb wrote me about the retreats she takes each year with her "two kindred spirit soul sisters." Their first retreat took place in an unheated cabin with no electricity or running water in the middle of winter. "With our 'feast' spread out and an incredible view of the valley sparkling in the moonlight we started stating our dreams, shy and reluctant to give voice to what we most wanted. It was quite an enlightening experience to hear each other, to say them out loud. We left that retreat with faint hopes that we might be able to create some real change in our lives." Fast forward a year. "This time, we stayed at a B & B. A bit more comfort, more permission to spend money on ourselves. We weren't so shy anymore. We spent hours sitting on the cobblestone courtyard between the main house and the summer kitchen, nestled in among the tall pines, discussing our authentic selves. It was quite enlightening, how we saw ourselves and how we saw each other. The owner of the B&B was working in her office and, unbeknownst to us, could hear us. She came out briefly to tell us that she was wishing she could be one of us. After this retreat, we were more sure than ever about what we wanted for our lives.

"On our third retreat, in a cabin with warmth, real beds and a real bathroom, we found we were well on our way to following our dreams and celebrating our successes. Your books followed us again, instructing us, guiding us, and supporting us in our endeavors. The power of retreats!"

If I could give you anything, I would give you the courage to listen to the whisper, the roar, the ache, that brought you to this book. If I could send you anything, I would send you the courage to venture into your inner world, to venture into the mystery of retreat. Be still and listen. Can you hear your story of retreat? Can you hear it calling to you? It knows exactly what you need. You need only listen.

Jennifer Louden
November 2003
Bainbridge Island, Washington

Acknowledgments

Once again the good people at Harper worked patiently with me to produce a well-designed and carefully edited book. Thanks to my editor Lisa Bach, whose careful eye and support were of great help to me. Copyeditor Priscilla Stuckey has been an intellectual wonder on each of my books. Production editor Mimi Kusch, Author Relations Manager Judy Beck, Marketing Manager Margery Buchanan, and all the rest of you fine people, you are consummate professionals. May corporate America stop yanking your lives around and start giving us all a break.

This book would not exist without the wisdom of a number of amazing women. Christina Baldwin, Marion Woodman, and Marcie Telander's interviews were priceless in their illumination of the subject. The wisdom of Deena Metzger, Clarissa Pinkola Estés, and May Sarton forms the foundation. Thank you.

To the many people I interviewed, who read my material and went on retreats, and who allowed me to experiment with them, "thank you" is but a pale approximation of what I feel. The gifts of your time and insight will illuminate many women's retreats. To Cynthia Anderson, Audrey Berman, Anna Bunting, Saral Burdette, Sara Moore Campbell, Jeanie Class, Lola Clark, Barbra Clifton, Rhonda Foreman Cook, Kristina Coggins, Nancy Brady Cunningham, Sandy Danaher, Mary Davies, Maggie Davis, Candace DePuy, Lucinda Eileen, Mary

De Falla, Susan Fisher, Jennifer Freed, Cynthia Gale, Dawn George, Don George, Kay Hagan, Jodie Ireland, Donna Karpeles, David Knudsen, Dennie LaTourelle, Diana Lieffring, McKenna Linden, Lola Rae Long, Paula Markam, Kim McMillian, Belleruth Naperstek, Rob Pasick, Carol Quest, Randi Ragan, Virginia Beane Rutter, Kim Schiffer, Diane Siegal, Barbara Shaw, Anne Simpkins, Barbara Walker, and Jack Zimmerman, my gratitude is immense. Thanks to the people who are not named because of their desire for anonymity and for those who allowed me to compose composite examples. I sure hope I haven't forgotten anyone.

My women's groups let me road-test some material and brought me back from the pit of despair too many times to count. You are unwavering heart sisters. I love you all.

To Michele, Beth, Mom and Dad, and to Anna and Ray, Julie and Diana, you continue to believe in me and be proud of me. You make me feel ten feet tall.

Anna, without your house to retreat to and your bookshelf to pillage, this book would lack heart. You are my definition of a true friend.

Barbara Moulton, you have listened to me kvetch for seven years now. You manage to remain calm and loving through all my ritually repeated doubts and triumphs. May we work together, and be friends, for many projects to come. And may I learn to trust this process somewhere along the way.

Chris, without your support in raising Lillian and your stalwart belief in my ability, I would never sit down at my desk. Your love is like a giant pair of arms encircling and supporting this book. I know this is a cliché, but I could not do this without you.

Introduction

If we don't get there, the mind will take us there anyway. We must retreat to survive.

Marcie Telandar, therapist,
writer, and ritualist

My interest in solitude and retreat has been one of the main threads running through my life. It was the way I used to hide from being connected to others. It became the way I located my authentic self and, in doing that, true connection to others.

Thinking, writing, and teaching about women's and couples' self-care has consisted of years of diving deeper and deeper into the subject and into my own psyche, each time surfacing with another fragment of understanding. After years of doing this, I had to ask myself, "Why am I so obsessed with this subject?" The answer was that as much as I immersed myself in trying to understand and explain the importance of self-care, it remained a mystery. I could never lay my hands on exactly why self-care was so important.

Until I took a retreat.

And met my authentic self. Only then was I able to grasp that self-care helps me to make daily choices that affirm me, thus allowing me to contact, hear, and eventually live from my truest self, what Alice Walker calls "the natural self." I am more and more able to choose a self-referenced life: looking inside of myself to see what I think, feel, and need, then looking outside of myself to see what others think, feel, and need, and then bringing the two together. This may seem like common sense, but for millions of women, including myself, it is nothing short of a revolutionary act.

I have always been in love with solitude. Some of my favorite childhood memories are of riding my bike in the winter wind alone, playing on a huge sand pile in our backyard alone, exploring empty lots alone. I lived alone for seven of the ten years between my parents' house and the house I now share with my family. When I was twenty-seven, I read everything that poet and lover of solitude May Sarton wrote. I seriously considered emulating her life-style. I filled files with information about writers' colonies, wilderness trips, vision quests, and yoga retreats. And yet, as wonderful as solitude was, for me it was primarily an escape. Anthony Storr in *Solitude: A Return to Self* described me when he wrote, "Other individuals find it difficult to be authentically themselves even in the presence of their spouses, lovers, or closest friends and relatives. Such individuals, whilst not going so far as to construct a false self which entirely replaces the true self at a conscious level, have an especial need to be alone which goes beyond the occasional demand for solitude. . . ." I was running *away* from intimacy with others rather than *toward* knowing my authentic self, both alone and in the presence of others.

It will come as no surprise, then, that writing this book on retreats was very difficult for me. After months of painful stumbling in the dark, unable to find the focus of the book, my psyche guided me by giving me one clue: *a woman's retreat springs from and is guided by her inner knowing*. Well, to be guided by your inner knowing, you have to stop moving, stop doing, and sit still, listen to, and trust yourself. Unfortunately, I found this to be a difficult process. Unable to make the leap of faith that what I was feeling was okay simply because I was feeling it, I found it difficult to hear or believe my inner wisdom. But, thankfully, from my research the remedy emerged: do it anyway and use a map.

"Do it anyway" is best summed up by my friend, the writer and feminist theorist Kay Hagan, in her brilliant book *Fugitive Information*:

> A counselor specializing in mid-life transitions for women startled me a few years ago when she confided that she had stopped telling her clients to love themselves. "That was absolutely the wrong advice," she told me. When I recovered from my surprise enough to ask what she was suggesting to women instead, she said, "I tell them to act like they love themselves. I realized if a women waits until she actually loves herself to act that way, it may never happen."

I leaped into retreating by pretending to trust myself, praying that with time, by emulating self-trust, I would someday soon truly believe it.

What also made the leap possible was expanding my definition of what constitutes a retreat. When I believed I needed to travel to distant realms (for me that always meant the wilderness) and be gone for at least a week (preferably longer) to locate my true self, I didn't have a chance. With a career and a young child, long trips simply weren't possible anymore. So I got straitjacketed into tight shoulder muscles, confused thinking, and my own litany of when-thens ("When Lily is older, then I will retreat. When there is more money, then I will. . . ."). I spiraled farther away from my natural self till it felt like every word out of my mouth was a whine. But in reading about women on retreat, in talking to women who retreat and women who do not, I discovered what makes a retreat a restorative healing encounter. *It is not where you go or for how long you go. You don't have to go anywhere.* It is all in your intention and commitment.

In finding and evoking the archetypal pattern of retreat, I could take a Saturday morning and render it regenerative by connecting with my authenticity. I could disengage from my externally referenced mind ("What should I be doing? What are others thinking of me?") and from my web of connections and commitment to others, and I could sit down for a cup of tea with this extraordinarily interesting, quirky woman who had always been inside me, biding her time. I would be, at turns, gleeful, philosophical, enraged ("Why had this break with her happened?"), and sad ("Why had it taken me so long to claim her?"). Slowly I would gain more peace and perspective. Images of whole loaves of fresh bread, mountain hikes, and the smell of clean sweat kept coming to me in this place of grace. Living the archetype allowed me to step out of ordinary time, off the gerbil wheel of endless responsibilities, away from the shoulds and have-tos I burden myself with and into what T. S. Eliot called "the moment in and out of time."

Once again, my psyche drew me to write about what I most needed to learn. Through practicing tiny daily retreats centered around listening, through mini-retreats of a weekend morning and a few weekends, my consciousness has shifted. I am more and more able to live Alice Walker's words:

> People have to realize they are really just fine, they are really just fine
> the way they are. The beauty and the joy is to be more that, to be more
> of that self. It is unique, it is you, it is a fine expression for this moment,
> for this time.

And through this, I'm moving into more authentic relationships with those I love. The myth is, when you focus on yourself you are being selfish. The reality is, if you don't know your true self and cultivate an ongoing relationship with her, you can't truly be with or give to anyone else.

A retreat, like each act of self-nurturing, is a radical leap into self-love. You retreat because you are yearning for something. That something may be ineffable, impossible to name, a whisper tickling your imagination. It might be a desire to know your true self, to be at peace, to find an answer, to bask in self-kindness. It might feel like a desire to touch something you can't quite name, a yearning to be held by something larger than yourself. No matter how half formed any reason for retreating can seem, each has a spiritual core.

How do I define *spiritual? To become spiritual is to choose to do only those things that contribute meaning and healing to one's life.*

I have no record of who uttered this wisdom, but to me it perfectly defines a spirituality that is life affirming and self-loving. How can you know what will contribute meaning and healing to your life? Through retreat, you contact and embrace what is most you. This is the prerequisite to embracing both what is within you and what is infinitely vaster and unknowable. I hope you will come to agree with one of the women I interviewed, Cynthia Gale, a ceremonial artist and retreat leader living in Cleveland. "I can't imagine life without retreat. These chances to reconnect when we've disconnected not only get us back on track and functioning, but ideally move us to higher places."

I hope the stories and practices you find here will enable you to make that leap into having faith in yourself and, by doing so, to reconnect with your authentic self and to connect authentically with those you love and with the Divine as you know it. Living with self-trust and self-love is a lifelong process. Just as in any relationship, there are times when we realize with a sickening pang that we haven't sat down and truly looked at our beloved for a very long time. And, thank God, there are those heady times when we fall in love all over again. Retreating, along with other tools of self-care like women's groups, therapy, meditation, and writing, brings on those heady days of love for ourselves and enables each of us to take another step along the spiral to wholeness. It is my prayer that with this book in hand you will regain what is most valuable to you, the treasure of your own wisdom and beauty, as part of your ongoing quest to know and honor your beloved self.

Namasté.

How to Use This Book

Like all my books, this is a reference book, a thesaurus of sacred solitude. It can be used to retreat in any amount of time, for any reason, and, hopefully, for many retreats. Most important,

There is no one way.

The instructions and practices offered here are *completely malleable.* Alter them, rewrite them, scramble them, use a bit of one practice mixed up with a fragment of another: write your own retreat book. Skip around; you *don't* need to read the whole book before you retreat, nor do you need to read the chapters in order. Read and do only what interests or compels *you.* If you love herstory, read A Woman's Retreat. If you want to jump right in, read A Retreat Outline. If you are struggling with the desire to retreat but are not able to make the time, read The Call to Retreat and Courage. If you are someone who hates instructions, skip to the section called Practices. When on retreat, if you start to feel lost, bored, or anxious, look at Uncomfortable Beginnings, Middles, and In-Betweens or jump into a practice that interests you. *Make the book your own.* Reinvent the retreat.

Overview

The book is divided into six parts. Naming, Shaping, and Saying Yes is the *planning* section. It outlines what a retreat is. In studying women's herstory and talking to various wise women and men, I found the archetype of retreat, the basic map, the container into which you pour the elements of retreat and cook them into your own unique gumbo. Here is where you choose what season or style of retreat you wish to do: a long retreat (two days or longer), a mini-retreat (one day or less), shared retreats (using a small group or a friend to support and frame your solitude), or a retreat in the world (retreats that take place partially or completely in public places).

Beginnings details how to create an opening ceremony. This section also gives basic retreat practices, the bread and butter of listening to yourself.

Practices offers exercises to help you address specific issues. These practices are called *practices* for a reason: they are never finished, nor is there a "right" way to do them. They gain meaning through repetition.

- You can follow a practice as written.

- You can use it as a jumping-off point and move into creating your own.

- You might mix two practices together.

- You might take one practice, say, the beginning of Contemplations, and blend it with an exercise from another book, tape, or video you've wanted to study.

- You will undoubtedly integrate your own spiritual practices and physical play into your mix.

Tips on what practices work well together can be found in Retreat Plans, and in the Intention Chart in the middle of the book. Each practice also includes instructions at the end of each chapter for expanding it on a long retreat, for condensing into a mini-retreat, for exploring it on a retreat in the world, and for adjusting it for a shared retreat.

A few practices require a degree of preparation. Before you retreat (especially if you are planning a long retreat or are traveling to your retreat location), read Prepare under the practices you might do. If something feels like too much bother, shorten or skip your preparation time. The basic supplies to have on hand are listed under A Retreat Outline. Experiment. Take one retreat in which you do little or no preparation. Then create one in which you slowly, deliciously, explore each preparation step, intuition in hand. What is the difference for you? Whatever you do, please, don't use getting ready as an excuse not to retreat.

Ending is about bringing your retreat home. This is the most neglected area of retreating and one I hope you won't skip over. It is crucial to give time and energy to ending your retreat experience, even if it has been very brief and seemingly uneventful. You also need to bear in mind your reentry into ordinary life. *Read Returning Home before or on your retreat.*

Retreating with Others is about retreating with a friend or small group *as a support and frame for your solitary retreat.* When I created this section, I imagined you would be doing the bulk of your retreat alone and then joining others for ceremony, reflection, discussion, and support. That said, you could adapt these practices for any kind of retreat you like or for a retreat with a lover.

Retreat Plans includes eleven retreat blueprints. These blueprints outline a few ways you could combine practices, play time, and your own spiritual discipline. If you are feeling overwhelmed about doing a retreat on your own, you could choose the plan that most closely fits with your intention and use that to help you get started. Included in this section are several ultrashort retreats especially designed for busy women.

The suggestions offered here reflect my research, the areas I and others have been led to address through retreat. These suggestions do not exhaust the possibilities for retreat, which are endless. To provide you with other ideas, I put together Resources, a compilation of books, tapes, videos, and other sources.

The Intention Chart can be used as an index to find a particular section within a chapter, if you are having trouble forming an intention, or when looking for practices that fit your intention.

What will hopefully emerge from these offerings is your own patchwork quilt of retreating, your own singular style of sacred time, sitting and talking with your authenticity. I hope you will spiral through this work again and again, fashioning and living new perspectives each time.

Naming, Shaping, and Saying Yes

A Woman's Retreat

For each of us as women, there is a deep place within, where hidden and growing our true spirit rises. . . . Within these deep places, each one holds an incredible reserve of creativity and power, of unexamined and un-recorded emotion and feeling. The woman's place of power within each of us is neither white nor surface; it is dark, it is ancient, and it is deep.

Audre Lorde

The woman who is virgin, one-in-herself, does what she does—not be-cause of any desire to please, not to be liked, or to be approved, even by herself . . . but because what she does is true.

Esther Harding, *Woman's Mysteries*

When I started my research, I thought I knew what a retreat was. But as I con-ducted interviews and read books, my idea kept broadening and shifting. The continuum of retreat experiences was so wide, the content and mode of re-treats were amazingly varied, and the history of women on retreat stretched to the beginnings of human culture. I was enthralled by images of women at the ancient descent of the Thesmophoria in Greece. I found myself exhila-rated by stories of women on arduous wilderness retreats. Rereading *Journal of a Solitude* by May Sarton made me want to go live alone, preferably in Maine. Stories about the medieval mystic Julian of Norwich's life as an an-choress made my small office, where I retreat daily, seem spacious, especially because the door opened. Pondering the literary and artistic accomplish-ments of George Sand, Emily Dickinson, Georgia O'Keeffe, Louisa May Alcott, Willa Cather, and others amazed me. These were accomplishments made pos-sible only because, going directly against the grain of society, these women lived in retreat. Talking to Buddhist women about three-month silent retreats conjured awe and terror in my heart. Recalling the "No Boys Allowed" club-house and indoor tents scrabbled together from dining room chairs and quilts brought back childhood memories of retreat.

The idea of retreat kept expanding. Is solitude important? Is solitude alone a retreat? Do you have to be silent? Do you have to meditate? Must you be serious? Do you have to be in pain or in crisis? Must you leave your home? Do you need to fast? Is only a whole day or week or month a real retreat? Do three hours count? Three minutes? I became more and more confused, uncertain how to help women create a retreat experience for themselves. What makes a retreat a retreat? I searched for the common threads among women's experiences, both historical and literary, as well as ones I gathered through interviews.

Then it struck me. My title. *The Woman's Retreat Book*. Why a *woman's* retreat? What distinguishes a woman's retreat? Why had I been drawn to write only to women?

After writing and reading and agitating for six months, one afternoon it came together. *A woman's retreat springs from and is guided by a woman's inner knowing.* A woman's retreat is about stepping out of your ordinary existence to *listen* and *attune* to your truest, most authentic self. It is about being self-referenced to become self-restored. It is about trusting what you experience as sacred without the need for external sanction. It is setting apart time to tend the hearth of your inner life, feed your muse, reclaim your dreams. A place to reaffirm your values by giving yourself permission to do what you need when you need it, not when you think you should or when someone else thinks you should. About using *loving* self-discipline to push past limiting beliefs, to instigate change, to bring closure.

Cycles

Each of us has a personal periodic, an internal tide, an instinctual cyclical rhythm that alternates between an accomplishing, energetic, doing time in which you engage with the world, dig ditches, get degrees, bake your ideas, and sell them and a retreating, reflective, being time in which you detach from the world, stare out the window at the rain, plant fat spring bulbs, and breast-feed your imagination. When we do not value or attend to the retreating cycle as much as we do the accomplishing cycle, we betray our basic rhythm and risk becoming walking zombies, with no life to speak of. We have not allowed time to replenish our inner world. As May Sarton wrote in *Journal of a Solitude,* to do without solitude "is even worse":

> I lose my center. I feel dispersed, scattered, in pieces. I must have time alone in which to mull over any encounter, and to extract its juices, its essence, to understand what has really happened to me as a consequence of it.

Right now, too few of us are tending to our cycle of being, of going within. We are suffering from *hambre del alma,* a starving soul. By not recognizing and feeding our longing for retreat, by not declaring "I need to do nothing" or "I need to knit or clean my closet or simply be alone," we diminish ourselves. By believing that if we take time for ourselves, our kids will starve, the cat will die, or our company will go bankrupt, we starve our lives into efficient skeletons. One question almost always presents the biggest obstacle: Do I believe I am worthy of a retreat? Is all this fuss necessary? Can't I just take a pill?

You, me, each of us must value the retreating, going-within cycle as much as the accomplishing, out-in-the-world cycle. Can you believe that being alone for a day is as important as going to work? Do you dare believe that making retreat a regular part of your life is as important as making a million dollars?

To come to this new belief we must learn the value in retreating. We must discover firsthand how solitude can allow us to locate our juice, our authenticity. Marion Woodman noted in her interview in *The Feminine Face of God,*

> One of the problems women have today is that they are not willing to find the river in their own life and surrender to its current. They are not willing to spend time discovering themselves, because they feel they are being selfish. They grow up trying to please other people and they rarely ask themselves, who am I? Rarely. And then life starts to feel meaningless because they live in terms of pleasing, rather than in terms of being who they are.

Since I was little, I have imagined canoeing down the underground river, the aquifer that runs under northern Florida. Finding the river of your life is as mysterious and mythical as imagining. To locate our personal rivers we must be willing, as Kim Chernin writes in her book *Reinventing Eve,* to "peel back layer after layer of pretense, compliance, and accommodation so that I could stand naked before myself as a woman."

Finding your river is a subtle and maddening undertaking, like trying to shape iron with tweezers. It is also terrifying work, for it requires surrender. Not only do you have to dig underground to find the water (which many of us believe does not exist), but you also have to jump into that murky water and swim! My friend Jeanie asked, "Why are you calling it a retreat? What are you running away from?" Finding your own underground river means running away from the external, "the torrent of daily have-tos," as my sister-in-law Diana names it. It is a running toward yourself, toward a place (it can be both internal and external) of seclusion, privacy, and contemplation.

We can see this in Kim Chernin's account of her own initiatory retreat in *Reinventing Eve*. She was bored and restless, depressed and despondent, and she had driven up into the mountains above Dublin, stopping at an old estate she had never visited before.

> An old man came out of the gatehouse; he was surprised to see me, touched his finger to his cap, showed me the bell on the gate. A scrappy dog growled and came toward me, tugging at his rope. I had several cookies in my pocket. I threw one to him. . . . The gate swung back a few feet; I walked through and turned to wave at the old man, who locked it behind me. . . . From the moment the old man disappeared into the gatehouse again I felt a panic of loneliness. . . . I wanted to run back to the car and head out for Dublin. . . .

She went forward with her walk and experienced a transcendent time out of time in which she grasped that nature, "which I'd always imaged as a brute force, had some kind of vivid life to it." She had to face a question: was it possible that her rational worldview, "everything I had been told about the universe was simply an assumption, a style of perception, rather than truth?"

> It was too late to flee from the place. I, the rationalist, was in the grip of extreme emotion. I could fight it off, run away, or surrender and find out what it meant. I found myself before an immense tree. Near the bottom it had been split almost in two by lightning and in the charred, concave base, a brilliant green-and-yellow lichen was growing. I stared at the tree, a natural altar. I tried to distract myself with this thought and meanwhile my body was doing something peculiar. I noticed it, thought I should fight it, was doing it anyway. Then it was done. There I was, on the ground in front of the tree. Tears streaming down my face. I, raised in a family of Marxist atheists, down on my knees, worshipping?

Chernin's story is echoed again and again in women's stories of retreat. Separated from what is normal, we are brought to our knees before all that is holy and meaningful.

We may retreat for many reasons throughout our lives, to reflect on our lives, to celebrate our wisdom, to mourn, to create, to recuperate, but the underlying one is to recontact our purpose in life. Life becomes dull and meaningless not because of what we are doing but because we don't know why we are doing it, because it has no resonance with our inner world. "I believe what a women resents is not so much giving herself in pieces as giving herself purposelessly. What we fear is not so much that our energy may be leaking away through small outlets as that it may be going 'down the drain,'" wrote Anne Morrow Lindbergh in 1955 in *Gift from the Sea*. "Every person, especially every woman, should be alone sometime during the year, some part of each week, and each day. How revolutionary that sounds. . . ."

A retreat is the restorative by which you walk away from being a woman who exists only in relationship to others and walk toward a self that relishes and enjoys her relationships because she has a strong center from which to relate. Creating your own retreat allows you to encounter your deepest needs, feelings, and impulses *away from the voices and needs of others*.

But here we get trapped in the feminine crucible. Here is the place where the social messages about what makes a good woman, the economic realities, the inner beliefs of worth, and the family responsibilities meet the call to retreat with a heart-wrenching, forward-momentum-stopping crash. A retreat simply feels impossible to do. For some of us, even an hour alone in the bathtub feels like a hopeless desire. It can take massive amounts of courage to believe that you must have time to muse, to fling open your dusty hope chest crammed with notions, recollections, fancies. To picture your future. To pore over and release the past. To retreat. "Women are, by nature, disposed to relationship and connectedness; yet true relationship cannot be embraced until a woman has a deep sense of her at-one-ment. Without this essential independence from all roles and bonds, she is a potential victim for servitude," Marion Woodman cautions in her book *Dancing in the Flames*, co-written with Elinor Dickson. To be connected with and to nurture others is a precious, delightful, integral part of our lives. We are constantly giving in a personal and emotional way. We want to do so, some of us *must* do so, but we also must take time to be in solitude, to find and tend our selves, or we risk becoming ensnared in a tyranny of relationships, unable to locate our authentic core. When this happens, we risk losing not only the meaning in our lives but our very selves, the deep-rooted, innermost knowledge of who we are and why we are here.

It often takes massive amounts of courage to take that first step.

I cannot give you that courage, although as I write this I imagine incandescent energy and fortitude shooting directly into your heart. I imagine performing a Vulcan mind meld to convince you in the most visceral way of how important it is to take this time, not once in your life, not once a year, but as often as your life cycle demands. I have lived in my own deserted spirit and have seen the devastation that comes from staying too long in the accomplishment/pleasing others/hoping-to-be-good-enough mode. *Cantadora* Clarissa Pinkola Estés, in *Women Who Run with the Wolves*, describes it this way:

See Courage.

There is a quality of mourning to it all. There is angst. There is a feeling of loss, of being bereft. There is wistfulness. There is a longing. There is plucking at threads in one's skirt and staring long from windows. And it is not a temporary discomfort. It stays, and grows more and more intense with time.

You can put on your coat, pick up your purse, and say as you shut the door, "You'll be fine without me." Go. Claim your right. Forget waiting for permission. Carve out the time. Notice I do not say *find* the time. That is an absurd and dangerous phrase. Time is never lying around waiting for us to find her. She is elusive. She wants you to sculpt her like clay, to mold her into exactly the form you desire your days to take. If you refuse to do that, if you spend your mornings worrying and your afternoons catering to others, always hoping there will be a few minutes left for you, time will play you like a sucker, making you run harder and faster with each passing week. Time wants you to realize that she is the most precious and irreducible fact of your life. Make her into what you will.

A New Path

Creating a self-led retreat can be frightening. There is no prescribed path to follow. I give a bare beginning here with suggestions and ideas, but you must make your own way *because that is what is required to meet your authenticity*. Am I suggesting we discard all the other retreat traditions, from Zen Buddhist to Benedictine—ancient traditions based on obedience and discipline? No, what I am proposing is that we need our own path, our own way to slow down, go within, and listen, a way *that is germane to our lives and is created through our women's understanding*. When I learned that *obey* and *listen* are etymologically related, I realized that what I am proposing isn't so radical, even from a traditional view. I am asking you to obey: to listen to and obey your own heart.

What Do You Need a Book For?

If a woman's retreat springs from and is guided by *your* inner knowing, why do you need this book?

I remember being on my first self-led retreat and not getting anything out of it because I didn't know what to do with my time. I took myself away to my friend Mary's bed-and-breakfast in Inverness, California. I brought with me a vague desire, several excellent books to work with, and my journal, and I was in one of my favorite places. My experience had moments of beauty and relaxation, highlighted by watching seals in a cove and having dinner with Mary. Repeating to myself "I am on retreat" was comforting and made the time feel somewhat shining and extraordinary, but it wasn't enough. I didn't know how to move deeper. I kept asking myself, "What do I do next?" I was plagued by guilt, boredom, and confusion. My time apart lacked the intensity and purity that I had experienced before in organized group retreats. I was disappointed and not renewed.

I didn't retreat on my own again for years. It felt kind of pointless.

Sometimes it is enough simply to go away by yourself and listen. But often you need some guidelines, an outline to refer to, a framework to build within, an alchemical vessel into which to pour your self for generous simmering. The longer we have been out of contact with our truest selves—the busier we have been, the more wrapped up in other people's lives—the harder it is to slow down and be with ourselves. The purpose of this book is to provide one way to begin doing just that.

The Archetypal Pattern

Retreats have been with us since the very beginning of humanity. From menstruating women living apart in huts to the biblical Ruth and Judith to anchoresses walled into a room to Emily Dickinson to Georgia O'Keeffe to Annie Dillard, there is a history, albeit slim and barely recorded (when compared to the sagas of men on retreat), of women alone, women turning within.

The first retreat took place when menstruating women separated from the rest of the tribe. The reason menstruating women first separated was probably for survival, hiding in trees and caves from animals who smelled their blood. Why, after this was no longer necessary, did the cross-cultural practice of ritual menstrual seclusion persist? The reason was certainly not to give women time alone. Nonetheless, over hundreds of thousands of years, alongside our emerging consciousness, grew the idea of women alone, women outside of ordinary space and time: the retreat archetype.

We can readily detect this elementary pattern's three parts: ritual separation, liminal space (on the threshold, a timeless, in-between place), and return.

First there is ritual separation. One of the meanings of the Sanskrit word *r'tu,* which translates as "ritual," is menstruation. Menstruation gave us ritual. Through ritual, menstruating women were taken out of ordinary tribal life. The ritual signified that *an essential shift in consciousness was occurring,* which is the purpose of retreat. Ritual enabled women to separate their minds from their everyday responsibilities. Ritual separation caused women to step out of profane space and time and into a secret, set-apart world: betwixt and between, liminal space, time out of time.

Menstrual seclusion often wasn't comfortable; some tribes bound girls in a hammock and hung them above the ground for days or even weeks; others covered women in dirt up to their necks. Yet the often extreme conditions—the most universal taboos being that women could not see the light or touch water or themselves—forced women to focus inward, giving us the second part of the pattern, a way to listen to the innermost self. Notes therapist Marcie Telander,

> That's the way to focus attention for the human animal. Sensory deprivation (which can also mean sensory overload) tricks the outer attention into focusing. Everyday attention can't focus us in the same way. Placing your attention on a stone, mandala, stream, candle, baby's face, flower, cat, helps to exclude the internal voices and pressures and turn you inward to what you are knowing.

Not allowed to participate in ordinary life, women were compelled to enter liminal time, the betwixt-and-between world where time and ordinary life are suspended. They are neither one thing nor another, neither who they were before nor who they will be after they emerge. They focused their attention by memorizing tribal history, by gathering herbal knowledge, by learning to weave baskets, or simply by being still.

The third piece of the pattern is the return to ordinary space and time. When the menstruating woman left the hut, it was with acknowledgment of her changed status, often through "a feast with relatives and friends, who made offerings to ancestors and spirits, as well as a number of rites similar to those for weddings," notes poet and cultural historian Judy Grahn in *Blood, Bread, and Roses.*

Here is the archetype, as old as human consciousness. Here are the elements you can reenact, alone and with others, to enable you to *separate* your minds from others, to sanctify your time for a larger purpose.

Intention and ritual separation thrust you into the betwixt-and-between space. Focusing the senses through various means allows you to maintain that space and hear the still, small voice of your wisdom.

Conscious return to ordinary time integrates what you learned through listening by acknowledging that your consciousness has shifted, enlarged. You have been changed.

Archetypal Herstory

Looking at a few examples from prehistory, we find the archetype being cultivated. The Thesmophoria was a three-day women's festival of rebirth, dating from at least 6000 B.C.E. and maybe much later. In *Uncursing the Dark*, Betty DeShong Meador tells the story of this ritual:

> The ritual of Thesmophoria begins with three days of preparation, during which the women observe rites of purification. . . . The women abstain from sexual intercourse. . . . Thus they begin their withdrawal from men. In their houses, the women sleep alone. . . . They begin to enter wholly into the femaleness of themselves. They eat garlic to repel the men by the unappetizing smell of their breath. . . . At dusk on each of the three preparatory days, the women gather at the chosen fields. . . . There they build the huts in which they will sleep. . . .

On the first day of the ritual, the menstruating women "carry down into a chasm newborn suckling pigs" and sacrifice them to the snake deity by slitting the pigs' bellies. They then carry up rotting pig flesh (no one has adequately explained how the flesh rotted in less than a day). On the second day they mix the rotted pig flesh with seed, make "images from cereal paste and carry them down in baskets into the chasm," fast in silence while sitting on the ground bleeding, and at night have a kind of tribal encounter group in which "what has been tolerated, ignored, hidden is exposed. The shouting exposes secrets, shatters pride, levels the women to a common ground." On the third day, each woman buries the seed-flesh in the newly plowed fields, and together they sing praises to the snake deity before returning home.

While I'm not suggesting you visit a farmer and bring yourself home a little piglet for your next retreat or eat a lot of garlic to discourage your partner ("Just go. I can't stand the smell anymore!"), this ancient ritual does apply to modern life. We cringe at the sacrifice of little piggies. Perhaps the sacrifice symbolically represents what we each must do to carve out time for retreat, how difficult it is for us to extricate ourselves. "She sacrifices the claims of family, children, village. . . . She acts out of a vision beyond the habits of caring, beyond the safe structures of society," as Betty Meador interprets it. The Thesmophoria also illustrates the descent into the parts of ourselves we would rather not see and the descent into mystery, into letting go of control, expectations, and outcome.

> Before a woman of our time can . . . realize her creative powers, she must participate in the downgoing. She must gather herself together. She must remove herself from the ongoing of her daily life. She must descend into the chasm.

Women on retreat, even mini-retreats of a few hours, often experience a feeling of descent. It is an integral part of the process. It forces us to stay fresh and humble, to disassociate with our overachieving, perfectionistic side, and to embrace our limitations. This is often the initiation that we must survive before we can hear and feel authentically. The Thesmophoria shows us that for nine thousand years women momentarily cut away the tethers of connection and descended into their darkness and returned reborn. If they could do it, so can we. And we don't even have to sink our hands into rotted pig flesh.

In countless times and places of prehistory we can picture women retreating. No one knows how the vast underground temples (more than thirty) on the islands of Gozo and Malta in the Mediterranean (ca. 3500–2500 B.C.E.) were used. Perhaps they were used for religious rites, burial, even grain storage— no one knows exactly. Yet from descriptions of the ruins, it is easy to imagine women on retreat within these shrines. The Hypogeum is the most spectacular of the sanctuaries on Malta. Imagine six thousand square meters of interlocking egg-shaped chambers, a main hall with vaulted ceiling and highly polished ochre-stained walls, chapels, burial rooms, and a room with a hole in the wall. When you speak into this hole, your voice echoes throughout the entire Hypogeum. It is speculated that people came to rest and be healed within the Hypogeum and to hear a priestess in the form of Oracle divine for them, perhaps through interpreting their dreams. Scholars believe it is quite possible that priestesses went to Malta to be schooled in the divine arts. Perhaps for thousands of years, female shamans and priestesses secluded themselves in such temples, and before that in the forest and in caves, to be alone and to receive wisdom they could use for others.

Imagine an opening ceremony that includes passing over a huge threshold adorned with a giant spiral into an inner sanctuary lit by oil lamps, where you are greeted by priestesses trained to help you relax and prepare to hear your own wisdom. Feel yourself curling up in one of those egglike chambers, literally held by the earth, your senses restricted to the sound of your own heartbeat. What would it feel like? What might you learn?

The Cost and the Struggle

Moving into recorded history, we could find countless examples of the archetype being evoked. But perhaps the most stunning is the medieval tradition of the anchoress. This piece of history does more than show us an extreme version of retreat. It illustrates the immense struggle we have endured to be alone. The history of women on retreat, women in solitude, is also the history of women struggling for autonomy. You cannot relax and listen to your deepest self, let alone transcend that self as the great contemplatives have counseled, if you don't have a life of your own in the first place. For almost all of recorded history, women have not had the freedom, opportunity, income, time, or energy to learn to read and write, let alone to go off and ruminate in some cave. Being alone, especially living alone, got us ridiculed ("old maid"), exiled from the relatively safe life of our father's house or marriage, thrown in prison, or even killed.

There are glimpses of women on retreat in early patriarchal history. Marion Woodman and Elinor Dickson in *Dancing in the Flames* offer an example from Hellenic times:

> It was not until Hera finally decided that she had had enough of Zeus's promiscuity that things began to change. She left Zeus and returned to her birthplace in Euboea. In aloneness she came to terms with her own essential oneness.

It is also told that Hera bathed ritually in the ocean each year to renew her virginity, her at-one-ment. Ruth in the Bible spends a lot of time reaping in the fields by herself. Judith is the patron of anchoresses because she "virtuously" stays alone in her chambers. But by and large, "the kind of autonomy which we think of as providing the opportunity for sustained solitude, was not available to women. They were ever under the authority of a male," writes Philip Koch in *Solitude*.

Early Christian convents give us a well-documented account of this struggle. In roughly the ninth through the twelfth centuries, women founded a way of life that allowed them time alone and a way to follow their inner wisdom. In an interview, feminist historian Barbara Walker said, "Under a sort of guise of being Christian virgins, women went into the convent and there they could have time to consult their own thoughts. In the beginning, when the convents were not too domineered by the church, a lot of noble women went into convents simply to have some time to themselves." One such movement was the Beguines. The Beguines formed no permanent order, did not enclose themselves, did not follow a leader, and did not renounce their own property (which later became a big sticking point with the church). In some places, the Beguines created whole towns that were entirely run and owned by them, as well as numerous hospitals and homes for the elderly. The Beguine lifestyle offered great freedom, and one of its gifts was time alone. So, inevitably, the Beguines were outlawed. In 1312 the monks of the Inquisition deprived the Beguines of their lands, houses, and freedom because they are "afflicted by a kind of madness, discuss the Holy Trinity and the divine essence, and express opinions on matters of faith and sacraments. . . . Since these women promise *no obedience to anyone* and do not renounce their property or profess an approved Rule . . . their way of life is to be permanently forbidden and altogether excluded from the Church of God," quotes Barbara Walker in *The Woman's Encyclopedia of Myths and Secrets* (italics mine).

Medieval women did not give up. Here is where the anchoresses come in, during the early thirteenth century or slightly before. An anchoress was *voluntarily* enclosed for life within a small cell attached to her local church. The door was bolted or bricked up from the outside after an awesome ceremony of enclosure, which in essence was a funeral. The young woman could not leave her cell during her lifetime without being excommunicated from the church. Carol Flinders in *Enduring Grace* describes Julian of Norwich's cell as "a very sizable room, reasonably comfortable, which opened (via windows) into the church and out into an enclosed parlor where people would consult with her." What led women to such an extreme measure, unthinkable by our standards? "A room of her own, a door she could close. Women have regularly been willing to pay a very high price to have that condition. . . . Maybe it was possible that the whole dramatic ritual that accompanied the closing in of an anchoress was meant to guarantee her safety, to define it as a sacred space that no one else dare enter," proposes Flinders.

An anchoress was safe, revered as a spiritual icon by the rest of the community and consulted by them as a spiritual guide. What about the women burned as witches? The infamous treatise for the detection and punishment of witches, the *Malleus Maleficarum,* says, "When a woman thinks alone, she thinks evil." E. William Monter, who has studied trial records of the period, concludes, "It is almost certain that fewer than half of all women accused of witchcraft were married at the time of their accusation. It is no accident that the typical witch of folklore should be an old woman dwelling by herself off in the woods. . . ." The witch persecutions covered two continents and persisted for more than three hundred years. What lessons regarding the danger of solitude and retreat sank into our Western psyches? How it illustrates the collective fear of women alone!

Of course, women still found solitude. We have the great women mystics, such as Teresa of Ávila, who insisted that every one of her nuns have a door "that no one could open without her permission, a real precedent to Virginia Woolf's a room of one's own," as Carol Flinders sees it. Scholastica was St. Benedict's twin sister, who founded her own convent. Hildegard of Bingen no doubt provided sanctuary for many women and produced numerous master-pieces from her solitude. But perhaps the early part of Catherine of Genoa's life is more representative. Trapped in a loveless marriage and a noble lifestyle she detested, she prayed to become slightly ill for three years. It allowed her three years to undergo a series of visions that radically changed her life and the lives of many, many others.

Illness has often been women's only recourse to retreat. Think of Victorian women on their fainting couches. Anthony Storr in *Solitude: A Return to the Self* notes,

> The Victorian lady used regularly to retire for a "rest" in the afternoon. She needed to do so because convention demanded that she should constantly be empathically alert to the needs of others without regard to the needs of her own. Her afternoon rest allowed her to recuperate from the social role of dutiful listener and ministering angel; a role which allowed no scope for self-expression.

She might use a ritual phrase to retire ("One of my headaches is coming on. Nanny, you take the children"). Then she might close the curtains and fold down the bed just so, perhaps placing a cool cloth over her eyes. Let her mind wander, perhaps do a little writing or needlework. Repin her hair and open the curtain before returning to daily life. Of course, this was a refuge available only to upper-class women. Think of the vast majority of women, denied even this modicum of silence and time for the self.

Even Florence Nightingale developed an illness that liberated her from the endless round of household duties, giving her time to study and write in the solitude of her bedroom. Ceremonial artist and retreat leader Cynthia Gale discovered in her illness a gift.

> At 30, I was dean of admissions at Sarah Lawrence. I was working 100 hours a week and also exhibiting as a fiber artist in New York. At 31, I had MS and was legally blind. What started for me was a long healing process. I had to heal my life on every level. My illness was my great re-treat—not my first retreat but my longest. It afforded me quiet. I spent

hours and hours in bed, not able to read, not able to engage in life in the way many people do.

Her illness was an initiation, offering a radical and unrefusable separation; her pain and blindness placed her in liminal space; her intent to listen and heal created her vehicle for listening. This "retreat" turned her life around. She started shamanic studies, and "the ceremonial art began to pour out."

For centuries women have searched for a physical place to separate, a room of their own. H. G. Wells wrote about his wife Jane's desire in his autobiography. "She explained what she wanted and I fell in with her idea; and in this secret flat, quite away from all the life that centered upon me, she thought and dreamt and wrote and sought continually and fruitlessly for something she felt she had lost of herself or missed or never attained." Doris Lessing's heartbreaking story *To Room Nineteen* depicts an upper-middle-class English woman who yearns and tries so hard to find her own room and thus a place to locate her lost self that when she fails, she kills herself. The church has provided a shadow of this function for millions of impoverished and oppressed women. Clarissa Pinkola Estés relates a story to this effect from her childhood in *Women Who Run with the Wolves:*

> Many devout women rose before five A.M. and in their long dark dresses wended their way through the gray dawn to kneel in the cold nave of the church, their peripheral vision cut off by babushkas pulled far forward. They buried their faces in their red hands and prayed, told God stories, pulled into themselves peace, strength, and insight. From time to time, my Aunt Katerin took me with her. When once I said, "It is so quiet and pretty here," she winked as she shushed me. "Don't tell anyone; it's a very important secret." And so it was, for on the walking path to church at dawn and in the dim interior of the church itself were the only two places of that time where it was forbidden to disturb a woman.

Women did find a way to be alone, and their stories show us the final element needed to retreat: great determination. Emily Dickinson, Alice James, Louisa May Alcott, Aphra Behn, George Sand, Anne Morrow Lindbergh, May Sarton, Alice Koller, Anne Bastille, Annie Dillard, Gretel Ehrlich, and Terry Tempest Williams are examples of creative women who listened, who bent, carved, hacked, changed, and otherwise defied convention to survive.

Georgia O'Keeffe's winter of 1928–29 illustrates this struggle. She had just enjoyed the most successful year for her paintings. She had considerable income of her own now. But she was finding herself increasingly without time to herself. She had become quite well known not only for her paintings but also because of Stieglitz's photos of her, primarily stunning and erotic nudes.

She was reviewed first as a woman painter, then as her persona in Stieglitz's photographs, and only then were her paintings reviewed on their own merit. This greatly disturbed O'Keeffe, and she regularly became ill after her yearly shows. Also pressing on her privacy and time was their hectic society life, the constant strain of being "on," and the busy summers at Lake George with the Stieglitz family and guests. "Stieglitz's mother had died and Georgia, as wife of the eldest son, supervised the summer housekeeping for the large family. This, in addition to her painting, was a tremendous task for one so meticulous," her friend Anita Pollitzer writes in *A Woman on Paper*. O'Keeffe determined to buy a house of her own at Lake George, "so that she could have the quiet she needed." But Stieglitz opposed the idea. It was too foreign to his concept of family and family summers. Georgia became increasingly ill and run-down. Out of three physicians consulted, one suggested she was close to death, but another was insightful enough to prescribe "real rest and time to live at her own pace." Because of this, and the advice of another prominent doctor "to stop expending herself in the busy summers at Lake George," the idea to spend the summer in New Mexico was born. Stieglitz told all who would listen that "the most dire of calamities has befallen them. . . ." Georgia, too, was troubled, but she felt "much was at stake for her." She told Anita, "Going West was the hardest decision I ever had to make." In New Mexico, Georgia and her painting blossomed. Except for 1939, the year she made a trip to Hawaii, she spent every summer, and eventually the rest of her life— long stretches of it alone—in New Mexico in nature.

You may be saying to yourself, "I'm not a brilliant painter. It is not important that I retreat." Because the examples we have of women on retreat and living in extended solitude are almost exclusively from women of great courage, talent, and at times wealth, it is easy to feel you aren't worthy or that a retreat is beyond your means. But in *Gift from the Sea,* Anne Morrow Lindbergh brings the archetype into modern life and the scope of solitude almost down to size.

> Total retirement is not possible. I cannot shed my responsibilities. I cannot permanently inhabit a desert island. . . . I must find a balance somewhere between . . . a swinging pendulum between solitude and communion, between retreat and return.

Three weeks alone in a cottage by the sea. What heaven, we sigh. There are no sacrificed pigs, no praying for illness. She doesn't need a twig hut or a tribe of people to toast her when she emerges. Yet the retreat pattern emerges. She separates from all that is familiar.

> For me, the break is the most difficult. Parting is inevitably painful, even for a short time. It is like an amputation, I feel. A limb is being

torn off, without which I shall be unable to function. And yet, once it is done, I find there is a quality to being alone that is incredibly precious. Life rushes back into the void, richer, more vivid, fuller than before.

She lives in liminal space fashioned from solitude, the sound of the ocean, meditation on shells, and writing. She plans her return, acknowledging how difficult it will be to retain the calm perspective she has gained. She brings home talismans to remind her of what she has learned ("The shells will remind me; they must be my island eyes"), placing them in her sisal bag as part of her closing ceremony.

Enlivening the archetypal pattern in a way that fits your life and makes your time apart—even five minutes sitting in your car—numinous and renewing doesn't involve much more than your willingness to take the first step. As Lindbergh said, "If women were convinced that a day off or an hour of solitude was a reasonable ambition, they would find a way of attaining it." Are you willing to believe this is a reasonable ambition for *you*? Are you willing to dedicate your attention to something out of the ordinary, to step away from the safe definitions of daily life? Are you willing to take the first step?

A Retreat Outline

We withdraw, not only from the concerns of the world and its preoccupations but from the incessant monologue and concerns within ourselves, in order for something else to come into being.

Deena Metzger, *Writing for Your Life*

Here is an outline of what makes a retreat a retreat, the steps you will repeat each time, even on very brief retreat. It is a shorthand way of bringing the archetype to life. Refer to it when planning a retreat or if you are ready to get going right now and want to skip the details.

See A Woman's Retreat.

- Prepare

Set an *intention*. Intention is what distinguishes your time off, makes it more than a vacation. Donna did the exercise in Intention not even knowing that she wanted to retreat and was astonished to learn she hoped to find a new direction for her life. Setting an intention requires setting aside time to prepare (often taking only a few minutes). This preparation sends a signal that you are serious about your time apart, that it is going to be uncommon, mindful, loving, and intentionally focused on you. Preparation also starts the process of slowing down and turning inward that is crucial to retreating. Even daily mini-retreats and retreats in the world benefit from a moment of preparation at the beginning of your time apart. To set your intention, complete the following statement:

On this retreat, I intend to ask myself . . .

See Intention for greater detail.

Keep it simple, open, and loving.

- Withdraw from Ordinary Life Through Ceremony and by Creating a Container

Withdrawal from ordinary life happens through symbolic action and by creating a safe space, either physically and/or emotionally, into which to withdraw. These are the signals to your psyche that you are entering altered time. Cynthia Gale speaks about her retreats this way: "What I try to do is make sure everything I do matters. So when I sit and have a cup of tea, I don't just have a cup of tea, I think about what tea I'm going to have, where I'm going to sit, what direction I'm going to sit in, how that ten minutes is going to be different." This effort at disengaging is especially important because you are not always able to leave, to go someplace, for a retreat, especially when working or when raising young children. You may have only a few minutes or hours to yourself. *Withdrawal isn't about the amount of time away or even your physical proximity to others. It is how much they occupy you when you don't wish them to.*

One of the great benefits of evoking the retreat archetype is the ability to withdraw into your own interior, sacred space. Choose or create such a space, your container. It could be your bed, your garden, a visualization of a place you love in nature, the crook of a tree, taking the phone off the hook and closing your office door, or a prayer of protective light and love surrounding you. Next, perform a symbolic ceremony to separate. This ceremony can be as involved as a sweat lodge or as simple as a purifying soak in the bath, slipping on a special shawl and staring at a candle, or reading a poem you love and then stepping over the threshold of your front door to go for a walk.

See Opening Ceremony and Where Will You Retreat?

- Listen in Sacred Space

Being in sacred, liminal space is perhaps the hardest part of the retreat to maintain in our modern world, especially when you are retreating in the world or for only a short period of time. Yet it is the heart of retreat, the place where the work of transformation takes place. You remain outside your daily life. You don't do the dishes, answer the phone, take care of others, work, watch TV, listen to the news, read magazines, or do other everyday things. You arrange your time differently, doing what enlarges your intention and enables you to listen to your inner knowing. This can be done in a myriad of ways. You might ask yourself thought-provoking questions, write in your journal about how you are feeling or why you are retreating, move to music, meditate on metaphorical words from poetry or the psalms, visualize your Divinity blessing you, paint, walk on the beach, knit, or lie on your couch listening to music. The end result always places you gently in your center, working toward a truer and more authentic relationship with yourself. Si-

See What Will You Do, Courage, Contemplations, Good Ways to Listen, and all the Practices.

lence and solitude have their place here. You can't contact your wisdom and come to accept yourself without spending time alone in silence.

Another way you maintain sacred space is to push yourself out of your habitual comfort zone. By doing so, you shift your view of yourself and your life. For example, leaving your comfort zone might entail hiking alone on a local trail or being alone at your home with no TV and no phone. Shifting out of your comfort zone often creates anxiety and fear. Encountering your fear, not running from it, brings great richness to the retreat practice. That doesn't mean putting yourself in danger, but it does mean leaving deadening comforts behind and being willing to take risks.

- Reemerge into Ordinary Space and Time

Reemerging into the world at a new place is the final act of retreating. It may seem the most straightforward and easy, but it is fraught with the difficulty of leaving sacred space and returning to ordinary space. You must acknowledge what you have done and where you have been and that you have been changed, even when your retreat has lasted for only a few moments. You can simply say, "I am returning from my retreat. I have done this, and this is why _____ (fill in your reasons for going or what you learned)." Give some thought to your reentry so that you don't lose the gifts of your retreat too quickly in the daily array of demands. Bring back a talisman from your retreat—anything from a small rock to a vivid memory. Give thought to how you will communicate your experience to those you love, how you will physically reenter your work or home life, what would make the reentry easier.

See Returning Home, Closing Ceremony, and Living Your Retreat Every Day.

Good Supplies to Have on Hand

Here is a list of universally good retreat items to bring along. *Don't* stress out over this; you can always improvise, do without, or change your mind. *Keep it simple.* Don't let this list overwhelm you—a walk with nothing can be a retreat!

In addition to these, look under Prepare in each practice.

- Your journal and a pen.

- Basic drawing supplies—anything from markers to colored pencils to water-based paints. Whatever you have, want, and can afford.

- Big paper, ideally eleven by fourteen inches and thick. But any paper will do fine.

- Music that relaxes you and encourages your imagination; music that makes you want to move your body; music that puts you in touch with your deepest, wildest feelings, even grief.

See Resources and Grieving for suggestions.

See Resources.

- A way to play the music in your retreat space—a personal stereo or small boom box. Borrow one if you don't have one.

- A book or two of metaphorical, spiritually sustaining, exquisite inspirational writing.

- A camera and film. Take pictures of yourself, of the light pouring through your living room curtains, the trees arching toward the sky, whatever captures how you are feeling in that moment, whether that is particularly wonderful or particularly awful. Create emotional snapshots to paste up in your life after your return.

- Nature, in the form of the wilderness, a park, a houseplant, a backyard, a bowl of rocks.

- A drum or rattle. You can make a rattle by putting small stones or gravel in a tin (tea tins work great). If you have children, borrow their musical toys. Jodie contemplated borrowing her son's Curious George drum. Drumming may seem too New Age, Robert Bly, warm and fuzzy weirdo nonsense. It has been lampooned in more places than I care to think about. Yet it remains an ancient and extraordinarily powerful way to get out of your mind and into your imagination, to get your juice going. There is no right way to drum or rattle—allow yourself to experiment and take your time. It may take you a few minutes to get into a beat.

- Self-nurturing goodies like fresh bread, soothing lotions, delicate flowers, a velvety bathrobe.

- Special clothing. In Ann Linnea's book *Deep Water Passage,* Christina gives Ann a magnificent purple wool sweater to wear on her kayak adventure-retreat. Ann is surprised because she has never worn anything so nice when camping. Christina reminds her, "Annie, you're not just going camping. You must mantle yourself for the journey." How will you mantle yourself for your journey? In what clothes will you feel creative or secure or luxurious or sensual or energetic or courageous? A fringed shawl, silk scarf, floppy hat, well-worn hiking boots?

- A touchstone, talisman, or other meaningful object that, by being held, worn, or seen will comfort and remind you of the love in your life, whether that love be from a lover, a child, or the Divine. Frankie fingered a tiny soapstone bear fetish in her pocket that reminded her of her lover. Sandy anchored her retreat by wearing an exquisite amulet given to her by a dear friend. A tiny wooden Buddha accompanies me. Georgia O'Keeffe carried at least one perfectly round stone.

- Mini-retreats and retreats in the world might benefit from a retreat bag or box that you keep with you or close at hand. In it go the things listed above as well as a bottle of water and whatever else you might need.

What Not to Have on Hand

- Work. No bill paying. No making a few phone calls or checking your e-mail. Not one contract or brief or bit of typing or student papers or mending or child's costume to sew. NO! If you are retreating in the world, get away from your work, even if it means clearing off your desk or leaving your home.

- A phone. If on a long retreat you need to be available because of your children and business, ask whomever might call you to ring once, hang up, and ring again. Otherwise, unplug or hide the phone, even if you are only retreating for a few minutes. No beepers, faxes, or cellular phones, either.

- A watch or clock. You can tell by the sun when you need to return home. If you are living in Alaska in the dead of winter or in a skyscraper where no sun penetrates, or if you have only a few minutes or hours and must break at a very specific time, set an alarm. On a retreat in the world, take off your watch; even if it's only for a few minutes, it helps.

- Newspapers, TV, talk or news radio, gossipy magazines, escapist novels, video games, computers, anything that will break the retreat spell. (You may choose to watch *Oprah* or read a fat Regency romance. Fine, as long as you are *choosing* and not avoiding, staying stuck in comfortable but outmoded patterns. Remember to check, "Does this support my intention?")

See What Will You Do: Check-in and Good Ways to Listen: Shadow Comfort.

- Negative people. Some of you will be using this material with a friend or group, or you may choose to have someone be your check-in person or retreat coordinator. If so, be sure this person is truly supportive. Or are you choosing or going along with a friend because you don't want to hurt her feelings? Don't waste your retreat time around people who drain, depress, or derail you. On the other hand, recognize that in almost any group situation, there will be tension, anger, misunderstandings, people you don't like. If seen correctly, this discomfort can provide invaluable insights.

See Courage: Support on Retreat.

See Retreating with Others.

- Emotional baggage. I'm joking, but only a bit. What if you could leave behind a certain obsession, emotion, or worry? Which one would you choose? Write this baggage on a piece of paper, tie it around a rock, bless it, and leave it behind.

The Call to Retreat

*Close to the bone, there had to be an inner stratum, formed and culti-
vated in solitude, where the essence of what I was, am now, and will be,
perhaps, until the end of my days, hides itself and waits to be found by
my lasting silence.*

Doris Grumbach, *50 Days of Solitude*

What was your first thought when you picked up this book?

I need this!

This sounds great, but I'm too busy.

What is a retreat exactly?

Sounds too extravagant and expensive. I'm too practical.

I've been on retreats before, but I'm looking for something deeper.

I'd consider it, as long as I'm not just sitting around. I need to be accomplishing something.

Sounds scary. I don't know if I could be alone.

Name your reaction(s) right now. This is the beginning, the process of asking
and listening. Write them down or speak them aloud.

The call to retreat is your signal to go. You've been in the doing cycle of your
life long enough (way too long, you may be muttering). It is time to turn
within.

Can you hear the call? It may be very distant and weak at first, but it *is* there.
It may be a small voice begging you to attend to your inner life. It may be im-

ages of nourishing moments in nature. It may be a snatch of a poem or song. Take a moment to sit quietly. Right now. *Make no effort to do anything.* Only breathe slowly and deeply and listen.

• • •

What did you hear? Sometimes you will hear a bellow, a clear "yes" or "no" or "soon." Your voice may be loud, telling you exactly what you should do. "Jump off this gerbil wheel of a life for a moment, for pity's sake. You need a breather! You need fresh air and solitude." Great. Respect what you hear. Too often, we get clear messages from our inner selves about what we need to do, silvery treasure maps with the location of the treasure marked in fire engine red, but we don't act on what we hear. When you hear, *listen.* To retreat doesn't have to mean a week at an ashram; it may mean an afternoon alone. Listen.

Sometimes sitting quietly and listening makes us ache. It feels like returning home, déjà vu, "Oh I remember this! I haven't done this since _____ (you fill in the blank: since I was seven or since I was in college or since the last time I was sick)." You might remember the promises you made to yourself in the past, all your well-intentioned plans to take better care of yourself. You wonder how you got distracted. Again. It feels good but scary to make another promise to honor your needs.

Do you dare risk it again? Yes, you must. For the cycle of being-doing is also the cycle of remembering-forgetting. Like Persephone in the myth of Demeter and Persephone, you blossom, you die, you are reborn again and again. You contact the knowledge of who you are and what you need, and then slowly, bit by bit, you forget, eaten up by life again. Then you descend and reconnect with yourself. You come back from a week's retreat full of love for yourself, your life, and your relationships, and for a few weeks you meditate every morning, you eat well, you take a few hours once a month to be alone, do yoga, and write in your journal. But then you forget, get lost, lose consciousness. That does not make retreating worthless, nor does it mean you have failed. It is an organic spiraling process, and each time you retreat you retain another piece of knowledge, courage, and purpose, slowly honing your life into what you want. It literally takes a lifetime. It is the process of life.

See Living Your Retreat Every Day.

Sometimes when you listen for the call to retreat, it is very hard to sit still. You sense nothing. That is okay. I have been there. Most of us have. It is still possible to discern your invitation. You just may need to listen for other languages, such as the language of perpetual fatigue or recurring minor illnesses. Perhaps the message will come as piles of resentments blocking the doorway to your heart, like so much junk mail, as in, "If I just didn't have so much work to do" or "If my kids were just older, then. . . ." The summons might come in the form of feeling like you are "living just for next month, just till this semester is past, can't wait till winter is finally over . . . waiting for a mystically assigned date somewhere in the future when [you] will be free to do some wondrous thing," as Estés writes in *Women Who Run with the Wolves*. I call this the "when-then whine": "When I'm done with my Ph.D., then I'll take some time off," or "When the kids graduate from high school, then I'll go on a retreat." The call to attend your deepest self speaks in the tongues of yearning—how you drive yearningly by the dance center or obsessively read the adult education class schedule or stare at the patch of woods you can see from your office window. What are you waiting for? Ask yourself. Stop reading, close your eyes, and ask yourself, "What am I waiting for?"

One of the questions or fears that often arises after you hear your call to retreat is, "Won't I want to retreat all the time? Won't I want to quit work, abandon my children, go live in a hut in Tibet?" Another reaction can be, "This feels like another should. I don't need one more should to cause me guilt." Both are valid. It can be comforting to know the different cycles of retreating, cycles that vary from person to person and also through the different stages of life.

Courage and Uncomfortable Beginnings, Middles, and In-Betweens will help an extrovert slip more easily into a solitary retreat.

Extroverts need fewer and shorter retreats and may find being alone, especially in the beginning, the most difficult part of retreating. Extroverts may find themselves getting more and more tired as they move deeper into their retreat, for they are making the switch from projecting their energy out to turning their energy inward. Extroverts may find themselves feeling trapped and anxious. Having support on your retreat, in the form of a friend or group, is another good choice.

See For How Long Will You Retreat?: Seasons of Retreat and Retreating with Others.

Introverts, on the other hand, may find themselves wishing they could retreat half of every month, preferably to someplace remote like the Galapagos Islands. Introverts struggle less with the fear of being alone and more with the need to go often and for longer periods of time. Of course, most women are a blend of introvert and extrovert, and your experience will lie somewhere along this continuum.

Your age also influences how you respond to your call to retreat. In *Jubilee Time*, Maria Harris takes the biblical Sabbath of the Jubilee—a two-year period from the forty-ninth through the fiftieth year known as the "Sabbath of Sabbath"—and uses it as a model for older women. Through it, she says, we can both reclaim the wisdom and dignity of age and fill our ache for stillness and quiet. In her sixtieth year, poet, teacher, and therapist Deena Metzger took four retreats. On the winter solstice, she spent ten days at the Arctic Circle. The spring equinox found her near a cove in Hawaii where dolphins swim. Back to the Arctic for the summer solstice, and she then spent the autumnal equinox on Mount Sinai.

> In each corner of the circle, I'm addressing a question I spent a lot of time formulating: "What is appropriate for me in the next third of my life?" I don't want to try to relive the first or second half of my life, I want to know how I can live my life right in this time.

In *Dancing in the Flames,* Woodman and Dickson note,

> In the first half of life we live mainly in terms of doing. We find out who we are through going to school, pursuing a career, marrying, having children and raising them. In the second half of life, we are pushed toward a deeper consciousness of who we are, an identity in terms of being, an identity based not on the ego but on the soul.

This is not to say that young women can't or don't need to go on retreat. In an interview, Woodman said,

> Most young women go on retreat because they are so driven by their jobs, and so busy, that they yearn for some kind of peace. They may find it harder to be quiet than an older woman. Young women who choose to go on a retreat want being, they want to know their own reality.

In the doing stage of your life, the need to withdraw may feel sporadic, easy to dismiss as not as important as moving up the career ladder or finding the right relationship, and yet your need for sacred time may be the greatest.

Whether young or old, if you have neglected your inner life for too many years, you may find retreating a terrifying prospect. Start small by scheduling mini-retreats, retreating with a friend or a group, and gradually learning to listen to your inner knowing.

See Courage and Retreat Plans.

Intertwined with our personal rhythms are the universal cycles of retreat, rhythms that run through each woman but are mediated by your own personality. The most familiar cycle may be the daily or circadian cycle, a sometimes subtle, sometimes screaming need to be quiet, to be alone, to sift through the emotional impressions of the day, to catch up with yourself. You may be honoring this cycle now by taking a long bath or shower, exercising alone in nature or with headphones on at the gym, napping when your baby does, or reading before bed while not really concentrating on the words. Some of us need (but rarely take) several retreats within a day, especially if we are under a lot of stress or working at a job we dislike.

See For How Long Will You Retreat?: Mini-Retreats.

There is a monthly need for retreat, which in younger women may be linked to menstruation or premenstrual syndrome. This cycle may call for a longer retreat, an afternoon or a day. You might be meeting this need now by escaping to do errands alone or shopping alone (the car is a popular refuge), watching a movie alone in a dark theater, or getting just sick enough to let yourself stay home in bed for a day.

Then there are yearly cycles, a yearning to go within that might recur every winter or at the anniversary of the death of a parent or on your birthday. Perhaps there is a pilgrimage built into your life, like a trip home to see your parents and swim in the quarry of your childhood or a hike to the same peak each year with your best friend from college.

Beyond these are once-in-a-lifetime cycles, which may occur during periods of crisis or transition, like a "big" birthday or the passage from one stage of life to another. At these times you feel a need to look at where you've been and decide where you want to go. Grieving the death of someone you love, the offer of a new job, or a divorce will create a strong need to separate and look within.

When these cycles are noted and treated with respect, without creating another should in your life, when you recognize your call to retreat and answer it in a way that truly nourishes you, you invite balance, contentment, health, and inner simplicity to inhabit you. By consciously setting aside time, forming an intention, and moving through a few simple steps that help you to wholeheartedly declare yes, you drink from your own inner spring of water, the water of life.

Stories

In *The Feminine Face of God* is a story of Patricia's call to retreat. It movingly illustrates the need to listen to your inner voice, even after you have decided you will retreat. Patricia had already planned her retreat for the week before Easter at a retreat center run by a French order of nuns.

> Then a month before I was to go, something unusual started to happen during my regular meditations. Every few days I would hear an inner voice say, "You need to do the spiritual exercises of Saint Ignatius." Not being Catholic, I was not familiar with these exercises. . . . But the message persisted. So the first thing I did when I got to the center was to ask Sister Mary W., who was in charge of my stay, if we could somehow incorporate these exercises into my retreat.

She seemed both pleased and surprised by my request. . . . Then, looking me straight in the eye, she asked if there was a particular problem I wanted to work on. The question caught me off guard. I had certainly not come with any problem in mind. In fact my life had been going along pretty smoothly, I thought. Yet after only a brief hesitation I heard myself say, "Yes, there is. You see, I had an abortion twelve years ago, and I have come here to be healed."

See Contemplations.

Patricia went on to do active imagination with the story of the paralyzed man who was carried by his friends to Jesus to be healed.

As my meditation deepened I actually experienced the sensation of being borne along on a gurney by three very close friends, one on either side of my head and the third at my right foot. Although I knew someone had to be holding up the left end of the gurney, I could not make out who it was. Then raising my head up in order to see better, I made a startling discovery: it was not "someone" who was holding me up but a delicate gold cord which seemed to be attached to something in the sky. As I followed the cord upward I could see that the end of it was being held in the hand of the tiniest yet most perfectly formed infant I had ever seen. And hovering behind this ethereal cherub, protecting and enfolding it in outstretched wings, was an exquisite angel.

Suspended in this timeless moment . . . [I] heard a voice speak these words: "The light of this unborn child is leading you home. This is a deep mystery which you cannot penetrate, but know that you are healed."

Later that afternoon as I waited in the dappled sunlight beneath the leafy branches of a graceful oak for Sister Mary W., the truth of those words vibrated through my entire being. I had found my soul. I was well again, whole again, and through this healing I was awakened to the power of prayer and the meaning of grace.

Intention

Intention is the power of the experience.

Cynthia Gale, ceremonial artist

Why am I going on retreat?

What will I actually do?

How can I possibly take the time and go?

If you answer the first question, you will find it much easier to answer the others.

> Retreat is not about a statement, it's about a question. Most of the work of giving yourself a fruitful retreat is in understanding what your question is. That question is an articulation of an inarticulate longing.

So says Christina Baldwin, author of *Calling the Circle* and teacher of Peer Spirit Circle workshops. "Understand what the longing is." Investigate the yearning.

I knew that intention was crucial to creating the container of retreat, but I envisioned intention as a statement. For instance, you might state your intention as "For the next twenty-four hours I intend to be kind to myself." Through a very helpful conversation with Christina, I learned the more fertile route, better suited to the essence of a woman's retreat: forming your intention by identifying the most passionate, heartrending, or irritating longing in your life and then placing that longing in the context of a question. Now imagine a retreat in which you state your intention as "For the next twenty-four hours I intend to ask myself, How can I be kinder to myself?" Can you feel a difference? The first intention feels positive but closed, almost a should, and it doesn't inspire the imagination nearly as much as the second intention, which feels open-ended, expansive, encouraging, even tantalizing. An intent in the form of a question gives form to your needs and longings, yet remains open to the unknowable, the feelings and experiences that will arise during your retreat. Ultimately, a retreat takes on a life of its own, and its own direction. When you remain flexible, open, and yet focused, that direction will lead you to priceless treasures and marvelous interior visions.

A loving, questioning intention gives your inner knowing something precious to gaze on, the illuminated essence of your retreat. "Why am I on retreat? Oh, yes, because of this yearning, because of this question." Your intention is a still point of purpose to refer back to when you feel lost, unmoored from your ordinary life, or anxious or selfish or guilty. It helps you to concentrate your time in a way that has heart and meaning, which is especially important on mini-retreats. Whether you have five minutes or five days, intention helps you make the most of that time.

Intention can also be a catalyst, prodding you to overcome all the reasons you shouldn't retreat. It can provide a cover, an "excuse" of a purpose when you need to wave something around someone's nosy nose. It eases fear of the void, the fear that arises when you leave behind the rituals and distractions of daily life and face the raw possibility of time with yourself. You can hold on to your intention question as if it's a personal constellation helping you navigate home across a dark ocean.

What an Intention Is Not

An intention is not a goal, although you may present it to others as one. Intention is an aim that guides action. A goal, by contrast, is the purpose or objective toward which an endeavor is directed. Intention is gentle and keeps you in the moment, focused on unfoldment. Goal is driven and keeps you in the future, focused on finishing, on doing it all, doing it right. Forming an intention in the shape of a goal would defeat the purpose because it would take you out of being and into doing. The word *intention* comes from the Latin root *intendere*, meaning "to stretch toward something." Say Woodman and Dickson in *Dancing in the Flames,*

> Intentionality in itself does not lead to an enlightened heart. It is better thought of as a way of giving meaning to experience. It is open to both conscious and unconscious information.

Your intention should not foster lavish expectations or rigid agendas. Both of these can hog-tie your intuition, exhaust your creative juices, and fuel your chattering self. E. A. Miller, in her essay "Equipment and Pretense" in *Solo,* thought that "to prove my solitude, I had to experience a miracle—hear the voice of my mother (dead for five years now) laud me for my independence; wake to write an inspired masterpiece by sunrise; remember, in the light of the campfire, a long-forgotten commitment to dedicate my life to the poor." Bound up in expectations, you will be hounded by a voice asking, "Am I doing it right?" "Is anything happening yet?" "Why hasn't anything happened yet?" Such questions will block the sweet unfoldment of going within, of trusting your experience to be exactly what you need. As author and anthropologist Angeles Arrien elegantly states, "Be open to outcome, not attached to outcome." By crafting a simple intention as a question, one that invites outcome but doesn't force it or encourage expectations, you sidestep disappointment and are more able to receive the gifts of your retreat.

Movement in the spirit or inner realm is subtle and can sometimes take years to fully apprehend and appreciate. A shift always happens when you retreat, there are always insights and blessings, but they can sometimes seem, at first glance, extraordinarily delicate and amorphous. Can you accept that retreating is essential for your well-being and that the meaning of your retreat lies in the unfoldment of the time itself, in living the questions, in turning within, not in any outcome you might be anticipating?

See Uncomfortable Beginnings, Middles, and In-Betweens.

I struggle with this one, especially as a mother, when time away is so precious, so infrequent and short. Will I arrange the right retreat? Will I pick the right place to go? Will I be enough? These worried rumblings are static that I must tune out before I can truly allow myself to retreat. I suspect these expectations are just smoke screens to prevent me from being present with my feelings and open to my experience. It is easier and more familiar to be worried and disappointed than it is to be open and alive. If I listen to my expectations, I hear the voices of other people or the parts of myself that are damaged, critical, mean. If I listen to these voices telling me what I should be doing with my time, I become externally instead of internally referenced, and I lose the essence of the retreat. I end up feeling exhausted and anxious instead of rested and rejuvenated.

Keep it simple and light. Hoping for a particular result is fine. Demanding, planning, or expecting one is not. Try to remain open to the mystery.

Forming Your Intention

Explore the statements below. Jot down whatever occurs to you. Take plenty of time. Don't edit. It helps me to set a timer for two minutes and to keep my pen moving, exploring a statement at a time. Do this exercise even though you may have no idea whether you even want to retreat or when or for how long or what you would do. This is the realm of pure possibility. It doesn't matter that you believe you have no time because you are the mother of three children under five or that you have never done anything remotely like this before. It also doesn't matter if you sit zazen every day and have been on two hundred retreats. This is about imagining what you need right now, in this moment. Fresh mind. Complete possibility. Spend five minutes right now.

Use these statements at the beginning of a mini-retreat to calm down and focus.

- When I hear the word *retreat* right now, I see and feel . . .

- What I most yearn for in a retreat right now is . . .

- What I fear happening on a retreat is . . .

- What I hope will happen on a retreat is . . .

Imagine these sentences as a net. At first you cast it out wide and fast, hoping to snare many fishes, but as you pull it in, only the biggest fish remains: your question, your intent.

Read over what you wrote. What jumps out at you? What terrifies you in a thrilling, positive way? What ideas are repeated? As you read, ask yourself, "What is the question of my life right now?" Or "What is most vital to me right now?" Or, as Angeles Arrien asks in *The Four-Fold Way,* "What has heart and meaning for me right now?" Try circling the words that tug, leap, beg you. Can you winnow out a theme? Do you want to?

Scan the words you circled. How do they want to arrange themselves into a positive, compelling, *simple* question? Completing this sentence may help:

- On this retreat, I intend to ask myself . . .

What happens now? What do you do with your intention? It all depends on how you feel. You may feel exhilarated, sure of what you need to do. Asking sharpened what you already knew. Then keep going through the next chapters. Perhaps you are surprised by this exercise, by the ideas that emerged. That's excellent. You have an inspiring road ahead.

*See For How
Long Will You
Retreat?*

Or maybe you are feeling overwhelmed, frustrated, or angry because the yearning to retreat has been awakened but you know it is impossible to *ever* get time for yourself for the next million or so years. If this is how you feel right now, stop reading and do something to thoroughly, healthily, totally nurture yourself like ride that forgotten bike in the back of your closet or string white lights around your bathroom and then soak in the tub as they twinkle above you.

What if you did this exercise and nothing came to you? Few rules apply to a woman's retreat, but this is one: don't stress. An intention is solely for you. If you can't quite get one, forget it for a while. It is not uncommon to begin a retreat not knowing what your intention is and to grab hold of it a few minutes or hours into your experience. In some retreat traditions, intention is eschewed altogether and is thought to be counterproductive to encountering spiritual guidance. Would it be more appropriate for you to have no purpose on this retreat? *When retreating without an intention, it is even more vital to construct a strong physical and emotional container for yourself through solitude and ritual.*

*See Opening
Ceremony and
Where Will You
Retreat?*

If you don't want to do this exercise, fine. If you hate the idea of following directions, invent your own. They certainly will be as valid. If you hate exercises, form your intention by deciding what you want to do first. Page through the book; see what practices appeal to you and what intention they suggest. Or check out the chart in the middle of the book. Look at What Will You Do?: Ways to Choose What to Do. If you live alone and can't figure out why anyone would want to go on a retreat to be alone, look at For How Long Will You Retreat?: The Four Seasons of Retreat and Retreating with Others. There is no one way to form intention; of that I am positive. I am also positive that the most important thing is to have the time apart to listen to yourself. If an intention won't help you do that, then forget it.

It is comforting to remember you are going on retreat to contemplate this question. *You are not supposed to know the answer yet* or the means by which you will explore your intention. It is comforting to remember that no one else need know what your intention is. When forming her intention, Rhonda wrote, "What if my intention isn't good enough?" No intention is better, grander, more spiritual, or more transformative than any other. We were all raised in a competitive society. It is so easy to compare ourselves to others, even on a retreat. If those kinds of feelings come up, ask yourself, "Good enough for whom?" and "Who is watching me?" Your intention is a starting place, not a measuring stick. Neither is it about fulfilling or completing or answering your intention. Remember: it's an aim, not a goal. You can't fail at this.

Nor is your intent written in stone. It is very common to begin a retreat with one intention and to find it changing, being refined, during your retreat. The night before Sandy was planning a Saturday retreat, she set the intention "How can I anchor my inner strength and come together with my true self?" During the retreat, her intention changed to "How can I deepen my self-love and learn how to nurture and honor myself?" The difference may seem slight, but this process of refining can be an epiphany, a bright light turning on in your heart. Susan formed these intentions, using clustering: "What new directions do I need in my life?" and "What do I need to do next in my life?" However, early in her one-day retreat she realized, "My intention is about doing or fixing something, exactly the opposite of what I said I yearned for. I needed to be quiet first to see the true intention for this retreat is 'How can I find quiet and stay connected to my inner self or Higher Being?'"

Try referring back to your intention from time to time during your retreat. Ask yourself, "Does this question still have heart and meaning for me?" You might do some spontaneous writing or drawing with regard to your question to help you discover what your retreat is really about. Sometimes, the process of retreating reveals your true intention—it isn't until the end of your experience that you know what you have been up to! That is part of the spiral nature of retreats, coming back, again and again, to the same territory. Pay attention to where you end up: it may reveal a fertile path for future retreats.

See Good Ways to Listen and Uncomfortable Beginnings, Middles, and In-Betweens.

You may also find you have more than one intention. While "Keep it simple" is definitely my retreat motto, if you want more than one intention, then, by all means, go for it. On longer retreats you might name an overall intention and then experiment with forming an intention for each day, to help you maintain your focus. Or you may form two intentions that complement each other, like "How can I practice deeper listening with myself and others?" and "How can I love the dark, jagged parts of myself?"

Use this exercise as a stick to stir your imagination. Use intention to point the way but not as a should, as a straitjacket on your wisdom.

Other Women's Intentions

It might help to read some intentions formed by other women, both women who have gone on retreats and those who never have.

The question I intend to ask myself is . . .

> Can I allow myself to relax and be?
>
> How can I love myself more?
>
> What do I need to do next in the area of spiritual growth?

How can I bring the fullness of me into my work life?

Is this the right place for me to live?

Is this the right relationship for me?

How can I make time for myself in my life?

How can I be more me as well as mother, wife, employee?

What can I do to make peace with my body?

How can I be a mother and an artist, too?

How can I recharge my creativity?

How can I create more health and lightness in my life?

Why is my chronic illness in my life?

How can I begin to accept my imperfections and the imperfections of others?

What is the best way to lift this sadness I feel?

Why can't I get on with my life?

What is my relationship with God right now?

What is appropriate for me in the next third of my life?

How can I live with cancer?

How can I let go of this relationship that has ended?

How can I heal from exhaustion?

How can I grieve not being able to become pregnant?

How can I stop overcommitting to everyone but me?

How can I celebrate turning thirty-three, forty-five, fifty, sixty-one, eighty?

How can I be comfortable alone?

What do I love about myself, and how can I celebrate what I do love?

Should I commit to this relationship through marriage?

How can I listen to and honor my own inner wisdom?

How can I live my own life, inhabit my own center?

How can I create structure/organization in my life that will help me to love and respect myself?

How can I change the direction I am going?

How can I get comfortable with aloneness?

You can see that the number of reasons for going on a retreat are as varied as the women who go on them. Some questions lend themselves to long retreats, others to one or several mini-retreats. If you haven't yet done so, take a few minutes to form your intent. Let it speak to your heart's desire. Don't kill an idea because you think it is impossible. Dare to hope. And dare to keep it simple. "How can I relax and simply be?" is a wonderful intention and a great place both to start and to return to again and again. *See Retreat Plans for ideas.*

Be realistic about how your intention fits with the amount of time you are willing to take. You may covet a month alone to ask yourself, "How can I begin my first novel?," but you may be able to retreat only for a long weekend. You might want to tighten the focus of your intention. On the other hand, be aware of cutting off possibilities because you feel fearful and out of control. Setting an intention is a give-and-take process between what is realistic and attainable and what is open and expansive. If you yearn to live with a bigger intention even if you don't feel you have enough time, trust yourself. In archetypal time, three hours, one day, two days can feel like a lifetime and can deliver the images, feelings, and epiphanies you need.

If you are feeling pressured or disappointed because where or what you are going to do doesn't seem grand enough to fulfill your intention, check out your expectations and remind yourself, "There will always be time for another retreat." Remind yourself also, "I am where I need to be, doing what I need to be doing."

You can live with a retreat intention for years. Some intentions require many retreats to explore fully. There may be one retreat intention that you return to again and again over your life.

Stories

I worked on this intention when I was considering how to spend a few days away from my daughter, Lily, for the first time in her life.

- When I hear the word *retreat* right now, I see and feel . . . sad, nature, alone in a cabin high on a ridge in Big Sur or in the mountains of New

Mexico, like crying, afraid, excited, the desire to be very alone yet have a teacher, yoga, hiking, loose jaw, no guilt, some kind of purpose, great, healthy food delivered to me.

- What I most yearn for in a retreat right now is . . . being taken care of, being led somewhere deeply calm and spiritual, meeting the good mother, being deeply, deeply nurtured.

- What I fear happening on a retreat is . . . wasting my time, being pushed by myself or someone else, not being pushed and giving in to monkey mind.

- What I hope will happen on a retreat is . . . I will talk with my truest, core self, be in *kairos* time, be able to reach calm, not be interrupted either inside or out.

I read over what I wrote, asking myself, "What feels *most* vital for me right now?" My intuitive mind takes over, I try to get out of the way, not to force or control. I can feel the answer emerging, not really in words, but as a longing. . . . I yearn to be truly, deeply cared for with lots of unbroken time to meander. . . . I yearn for solitude and nature. . . . Hmm . . . I slowly form my question:

On this retreat, I intend to ask myself, How can I take profound, loving care of myself?

Notice my intention is doable but also very expansive. It doesn't scare me with harsh expectations but invites me to fulfill it and be fulfilled in the process. It invites inquiry and brainstorming—how can I satisfy this yearning? It makes me feel curious, excited, a little nervous, a nice blend of challenge and reassurance. Notice, too, that I could have formed any number of intentions from my first writing. I kept looking for, sensing, what I most yearn for *right now*.

Notice, too, that the last two questions help me know both what to avoid and where I want to come out, but they also point out the fears I need to address and possible expectations to let go of.

Here is an example from Pam, a mother of two in her late thirties and an owner of a small business. She had no idea where, how, or when she would retreat.

- When I hear the word *retreat* right now, I see and feel . . . a cabin in a natural setting. Me alone with loose-fitting clothes and a face free of any cosmetics. I feel anxious and relieved at the same time. I feel a kind of pressure to use my time wisely, to get beyond the regularity of my days.

- What I most yearn for in a retreat right now is . . . aloneness, warmth, comfort, healthy foods, nature contact, a portable word processor, a chunk of time of five to six days, time to unwind and even unravel. To push myself into the dark areas of my psyche.

- What I fear happening on a retreat is . . . I fear fear. I fear feeling frivolous. I fear liking my aloneness so well that coming home is painful. I fear giving myself the opportunity to truly express and explore my inner life and then discovering I don't possess the tools or inspiration.

- What I hope will happen on a retreat is . . . I'd like to connect with myself alone, my creative self, my emotional self, and my physical self. I'd like to use writing as a medium of exploration.

- On this retreat, I intend to ask myself, Why am I so uncertain of my creative capabilities and how can I teach myself to trust my inner voice? On this retreat I also intend to stretch my body and look at the cycle of a day and night.

Now it is your turn. Articulate your inarticulate longing. Mold the process to you. It doesn't take long. There is absolute magic in naming what you wish to find. Things begin to fall into place, helpers appear, insights shoot down from the night sky. Come along. Now is as good a time as any.

For Experienced Retreatants

Your task in setting a retreat intention is to be very aware of your razor's edge, neither choosing one that is too comfortable (doing again what you have done before) nor pushing yourself overly hard because you do have experience, because you survived a three-day vision fast, or because you did a silent meditation retreat for ten days. You must come back to what has heart and meaning for you *right now*. Also, if you are an experienced retreatant who has never conducted a self-led retreat, be extra aware of your assumptions and expectations based on the container or support other people or retreat centers have provided for you in the past. It is one thing to show up at a monastery and be enveloped in a cloud of calm. It is quite another to create that calm at home. Both are equally valuable but very different.

For How Long
Will You Retreat?

The leisure of the monks is not the privilege of those who can afford to take the time; it is the virtue of those who give to everything they do the time it deserves to take.

David Steindl-Rast

When your thoughts turn to when and for how long you might retreat, consider the words above and also these from Kathleen Norris, a Benedictine oblate (associate) and poet who spent two nine-month terms living at St. John's Abbey in Collegeville, Minnesota. She writes in *The Cloister Walk,*

> In our culture, time can seem like an enemy: it chews us up and spits us out with appalling ease. But the monastic perspective welcomes time as a gift from God, and seeks to put it to good use rather than allowing us to be used up by it. A friend who was educated by the Benedictines has told me that she owes to them her sanity with regard to time. "You never really finish anything in life," she says, "and while that's humbling, and frustrating, it's all right."

What if, instead of approaching this experience saying, "I have this amount of time, what can I do in it?," you approach it asking, "How much time do I need to live my intention?" Yes, it may be an unanswerable question, but it is one that begs to be considered. We spend a lot of our lives cramming what has to get done into the amount of time available. We joke that work expands to fill the space available. Is that true? Or are we afraid of what might happen if we gave a task our full attention and all the time it needed? Our lives might change, our perspectives might shift, we might become angry or sad over how little time we spend in a meaningful way. What might happen if you considered, just this once, putting your yearnings first and the time constraints second?

Entertain the idea for a moment: "If I had all the time in the world to retreat, to explore my intention, for how long would I retreat?" Let yourself hear the answer.

Before you panic, consider this paradoxical thought: if you can enter into the kind of time that T. S. Eliot describes, you don't need much linear time at all.

> Moment, the moment in and out of time,
> The distraction fit, lost in a shaft of sunlight,
> The wild thyme unseen, or the winter lightning
> Or the waterfall, or music heard so deeply
> That it is not heard at all, but you are the music
> While the music lasts. . . .

When you are betwixt and between, time no longer matters. You pass into that mystical place of timelessness, *kairos,* as the Greeks named it, where you are no longer just listening to your innermost self but living, *being,* your innermost self. Once you are there, it doesn't matter how long you have because you are unaware of time.

Length of time is not synonymous with depth of experience. However long you choose to retreat is long enough if you say yes with your full being.

Ask yourself, If someone walked in the room right now and informed you that you have one year to live, would you still go on retreat?

This is your litmus test. Don't let it be hackneyed, for it isn't.

Yes or no: Would you go on retreat? No qualifiers.

If the answer is no, you may want to go back and spend more time with your intention, going back to the question "What has heart and meaning for me right now?" Or you may wish to get your feet wet with mini-retreats, or you may want to put this book away for a while. Or perhaps you want to expand your idea of retreat to include friends, children, family, or your partner.

If the answer is yes, you certainly would go on retreat even if you had only a year to live, you are now charged to make it happen. You will find ways to make it happen.

Before you throw down this book in disgust, thinking I am the Martha Stewart of retreats and am assuming you have unlimited time and energy for this, please realize that out of the four seasons of retreat discussed below, you will take more mini-retreats and retreats in the world than long retreats. Long retreats are indispensable, and I'm encouraging you (begging you on my knees) to make time for them. But when a half hour waiting in the car for soccer practice to end, an hour alone in the house on a Saturday afternoon, or ten minutes away from work is all you have, a retreat can be wedged in. Please, please know that a retreat doesn't have to be difficult, doesn't have to be a big deal, to nourish you or to shift your perspective. Nor are you warped if this isn't a struggle for you. At certain times and for certain women, it is easy to find time for retreating. If this isn't difficult for you, rejoice! If it is a struggle or daunting, know that getting started, doing your first retreat, is by far the biggest obstacle. It *will* become a self-loving habit soon.

The Four Seasons of Retreat

Over your lifetime, you will retreat in many ways. You will retreat with teachers, with groups, in ways that challenge you, in ways that soothe you. There are four ways in which to retreat: long retreats, mini-retreats, retreats with others, and retreats in the world.

Long Retreats

See Retreat Plans.

This is the place that is reclaimed each time I retreat. I recognize the space based on a childhood experience. . . . It was Easter, my birthday. My dad held me up to the sky and said, "Look at the world." It is this moment I look for in all retreats. The deep, deep place of being held. I recognize my littleness in all the bigness and feel great joy.

Marcie Telandar, therapist, writer, and ritualist

Two to three days is the classic layperson's container for a retreat. Two of our most ancient female myths, the Sumerian myth of Inanna's descent into the underworld and the Greek ritual of the Thesmophoria, are both three-day journeys. The two-day weekend and the one-day Sabbath as retreats are embedded in our psyche, perhaps woven into our DNA.

The advantage here is time: time to unwind, time to venture deep, time to get some distance from your life. It will amaze you how long two or three days will seem when you are untethered from clocks and responsibilities, adrift in your own universe. Time stretches like it did when you were a child and threatens when you dig into areas you have resisted looking at. True magic can happen when you "have been out awhile," as wilderness guides put it, even if "being out" is two days of silence in your home.

The disadvantage of a long retreat is the same: time. Making the time. The other disadvantage is the danger of going too deep on your own. This danger can be allayed by arranging self-led retreats that are appropriate to where you are in your life. If this is your first retreat or your first self-guided retreat, avoid biting off more than you can chew. A week alone in the wilderness with no phone, no running water, and no way home may be too much. It might be gentler to start with a day or two at home, with the phone turned off. Scrupulously avoid harsh or overly rigorous requirements. The inner voice guiding you must speak with self-love and self-respect, not a self-hatred that tries to drive you faster, harder, better. If you are experiencing a lot of fear of being alone, attend a retreat center or share your retreat with a friend. If you feel experienced or strong, then venture out alone and longer. The kind of retreat you choose has much to do with your intention. The more intense the issues you are working with, the more you need some kind of support or check-in person nearby.

See Courage: Support on Retreat.

Longer retreats are better suited to certain intentions or purposes than others. Gaining perspective, making a decision, healing utter exhaustion, or merging with the rhythms of nature often need the spaciousness and luxury of more time.

See Retreat Plans.

Stories

This is Saral's story from a one-month retreat.

> For my fortieth birthday I wanted to take an entire month off, no work or social obligations. My husband and friends were wonderful about it, even though not one of them quite understands my need for solitude. Turning forty felt like a big deal to me because part of it was deciding not to have children, knowing that probably was not going to happen.
>
> When I started my month at the retreat center, I talked to my retreat coordinator. "Should I be silent? What kind of structure should I have for a month?" She was really great about saying "Don't have structure, or have very little structure, don't be silent. See what happens every day, stay in the moment." Because of that guidance, I had two relationships, particularly one, that were perfect. I helped a man (another retreatant) begin to deal with his childhood abuse. I was a mother to this man. I got to experience mother-love in a way I never had before in my life. I

wouldn't have been available if I had been silent, and so what ended up being the most important part of that retreat only happened because I stayed open to anything happening.

Each week of the retreat had a kind of subcontainer. I spent the first week rereading fifteen years of journals and reflecting on my life, where I had come from and where I wanted to go. Then I spent the next couple of weeks reading books that I had chosen carefully. I also worked on the land and counseled other retreatants.

I had many days of silence, but I also spent some mornings at a coffee house in town talking to strangers and meeting new friends. Even though a coffee house and time spent socializing wasn't part of my original picture for my retreat, both ended up being important. I wrote loads of letters in that coffee house, which helped me to feel the wealth of my friendships.

The last week was spent preparing for a vision fast, three days of silent meditation, then twenty-four hours alone in the woods using a medicine wheel, no sleep, just wonder and reflection. After my silent retreat I had my best friends come up, one a day for three days, to spend an afternoon. It was a way to integrate myself back into my life.

The last day of my retreat was Halloween, Samhain. I sat by the fire and had a ritual end to my month. I walked down the mountain and back into my regular life, enriched beyond words, knowing that solitude will always be a vital and necessary part of my life.

Mini-Retreats

Stop looking for the sabbatical—or even the weekend when everyone is out of the house. Solitude is wonderful, but vast swaths of it can be like bolts of vintage silk—so lovely, so hard to come by we are reluctant to cut into them, and so they sit unused while we say we "could."

Julia Cameron, *The Vein of Gold*

For many women, going away for even a day can be next to impossible or can feel too uncomfortable. Yet the busier you are and the more you are giving to others, the more you must replenish yourself. That's where mini-retreats come in.

A mini-retreat can be ten minutes waiting in the dentist's office, a half hour baking bread, your lunch hour spent in a park, a car trip alone with no destination in mind, a bike ride, a yoga class. A mini-retreat can look like just about anything if it is embedded within the archetypal structure of retreat: ritual withdrawal from the ordinary, a way to be in and maintain liminal space as you listen to your deepest self, and a conscious return to ordinary life.

Mini-retreats can enrich your retreat practice in many ways. They can be life-savers during a crisis such as a vigil in a hospital for a sick family member when you can get away for only a few moments or hours at a time. They are in-dispensable during a frantic time such as a deadline at work, at the holidays, or when you have a new baby. Mini-retreats can serve as reminders, weaving the fruits of retreat into your daily life. You might find yourself attending an organized retreat once a year, conducting your own self-led retreat on another long weekend, and practicing mini-retreats once every few weeks. Mini-retreats can be done consecutively, using the same intention again and again. If you do this, try repeating the same opening and closing ceremony each time.

See Living Your Retreat Every Day.

See Where Will You Retreat?: Retreating at Home.

Can a mini-retreat be as meaningful as an extended retreat? Of course! But having less time to unwind and shift your perceptions can present a chal-lenge. However, sometimes mini-retreats actually work better because the stress of leaving for a long period of time, the discomfort of being away from family for long, and the comfort you take in your own home can make a mini-retreat remarkably fruitful.

Stories

This story is from Jasmine, a second-grade teacher:

> I have had to visit doctors a lot lately. I love it when I find myself stuck waiting alone in a waiting room. Instead of reading *People* I do a little retreat. I slip off my shoes, pull my special sweater around me, and imagine I'm at a place I visited years ago in Bermuda on a day I felt great. I use the same check-in question each time: "What am I feeling?" I find something to focus on, like a picture of dolphins in a *National Geographic* magazine, and I let my mind drift with my question. Some-times I also write or read my daily prayer book. I am always careful to return consciously, because once I didn't and I found myself feeling very spacey and not driving carefully. My signal is when I hear the nurse coming. I put on my shoes, take off my sweater, and say to myself, "I am in so-and-so's office, but I am in a different place." I acknowledge my retreat time as holy.

Retreats with Others

An important distinction can be made between working with a group and working with others who support you in your solitary venture. During a group

See Retreating with Others and Retreat Plans: A One-Day Retreat with a Friend.

retreat, you concentrate on learning from a teacher and learning about yourself through your interactions with the group. This can be invaluable for reaching a new level in your spiritual practice or as a way to let go of stale beliefs about yourself. But during the kind of retreat outlined in this book, you spend the majority of time alone. A friend or small group provides support and mirroring at different times or when needed, *but being and learning from others is not the main focus of your retreat.* Instead, being with and listening to yourself is central. You use the other(s) for support in your solitary undertaking. As Margaret Mead said, "Groups help hold each other together, they help to hold each other's dreams."

See Retreating with Others: Dream Circle.

An example would be three friends going off together to a small inn or remote campground for the weekend. Each has her own room or tent. They do a dream circle together in the morning, meditate in the afternoon, then come together for dinner. The rest of the time they spend alone. This style of retreat is a good choice for extroverts, giving you something in between total solitude and becoming lost in group dynamics. The group provides a gentle structure, a chance to goof off (perhaps during dinner), and a useful way to reflect on the experience (dream circle), yet the focus of each woman's retreat is up to her. You make few concessions to the needs of the group and can follow your own way most of the time. Yet if you start to feel lonely or restless or afraid of the time alone or you need to discuss your insights, you know you have like-minded companions nearby.

Why take a friend or small group along? Because if you don't feel safe, physically and emotionally, on retreat, nothing will happen. If you are afraid to be alone or if you want to spend time in a secluded place, it is often a good idea to have someone along. Anna and Sandy often retreat together at Big Sur, California, where they hike within whistling distance of each other but without speaking or interacting. If you are working out tough or scary emotional issues or are planning an extended retreat, having someone nearby is wise. If you need help with your motivation, a small group can make a difference (meditation retreats often work in this way, although the presence of an experienced teacher is usually an important addition). A tremendous sense of shared purpose and energy can be created when two or more people do retreat work together. In addition, you have someone to check in with when you are back home and your retreat experience begins to fade or you doubt a new path or decision. If you are doing a self-led retreat for the first time, having someone beside you who is doing the same thing can be very reassuring.

What are the disadvantages? Chatter. As women, we often distract ourselves through polite conversation. Chitchat. We take care of others through small talk. The pitfall in retreating with a group, with a friend, or even alone at a retreat center is that you will displace your inward focus and lose insight by chattering about unimportant things at the wrong time. Meals are a prime place to do so; it is easy to start chopping garlic together and end up talking about your weight or your old relationship instead of staying inwardly focused, in sacred space. It isn't always the act of talking that is depleting; it is more often the subject matter or getting caught up in "helping" another woman.

Another disadvantage of retreating with others is that when you are trying to regain a sense of your own rhythm, fitting into any kind of schedule and compromising with other women may feel too restrictive. You can waste time and energy taking care of the group or your friend instead of tending to your needs. When retreating with others, you must be constantly aware of where your attention and help are directed. Remaining aware in this way can provide a fantastic opportunity to learn about your own process, your moment-to-moment choices and self-talk, but it can also be incredibly tricky.

Stories

One of my favorite shared retreats was with my dear friend Barbra. We set aside one day to sit on the beach from nine to five. We chose an undeveloped beach where there were few people. We spontaneously created an opening ceremony together, drawing a circle in the sand, outlining it with shells and stones, making a sand shrine covered with things that represented our inner and outer lives, burning sage, and praying together. We called a deep listening circle to discuss our friendship, made sand sculptures, napped, swam, walked together and alone, and caught up with each other and ourselves. The time went too fast and we did not do a strong enough closing ceremony, but the feeling of being honest and reconnected persists.

The questions we used are in Retreat Plans: A Friendship Retreat.

This story is from *Turning the Wheel: American Women Recreating the New Buddhism* by Sandy Boucher:

In Marin County, California, on a summer weekend, thirty women who have come from Berkeley, Oakland, and San Francisco as well as Marin gather in a secluded house to meditate together. They sit in the large open living room of the house, they do walking meditation in the yard. Silence is strictly observed. There is no formally designated teacher present.

The Women's Sangha [the first independent, teacherless group of women meditating in the United States] had asked each participant to bring an item of food for the meals. Everyone signed up for chores on a job sheet on the wall.

For two days, the women sit and walk. Shinma Dhammadinna, visiting from Taungpulu Monastery, sits at the front of the room during the meditation periods. A movement session is led by a meditator who is also a dancer and performer. A Theravadin meditation teacher from Insight Meditation Society, who happens to live down the road, drops by to give a short, respectful talk.

At night, the women unroll their sleeping bags on the living room floor and go to sleep. On Sunday they take a silent hike up into the yellow foothills of Mount Tamalpais and sit for an hour in a high meadow. In the afternoon a woman leads some instructions in Vipassana meditation. To end the retreat, another woman guides the loving-kindness or metta meditation.

It is a peaceful, concentrated weekend in which women meditate and are silent together, prepare food, do other chores, each taking responsibility for some aspect of the retreat. On leaving, many women express their gratitude for this opportunity.

Retreats in the World

See Retreat Plans.

By far, my happiest memories when I was a teenager were when I was in the ocean. It was the ultimate retreat for me, the container that was bigger than anything I could put into it. The ocean became my solace no matter what I was going through, something vaster than my particulars. I have never been in one frame of mind, gone in the ocean, and stayed the same. It is a continual baptism.

Jennifer Freed, therapist and educator

Because our lives as women demand that most of us be embedded in a nourishing and sometimes debilitating maze of relationship, work, and commitments, we often find it impossible to carve out enough time for even a mini-retreat. At these times, we need a way to retreat in the midst of crying children, deadlines, and the subway. "Go on retreat with what you've got" is what writer and Peer Spirit Circle originator Christina Baldwin believes. If what you've got is the drive from home to work, a walk through your neighborhood with your infant nestled on your chest, a half hour stolen from a family holiday dinner to go to the market, or your lunch hour, then, as the saying goes, "Work it, girl."

Writes Clarissa Pinkola Estés in *Women Who Run with the Wolves,*

For myself, solitude is rather like a folded-up forest I carry with me everywhere and unfurl around myself when I have need. I sit at the feet of the great old trees of my childhood. From that vantage point, I ask my questions, receive my answers, then coalesce my woodland back down to the size of a love note till next time. The experience is immediate, brief, informative.

Last summer, walking on a crowded beach, I realized I could be open to and invaded by the presence of others, or I could draw into myself and be alone with the sound of surf. Wearing sunglasses and a hat helped, but my intention was what gave me solitude. Who hasn't had the experience of being deliciously alone in a crowd, of feeling that your seat on a darkened plane was a private chamber, of eating alone in a restaurant while the other diners receded out of your consciousness? Or of strolling through a museum, each person caught up in an individual, hushed reverence? The social constraints of most societies collaborate with you: you are not expected to talk to strangers, to share your table, to smile on a busy street. Lunch time, commuter time, even shower time can become retreat time if you conjure the retreat archetype, if you have intentionality.

These kinds of retreats work as a catch-your-emotional-breath time, a time to sift through your recent experiences. They sustain you on your spiritual path. They can enable you to work or to create. I try to approach my writing time as a retreat.

Some women carry talismans to help them feel that these retreats in the world are real. Fingering worry or rosary beads, writing in a purse-sized journal, reading a daily meditation book, wrapping a shawl around your shoulders, slipping on personal stereo headphones while playing soothing music —all these can signal to your heart, "This is a retreat, and no matter how brief, it is important."

These brief visits to the land of self and solitude feed our quest for richness of meaning and purpose. The creating of such unions between our outer persona and our inner life allows us to hear what our soul needs. Now that may sound grand, but in fact it is very simple. Who hasn't forgotten what her soul truly needed? When we don't listen to our authenticity, we become women who believe their souls are found in *Melrose Place* reruns, Macy's half-price sales, a child getting into Harvard, or becoming vice president in charge of production. Retreats in the world, for all their lack of romance and bravada, give us a chance to listen to our own souls. We may hear "You need to move your body" or "You are running away from something. If you don't start dealing with it, you are going to get sick" or "Way to go! Keep up the good work!"

Without these regular conversations, we are lost. When we open our lives a sliver for these mundane yet incandescent moments to blossom, we risk becoming the women we want to be, our inner lives blazing on the outside for all to behold.

Stories

This is Christina's story.

> One of my favorite retreats is to get in the car and drive eight hours in an unknown direction. It is a tremendously fruitful time. Either I do it alone or with someone who is very trusted, like my friend Ann. When we have to drive somewhere, we don't listen to the radio, we just have quiet time and talking time. It is a deep retreat. But if you did it alone, you could take that set of eight tapes on how to be a totally enlightened human being that you've never had time to listen to and just listen to it. Take along a little portable tape recorder and talk to yourself; make notes to yourself as insights occur. Don't listen to anything in the car that is polluting your mind. Silence, driving with the windows open and the wind roaring in, that white noise can be very amazing.
>
> I had an experience about ten years ago when I was driving through Minnesota in July going from one conference to another. Even though I had air conditioning, I didn't turn it on. I just sat in the roar of this white wind—heat, summer—and I just let my hair blow, and it was as if this breath was in the car with me. I drove through those high corn-fields and rolling hills, drenched in summer. About halfway to my destination I said, "Here is what I am going to do." I just spoke it out into the day. My intention was so purposeful that I do not remember one word of the actual promise; it was more like a transmission. But when I clicked back in to myself, I had lined up blocks inside of me some-where, and I followed those blocks. And every now and then, I would do something and find myself saying, "Oh, this must have been one of the things I promised myself."

What style of retreat you choose, how long you retreat for, and even what you do on retreat doesn't really matter. All that really matters is the simple act of committing. Of going with a big *"Yes, I deserve this, I need this"* in your heart. Of trusting yourself enough to get quiet and listen to your wisdom. All the rest is icing on the proverbial cake.

Where Will You Retreat?
Your Physical and Emotional Containers

*That is what is strange—that friends, even passionate love, are not my
real life unless there is time alone in which to explore and to discover what
is happening or has happened. Without the interruptions, nourishing and
maddening, this life would become arid. Yet I taste it fully only when I am
alone here and the house and I resume the old conversations.*

May Sarton, *Journal of a Solitude*

Where will you retreat? What kind of container do you need? Why do I keep
using that word *container*? Am I secretly running a Tupperware racket?

A retreat container holds and carries the energy of your experience. It is your
means of enclosing yourself and maintaining liminal space. Without a container, your retreat will either never come alive or never feel like a true retreat,
or the energy will slowly leak away, like air escaping a leaky tire. Your container also helps you feel safe, and safety is the precursor to inner work.

A container can be created in several ways. A convincing opening ceremony
creates a strong emotional container. Choosing a physical place where you
feel sustained and comforted, like your home or a place in nature, creates a
container. Solitude creates a container. Support from another person, either
before or during your retreat, creates a container. Prayer, visualization, a
beloved cape or hat, even your car can create a container. What is important
is that you feel physically and psychically enclosed, in a cocoon, set apart, betwixt and between. The boundaries of your container enable you to hold the
tension of waiting for your authentic self to communicate, to stick with the
work at hand, to journey deeper into your insights and feelings, to be comforted when you are buffeted by raw emotions, and to exult when joy blooms
in your heart.

How do you create a strong container?

Choose the Right Physical Setting

Your retreat surroundings are hallowed ground. I have retreated at retreat centers. I have retreated at home. I have retreated at my friend Anna's cottage. I have retreated in a canoe in the New Mexico desert and the Canadian wilderness. I have retreated in motel rooms, cars, trains, creeks, easy chairs. As Jack Zimmerman, a therapist and retreat coordinator at the Ojai Foundation, says, "The land shapes the retreat. Attunement to place brings shape." Some places fit some intentions and not others. Choosing or creating your container depends on what you want out of your retreat and what is available to you.

Consider a retreat center. Retreats I have done at the Ojai Foundation were informed by living in a yurt close to the land and by doing much of the retreat outdoors. While there, I know no one can reach me except in a true emergency. I participate in a morning meditation practice and talk with a retreat coordinator. I feel emotionally safe because I know if I become too lonely or unstrung, someone is nearby to reassure me. I am also comforted by feeling the energy of all those who have come to the land before me. That, too, adds to the emotional container.

See Resources: Books Listing Retreat Centers, Leaders, and Adventures.

Thousands of retreat centers around the world offer an amazing diversity of programs. Many are inexpensive or request a donation. Some are available for day use (good for a mini-retreat if you are nearby). When is a retreat center the right fit for you? When you would flourish away from your life; when you need something a particular retreat center offers; when you feel support would be emotionally helpful; when the newness of a place will help you gain perspective; when it feels like a retreat center offers the safest way to be in nature as a woman alone.

When isn't a retreat center a good fit? If being away from home creates more stress than you need; if being in a new environment or participating in a program is too frightening; if you might sabotage yourself by obsessing over finding the perfect retreat center and therefore wait three years to retreat because you don't have the money to fly to Thailand; if you are doing only mini-retreats or retreats in the world right now; or if your intention would not be served by peace and quiet. For example, if your retreat intention is "How can I live through my husband's leaving me?," you might not want to be welcomed by smiling nuns who envelop you in silence and kindness. You instead may need space to mourn, cry, shriek. Perhaps you want to be at home where you can make all the noise you want, or perhaps you want to stay at your friend's house in the woods.

What about a retreat at home? Home is free, familiar, and hopefully a comfortable place imbued with your spirit. It will require less energy to prepare, and there is no traveling time. Home is the perfect choice for mini-retreats. For many women, retreating at home is the ultimate in safety and comfort, and it supports intentions that spring from a need to nurture yourself, to make your home a retreat center, to bring your spiritual practice into your ordinary life, to slow down and shed stress, to face grief or disappointment. Home is the only choice when you wish to retreat in the few hours during your child's nap or on a weekend afternoon when the house is suddenly yours.

Retreating at home is more of a challenge if you are easily distracted, if you will answer the phone, if you have neighbors or family who will drop in, if your children, partner, or roommates will be in the house at the same time and their presence will inhibit or disturb you, or if you live alone and being alone in your home feels too mundane or depresses you. Retreating at home won't work well if you need outside help sticking to your retreat plan or staying away from energy dilutors like junk food, TV, phone calls, or work around the house. Also, if asking your housemates, partner, or children to leave the house will bring on waves of guilt, you must factor in the added stress. If you are going to end up waxing your dining room table or getting a jump on your taxes *and then regret doing so,* you need to go somewhere, *or* you need to let yourself wax while observing your process. Maybe you needed to use this time to get organized. Skip feelings of failure. And next time, take a retreat away from home.

See Retreating at Home, below, and What Will You Do?: Check-In.

A friend's house can provide a good middle ground between a retreat center and your own home. You (hopefully) won't feel compelled to wax her table. You've left home, so there is a feeling of separation from everyday life. A friend's home can offer wonderful features, like my friend Anna's cottage, an utterly feminine, pink place filled with candles, flowers, a garden with a hammock, and a view of the ocean. Retreating at a friend's house works well if there is something you want to learn or absorb from her space, if you are clear about what the distractions will be, if you can relax and not feel like you are walking on eggshells because you might track mud on the carpet, and if you need to get away from home.

Retreating at a friend's house might not work well if, as Christina Baldwin joked,

> Someone lends you their lake cabin and you think, oh this is wonderful. There is no phone, no TV, and you walk in and there are twenty years of *Good Housekeeping* magazines piled up. I don't know what you would do in that situation but I would have to take all that stuff and

stick it in a corner because I'm an addict about browsing through reading material. I have to do something to remind me that my intention is not to read 20 years of *Good Housekeeping* magazines. It's a foible many of us have, macramé of the mind.

Christina goes on to detail a wonderful way women can support one another.

> Say you have a friend who lives in a house with an apartment over the garage and she says you can hide out over the weekend. And you say, "Here's what I need. I need to know if you would bring me a tray of food that you leave at the back door. I need to know if it is okay if I do some screaming and crying and nobody comes to get me. I need you to remove any reading material." What if women could learn to provide this space for each other?

Massage therapist Saral Burdette has done just that, setting up a retreat for a friend, drawing a bath, giving her a massage, providing a beautiful place and a little structure. What if you did this for a friend and she reciprocated the favor a few weekends later? This is a loving way to support each other in creating time for retreat.

See Good Ways to Listen: Divine Landscape.

Retreats in nature have shaped my life. From camping alone for the first time on Anacapa Island off the coast of southern California to sitting in my backyard watching crows, the natural world restores me. I feel more emotionally held in nature than anywhere. Reading Annie Dillard, Terry Tempest Williams, Ann Linnea, Valerie Andrews, and Anne Morrow Lindbergh, among others, tells me I am not alone. Women in my workshops list nature and water as their best restorers. My first wilderness retreat introduced me to a whole new world. It was the first step in articulating my longing for solitude, sacred space, and making peace with my feminine self. A few years after that retreat, a friend asked, "When did you first feel you were a woman?" I named that retreat, even though I was twenty-five at the time of that retreat. It was my first experience of instinctual femininity, unconstrained by being a lady.

There are many ways to retreat in nature, from a trip led by someone else to a cabin in the woods to a tent on a friend's wilderness property to a visit to one of the more remote and simple retreat centers. Often, nature will be just one aspect of your retreat. Meandering down a country road listening to the trees, biking in the mountains, roller-blading through your neighborhood, wading in a creek, plucking brown leaves off your houseplants on your city terrace— each can renew you.

When is a nature foray best? When you are stuck in your life, dried out from the pace, sick of noise and pollution and despair. When there is a piece of nature, no matter where or how small—a park, a creek, a hollow—near you that you love (Annie Dillard's famous Tinker Creek is near a highway). When a wilderness adventure is a lifetime dream. When you can tend your houseplants, terrace garden, or Japanese Zen rock garden.

When isn't a nature retreat appropriate? When the weather is too harsh. If you, as many women do, feel unsafe being alone in nature. If your physical comfort is an important part of your ability to relax and venture inward. For most women, being too cold and feeling unsafe are the two things that block the ability to settle inward. Watch for these in your planning, but don't let them stop you from doing something you yearn to do.

See Courage: Support from Others for ideas to make being alone in nature safer.

Another set of retreat locations to consider is bed-and-breakfast inns, hotels, resorts, and spas. The cost of these settings makes retreating in them a rarity or impossibility for most of us. And in this kind of physical container, it can be hard to maintain discipline. You tend to feel you are more on a vacation than on a retreat. Everything is arranged to make you comfortable, pampered, waited on. For exhausted women, this may sound divine. But does it fit your intention? If you need luxury, quiet, breakfast in bed, or a variety of exercise classes, or are afraid to be totally alone, consider these comfy sanctuaries. If seeing people sipping wine at four on the terrace will distract you from your intention, choose a retreat center, call your friends, or rearrange your home.

Please don't neglect the places you can do a retreat in the world. Find a spot near your work or home that you can slip away to when you need to get out of your house for a mini-retreat or as part of a longer retreat. A rooftop garden, a window seat in your favorite cafe, a carrel in a library, a museum, your car, a fountain, a nature preserve, a historical home, a secluded *paseo* off a main street, a coffee shop, a seat at the back of the bus, a sleeping compartment on a train, a carriage ride in a park (ever done that alone?), a tennis court, an aquarium, a pier, a church, even the bathroom at work can offer refuge. Once you start looking for these places, you will be amazed at the nooks and niches that beckon to you. Almost anywhere can be a place to withdraw into yourself. If you are doing a lot of retreats in the world (say, to get away from a horrible job), retreat to the same place each time. This will make it easier to slip into an altered, interior state more quickly.

Create Emotional Containment

Emotional containment grows out of two things: your physical container (which often provides most of it) and your opening ceremony. On retreats in the world, when retreating at home, or when you just need to be emotionally held, you can strengthen your container with one or more of these ideas:

- Visualize yourself protected. If you begin to feel you are no longer on retreat or that you are wavering in your focus (this often happens on retreats in the world, especially lunch hour or work retreats), imagine yourself surrounded by a cone of incandescent light. See this light encircling your body and spirit in shimmering beauty. Feel it enclosing you in a cloister of peace. Nothing outside this cone can touch you emotionally unless you choose to let it in. The light moves with you wherever you go.

See A Woman's Retreat: Archetypal Herstory.

- Visualize yourself in a favorite place, a place you feel utterly safe, comfortable, energized, healthy, and capable. Or imagine yourself at an ancient retreat center like the Hypogeum or in the menstrual hut with other women. Or at your ideal retreat center. Take a few minutes to use all of your senses to enjoy your place. Indulge your imagination: let yourself have the massage, the hot mineral baths, the fresh meal prepared for you, the three-piece jazz band strumming in the corner, the view of the Rockies. Rest and enjoy your vision for a few minutes.

See Resources.

- Before you retreat, choose a poem, song, or meditation and memorize a few lines (or the whole thing if you wish). Choose words that bring you to your center, to your source. Recite these lines when you need to reinforce your container.

See Courage: Getting Support from Others.

- Contact someone, before or during your retreat, for support.

- Write in your journal. For many, the act of writing fosters containment. You could explore the statements "To feel contained, I need to . . ." and "I feel centered when I. . . ." Or you might describe your perfect physical and emotional container, imagining yourself in it as you do.

- Have a pair of sunglasses, a hat, cape, shawl, sweater, bathrobe, or other apparel that comforts and envelops you. Wear it each time you retreat. This is especially helpful when doing retreats in the world.

- Ask your Divinity for protection and refuge. Recite the twelve-step serenity prayer.

In the end, creating your container evolves from your intention, your choice of where you will retreat, and your opening ceremony. Give just a little thought to how you will enclose yourself, and the container will take care of itself as your retreat takes on a life of its own.

Questions to Consider When Preparing Your Place

If you need help choosing a place, reflect on these questions:

- If money and time were not considerations, where would you retreat? Where would you feel most supported, most able to explore and reach new depths? This may be a specific destination (Lama Foundation in New Mexico or Esalen in Big Sur or Omega in upstate New York for long retreats; a cottage near a lake for a one-day retreat; a river bluff near your route home from work for a mini-retreat; a bookstore for a retreat in the world). Or it may be an unnamed destination with certain specific qualities (good food, library of spiritual books, very quiet, in nature, close to home).

- What style of retreat are you planning?

- For how long?

- What is your budget? A retreat should not add financial anxiety to your life.

- What compromise between your ideal and your reality serve both your life and your intention? Where will you be sufficiently supported and held? If your physical container doesn't provide enough emotional support, what do you need to add to feel sheltered?

Deciding where you will retreat may take you five seconds, or it may require a bit of research. To find places, buy or borrow a book listing retreat centers in your area, brainstorm with a friend to think of places close by where you could go, and survey your home with a retreatant's eye.

All that aside, avoid getting caught up in where you retreat, because in the end the place isn't what matters. To be on retreat means to take time to step away from your ordinary life to focus on your inner life. It is the interior landscape you are most concerned with. Trust that wherever you retreat will be the perfect place with its own gifts and challenges.

Retreating at Home

Home is the place where you will probably retreat most often. It is also the most challenging place to retreat because it is inextricably entwined with your ordinary life. At home it can be more difficult to alter or transcend your ordinary perceptions—something you want to do on retreat—as well as to gain enough privacy and avoid distractions like cleaning or talking on the phone. Home can simply feel too ordinary a place for a retreat. If this is the case, it helps to transform your retreat area in your home into sacred space.

- Ensure your privacy. Before your retreat, ask people not to drop by, arrange for your family or roommates to be out, put a Do Not Disturb sign on the door, turn off the phone, and turn down the volume on the answering machine. Consider what your biggest obstacles to privacy are and address these specifically. It can take a lot of effort to do this if you live with others, especially if those others are very young, very old, or not very supportive of your retreating. If you are lucky enough to have a home with an area you don't usually use, such as a guest room, a barn, or your backyard, retreat there.

- Change the energy of your home. Before you begin your retreat, clean, get rid of clutter, and make sure there are no bills, paperwork, or unfinished craft or renovation projects in sight. Rearrange furniture, light candles, add flowers or plants, create a shrine, play music, or borrow a white noise or positive ion generator or miniature waterfall. Clear the area you will be using. Open a window or door (even a crack). Start in the eastern corner of your room and, moving clockwise around the room, paying particular attention to the corners, burn either incense, sage, cedar, or sweetgrass, or spritz water from a spray bottle scented with your favorite essential oil, or clap your hands or ring a bell. Sense where energy feels stagnant, whether from old arguments, illness, loneliness, or too many other people's emotions. Use the smoke, water, or sound to get the energy moving. Finish by invoking the kind of energy you want to fill your home during your retreat by reading a poem, praying, singing, or boldly stating your intention.

- Surround yourself with things that feed your retreat. If your intention is to explore relaxing, you might decide your bedroom is the best place. Make your bed with clean sheets, pull up a good reading chair and light, hang up pictures you love (even if that means moving your best print from the living room), and add a big vase of flowers and some of your favorite books. Or perhaps you need a place to grieve? You might want to clear a big floor space where you can move, put down a rug, blanket, and pillow, pull the drapes, and remove any objects that remind you of either happy times or what you are trying to let go of.

- When doing mini-retreats at home, store all your retreat supplies in a special "container" or basket, and use the same room consistently. Devise a simple way to restore your retreat space. For instance, you might always retreat in your living room. You might fill a box with your journal, candles, crayons, your intention written on a large piece of paper, several inspirational books you are working with, and a scent you love. When the door closes on your family and you are alone for an hour, the first thing you do is grab your box and claim your space, happy to see the items that remind you of your inner life. As part of your opening ceremony, you arrange your space. Lighting the same candle, smelling the same scent, and using the same supplies help you drop into retreat space faster.

Food

When preparing to retreat, ask yourself:

- How can food help me explore my intention?

- How can food sabotage my exploration?

- How can I nurture myself with food?

For some women, food is a no-stress subject. What you eat and how you eat on your retreat don't matter a whole lot. You could enjoy creating a three-course meal for yourself, or you could eat only raw carrots and drink rice milk. You don't need to spend much time on this topic, except to be sure the food on your retreat will be adequate, nurturing, and easy to prepare. You can just prepare a robust soup, rice and beans, steamed veggies, a fresh fruit salad, or a casserole before your retreat.

For the rest of us, food is a *big* subject. Some of us don't have issues with food, but we crave to be released from the nightly cry of "What's for dinner?" and from having to compromise with other people's tastes. It helps to consider:

- How does food fit in with your intention? For example, if you are going on a retreat to learn about being kind to yourself, you might want to eat foods that you always deny yourself. Saral enjoys chocolate, fine wine, and a pipe on her retreats. "Some people think it is not 'retreaty' enough, but it never tastes as good as it does on retreat." If you are going on a retreat to explore being healthier, you might want to avoid chocolate and wine. If you are planning a lot of physical activity, have food available that fuels you, especially high protein breakfasts like oatmeal with nuts and wheat germ, peanut butter on toast, fruit and nuts, or eggs.

- Is it important that you be fed? For women responsible for the food preparation in their families or who live alone, being released from shopping, planning, and cooking feels like being twenty-five and single with money in your pocket. Choose a retreat center that has a reputation for *really* good food. Or if you are retreating at home, ask a friend (not someone like me, whose cooking repertoire is macaroni and cheese and macaroni and cheese with tomatoes) to make you lunch or dinner and deliver it to your door. Or stock up on prepared salads or sandwiches from a gourmet or health food store. Or if you can find and afford it, order great take-out before your retreat, pay for it, and give instructions that it be delivered to your door at a specific time.

- For some, cooking is a way into the interior realms that is as profound as meditating in a Japanese Zen temple or canoeing five hundred miles down a wilderness river. When Alix Kates Shulman retreated over the course of many summers to her ramshackle seashore cabin, she found learning to make salads from common dune plants, to harvest mussels, and to scavenge fish dropped by seagulls an essential way to reclaim her sense of self and gain the courage to survive an acrimonious divorce and write again. Me, I prefer to be fed. When trying to forge a better relationship with food, you could do a mini-retreat around scavenging fish or more likely around cooking a luscious meal or eating out in a nice restaurant.

- Keep your food simple and light, and try to stay away from foods that you use to tune out your inner voice. For me that would be chocolate, wine, bread, pasta, and more chocolate. These are "container breakers" for me, like the old Tupperware commercials where they burped the lid: if I eat these things, I leak energy. To eat these foods with awareness, I must choose them from a place of self-nurturing and self-kindness, not from a desire to avoid uncomfortable feelings or to prove to my critical self that I can't be trusted to let go. If you do eat foods that are "forbidden," enjoy them. Guilt is not on your guest list during a retreat.

- If overeating or eating foods that don't make you feel good is not part of your intention, retreat where your food intake can be lovingly controlled, such as a retreat center or a friend's home where she has nothing more interesting in her cupboards than chicken broth and melba toast. If retreating at home, you could lock up everything you would be tempted to munch and post a sign in the kitchen that says, "How does eating enrich or hinder my retreat?"

- If you will be visiting a retreat center, be sure they offer food and that it fits your needs. If they put out cookies and tea in the afternoon and offer dessert after dinner, will that be a problem? If the food is bad, will your retreat be ruined?

- Beware of imposing a new or restrictive food discipline during your retreat. If food is comfort for you, and if you are retreating for the first time or you have chosen a challenging intention, make a food plan that allows you some comfort. (Just one wee bag of chocolate kisses. . . .)

- Fasting is a time-honored tradition on retreats but can be risky if you are retreating alone. Don't attempt this if it is your first time fasting, if you are doing any kind of strenuous exercise, or if you will be alone in a remote area. Fast only with adequate preparation and knowledge, and if you plan to fast for longer than a day or two, you need someone to check in on you.

Stories

Stories abound of special places that women have discovered and developed in their searches for spiritual solitude. Here are two of them.

During the very stressful and prolonged proceedings to receive tenure, Professor Elizabeth Ellsworth experienced a health crisis that helped her to see both the value of self-care and the importance of retreat and solitude in that self-care. This is from her essay "Claiming the Tenured Body" in *The Center of the Web: Women and Solitude* edited by Delese Wear:

> There is an old pasture close to the farmhouse that I live in (but out of sight and sound). I had saved six straight, ten-foot-long beams out from the bundles of slab wood that we cut into 18-inch lengths for burning in the wood stove. In April, I tied the beams, one by one, to the hitch on the beat-up orange John Deere garden tractor, and dragged them to the top of the pasture. I lined them up in the place I had begun to go to last October, where I sat on a straw mat intending to read or write, but mostly found myself listening to the wind that sounded like the sea and watching the leaves turn red or yellow at the end of each day of the new semester. Everything stirred and breathed.
>
> By April, I knew I wanted to spend much time in that place. I stacked the beams like Lincoln logs to make a low and level foundation under the eight-foot by eight-foot floor of bare cedar logs that I wanted there.

I pounded nails to the thunder, lightning, rain, mud, sun, and wind that flew through the pasture all within the same half hour's time—urgent and enthusiastic visitations by each of the four elements to this tiny platform retreat. . . .

. . . Casting a space in the world where I would go to hear my breath and my heart. Where I would choose to retire in solitude—a very different form and meaning of solitude than the isolation expected by the tenure track. I sat alone with my journal, in the sun, with pens, pencils, a box of craypas, and asked: What versions of myself-in-the-academy were literally and symbolically killing me—and what versions of myself-in-the-academy might sustain my life and support my passion for learning and teaching?

Writer Valerie Andrews, in her book *A Passion for the Earth,* writes about her retreat place as a child, beautifully depicting the instinctual nature of retreat and the role of place in it:

As a child I had a secret place. Every day at sunset I visited a grove of birch trees surrounded by a hedge of sweet-smelling privet. At the center was a mound where I would lie down and listen to the steady rhythmic heartbeat of the earth. For seven years I performed this daily ritual; even in the winter I could feel this pulse as though I were connected by a rootlike umbilicus to the dark core of the land.

The grove faced west and formed a kind of kiva or womb-like container. This enclosure had all the power of an ancient shrine; it was a place of dying and becoming. As the light intensified and left the sky awash in crimson flames, I learned a way of being in the world and in transition. Something within me changed as the earth underwent its own transfiguration and as the day's activity gave way to the long, slow respiration of the night.

What Will You Do?

*Whatever the timing or the place, then and there she is able to drift into
her own being, listen and hear her own voice. Whether it speaks in
whispers of love, in screams of pain or anger, in shouts of joy, or in
silent thanksgiving, the voice is hers, hers alone. She finds the depths
and limits of her own emotions, the clarity of her thoughts. She finds
courage in her strength and ebullience and resolution to inner turmoil.*

Virginia Beane Rutter, *Woman Changing Woman*

My friend Jodie called me one day, caught in one of those harried cyclones of dashing, driving, doing. "I want to know about that retreat you just did. I need to get away," she said. As I explained what had happened on my retreat, Jodie kept interrupting to ask, "But what did you *do* on this retreat?" The allure *and* the apprehension of a woman's retreat is that span of hours stretching before you in which you will follow your inner knowing.

What will you do?

You don't need to do anything.

And besides, you already know how you need to listen and care for yourself. You just may need a little help drawing that knowledge out.

Ways to Choose What to Do

Investigate with a fresh mind what you might explore on retreat, using your intention as your guide. Here are a few ideas.

- Sit still and ask yourself, "What do I yearn to experience on this retreat?"

- Using clustering, or webbing, a technique used by Gabriele Rico in *Writing the Natural Way,* write your intention in the middle of a piece of paper. Circle it. "Now simply let go and begin to flow with any current of connections that come into your head. Write these down rapidly, each in its own circle, radiating outward from the center in any direction they want to go. Connect each new word or phrase with a line to the preceding circle. When something new and different strikes you, begin again at the central nucleus and radiate outward until those associations are exhausted." Create a map of all the associations that spring into your mind around your intention. Fill the paper up. When you are finished, it looks like a spiderweb. Read it. What patterns do you see? What are the connections between your intention and possible action? Jot down a list of things to do and another list of things not to do on your retreat. When Rhonda plans a retreat, she does a cluster on the inside of a file folder, then fills the folder with a list of possible things to do, poems, maps, photos, and journal pages: anything she may need for her retreat. She can also put what she gathers during the retreat in this folder.

  With nascent ideas, ask yourself, "How can I make this into an action that supports my intention?" and "What could I avoid doing because it does not support my intention?" When you've gathered together lots of ideas (don't worry about having too many right now), take your ideas to the next section.

- If you have some idea of what you wish to do but these have not coalesced into an intention, jot down one or two descriptive words for each of your ideas. Use a pencil. Don't do this in list form. Dot your ideas all over the page, moving quickly, adding whatever occurs to you. When you are done, circle the ideas you've written and connect any that relate to each other. Erase any ideas that don't feel right. Working backward, see if the ideas you've recorded suggest any intention. You might want to refer back to Intention.

- If you have a clear idea of what you wish to do, such as astanga yoga and journal writing, consider how you can arrange that practice to explore your intention. Let's say your intention is "How can I recharge my creativity?" How does your yoga fit? You might ask yourself, "Should I practice alone? Should I attend a retreat? Or take my usual class? Or a new class? If I choose a class, what kind of environment do I crave? What kind of teacher?" Ask yourself the same questions about journal writing. Then ask yourself, "What else do I need to explore my intention?" You can do this with timed writing or by flipping through the book and seeing if any of the practices meet that need.

- Choose a design from Retreat Plans, adjusting it however you like.

- Use the Intention Chart to locate practices that fit an intention similar to yours.

- Include elements that appeal to you from Good Ways to Listen.

- Complete the sentence "I never have time to _____ anymore" fifty times. Then see which of these things nourishes your intention.

- Keep filtering your ideas through the question "Does this support me in living the question of my intention?" or "Is this what I need right now?"

- Look over Resources and see if any of the books, videos, tapes, or other things listed there inspire you, including a retreat led by someone else. Sometimes a self-led retreat is not what you need. If, while giving thought to what you want to do on retreat, you are drawn to work with someone or your intention feels too big to explore alone, by all means, find someone to study with. Be aware of the "smorgasbord phenomenon" as you look for a guided retreat. It is easy to get seduced by all the luscious settings and teachers. But if you know why you are retreating and what you are looking for, you can find exactly what you need instead of being swept away by the richness. Remember, too, that going on a guided retreat is not an invitation to give up responsibility. It is still necessary to check in with yourself regularly and to be sure that what you are doing fits your needs and is guided by your inner knowing.

- Do not feel you have to read this entire book! There is enough here for fifty retreats, and some of it won't fit you at this time in your life—skim only what you wish. Jump into your retreat whenever you feel ready. Remember, there is no one way to do this! Be guided by your inner knowing.

The Flow of Your Retreat

What might your retreat be like moment to moment? What is a good mix of planning and not planning, of doing and being, of being with others and being alone? You want to create enough structure to aid you but not so much that you feel you have to get things accomplished. Recall the underlying purpose: to listen to your own inner knowing. Here are some retreat designs to consider:

Check Retreat Plans for templates.

See Good Ways to Listen and the section below, Check-In.

See Good Ways to Listen: Being.

See Retreat Plans for examples of balance.

- Bring little and do little. Create a simple opening ceremony and then see what happens. Nap, rock, watch the sunset and sunrise, write in your journal, read the psalms or poetry. Do what Kay Hagan calls an "intuit trip," where you follow your inner knowing for a period of time with no tasks that must be done, flowing from one thing to the next. Interact with your environment. Let solitude and silence fill you and direct you. Locate your rhythm. This is a good choice if you are retreating to heal exhaustion, overwork, or busyness or if you have no idea why you are retreating except that you *must* go. Listening then becomes your main practice.

- If a stretch of unstructured time gives you the shakes, design a precise schedule. If you always have to be somewhere, forget schedules. If you are unemployed or underemployed or have plenty of free time in your life, a specific retreat plan is a good idea. Check in as you go along and after your retreat. A schedule does not mean you have something planned for every moment. Avoid overscheduling! "Less is more" is definitely true on a retreat. You don't want to feel harried, like you are rushing to get things done. If that happens, STOP everything, sit or lie still, and do nothing for a while.

- Prepare several practices or activities you wish to do that relate to your intention, do an opening ceremony, and then see what you are drawn to do when. Put yourself in a place filled with tools that support you in exploring your intention. This pattern works well for artist retreats and for people who won't get sucked into the void, spending their retreat alphabetizing their CD collection.

- Choose an anchor activity, like getting a massage, meditation, working with a group or a friend, journal writing, painting, and so forth. Decide how often you will do this activity—say, four specific times each day. Stick to these times, but in between, float, experiment, question yourself about what you want to do. On longer retreats, you could choose an activity or focus for every few days or for each week.

- Listen to great music, read something metaphorical aloud, move your body rhythmically, be silent, be in nature, rest, bathe, ask yourself good questions, and write, draw, or sculpt all the millions of possible answers.

And some additional thoughts on design:

- The longer your retreat, the more you need to pay attention to what you will do when.

- Experiment with different designs on mini-retreats to see what feels best.

- Ask yourself, "What is the best way for me to be fully alive on this retreat?" And, "What have I done in the past to avoid being fully alive when I had time to myself?"

- If you have ever attended an all-day or weekend workshop, when did you get tired? How long can you concentrate before you need to change your channel, take a break, eat, or nap? Keep this information in mind.

- An hour or so of inner work is pretty exhausting (there is a reason why therapy sessions last only fifty minutes). Ground yourself by alternating deep inner work with soothing activities like lying on the earth, snuggling under flannel sheets, eating icy strawberries, or sipping hot tea. Make time to inhabit your body.

See Good Ways to Listen: The Smell of Your Own Sweat.

- Transitions between planned activities can be uneven or feel not as important as the activities themselves. Yet every moment of retreat is precious. "Moving between activities became as important as the activities themselves. Instead of leaping up from my meditation cushion to hurry to my walking path, I let the journey itself become the practice," writes Sylvia Boorstein in her mindfulness retreat handbook, *Don't Just Do Something, Sit There.* Transition or in-between times provide regular checking-in reminders. They also allow you to realize each moment is an opportunity to learn about yourself (a truth that often makes me scream with frustration and head for the nearest Haagen-Dazs).

In the end, you don't need to *do* much. Simply reading a bit of this book, reflecting on your need to retreat, letting go of control, and *allowing* yourself to have it will bring your retreat to life. As Sandy said, "I had no idea at the beginning of my day that I would go to the beach, remarry myself, and play the piano for the first time in two years. Before my retreat, I thought, 'Put on music and dance with myself. Yeah, right.' But I did because it was what I needed to do. The retreat had a life of its own. All I had to do was listen."

Check-In

The best way to know what to do and what not to do is to ask yourself. Check-in allows your wisdom to inform your retreat, to tell you when to sink your toes into mud, when to shoot whipped cream directly into your mouth, and when to descend into your dark, fertile depths. Check-in is a reliable way to meet your authentic self.

See Living Your Retreat Every Day: Daily Practice.

I saw the need for this inner guidance on a wilderness trip I co-led. My transformational experiences in the outdoors had come through being pushed physically, so when I led a trip, I figured the same thing would work—challenge women physically and they would have a profound experience. I was right and wrong. Mostly, the women needed to be nurtured. They pushed themselves so hard in daily life and were already so competent and accomplished, they needed the awesome comfort of the earth holding them close and the gentle rhythms of life lived outdoors to restore their own inner rhythms. Yet they also needed to be encouraged to push past what they thought they could do, physically and emotionally, because this brought increased confidence and changed their beliefs about what they were capable of. What was missing was balance: between soft and hard, between rest and pushing. I learned the importance of checking in as a group and individually.

Checking in is very simple. You center yourself (close your eyes and take a few very deep breaths, perhaps sighing on the exhale; or use your usual ways of calming and gathering yourself). Then you ask yourself a question. Any question will do. Experiment. Pick one for each day of a retreat or one for each mini-retreat. Or use one for a year, a decade, a lifetime. Here are my favorites.

*See
Contemplations
for additional
questions.*

- How do I feel in this moment?

- Am I being true to myself?

- Is there something else I want to be doing?

- What do I yearn for right now?

- Is this what I need right now?

- What do I need right now?

- What do I need to do to be fully alive right now?

- Am I comfortable? Why? Why not?

- What thoughts, people, etc., keep entering my mind?

- What can I change?

- Is this a good feeling?

It takes only a few moments. It is deceptively easy. But remembering to ask and then listening to, trusting, and following what you hear without beating yourself up can be quite a challenge.

With all this talk about listening, it has probably occurred to you to ask, "How do I know if what I hear is reliable?"

Good question.

When you are in touch with a trustworthy part of yourself, you will never be led to do anything dangerous, shaming, or rash or that has consequences that would hurt you or someone else. You will not feel pushed, prodded, guilty, or rushed. You have many interior voices. You must distinguish between the critical, pushy, judgmental voices, the voices of others (father, ex-husband, teenage daughter, seventh-grade English teacher), the voices of old complexes (for instance, an unresolved need to be in less-than-nurturing relationships or a damaging desire to punish yourself), and the voices that lead you into a truer relationship with yourself. The voices you can trust resonate in your body with a resounding clarity, like a chime rung in perfect tune. The voices you can trust may bring with them memories of a time in your life when you were in balance, when you were healthy, determined, or on your own course, or when you were a young, confident girl. The voices you want to avoid listening to want the same things they always have—for you to remain in the same safe but deadening place, for you to cudgel yourself with shame, for you to be less than fully alive. One way to distinguish between trustworthy and untrustworthy voices is to ask:

See Retreat Plans: A Half-Day Trust Retreat.

- Have I heard this voice before?

- How does my body feel when I listen? Do I feel I am opening up or shutting down? (Therapist Belleruth Naparstek advises, "Go in and listen to your body. Pay attention to internal sensations. A yes is a subtle release, a no is a tightening.")

- Am I moved to do something that makes me feel good, centered, and alive or to do something that makes me feel that I can't be trusted or that I am bad, worthless, silly, or dumb?

This checking-in process can work in any number of ways throughout your retreat. If you are feeling stuck, panicked, or unsure of what to do, quiet yourself a bit and then ask yourself, "What would make me feel truly alive?" or "What am I afraid of?" If you are having a difficult time being present or enjoying yourself, stop and inquire, "Why am I not enjoying myself?" and "What am I getting out of not enjoying myself?"

When trying to decide between reading old copies of the *Enquirer* and eating a case of frozen Butterfingers or staying with your retreat schedule, stop and ask yourself a question: "If I _____ (read the *Enquirer* and eat a dozen Butterfingers), will I learn something I need to know?" Any number of things might happen. Sometimes, especially in the beginning, you practice check-in and you hear nothing. The big zero. If that is the case, you can eat the candy while reading about two-headed aliens marrying Michael Jackson, stick to your schedule, or randomly choose a practice that interests you. Afterward, check in with yourself, asking, "Did this make me feel good, better, more centered, more me?"

Or you might hear a crystal-clear "No Butterfingers." Follow that voice, and check in afterward.

Or you might hear, "I don't care what I learn, give me my gossip and my Butterfingers." Stay put for another minute, see how this suggestion makes you feel. Do you feel relaxed, centered by this idea? Or do you feel guilty, uneasy? Ask more questions: "Do I feel relaxed because chocolate is a way out of looking at difficult stuff or because, for once, I am allowing myself to do what I wish?" Check how your body feels. Does this suggestion of candy (or of a nap, reading, or quitting and going home) make you feel you are being led into a deeper, more nourishing place? Is your body relaxed more by the suggestion? Or does your jaw tighten, your shoulders crunch? Descend through the levels of check-in. It takes practice to know what your body and spirit really need.

Another way to use this tool on retreat is to set a timer (with a nice low ring or beep) to go off at whatever interval feels good to you: every hour or perhaps four times a day. Or designate a sound in your environment that you hear fairly often (a train whistle in the distance, the caw of a crow, wind chimes). When you hear the sound, stop, center yourself however you choose, and check in with yourself using a question of your choice. As with the ancient practice of a mindfulness bell on a meditation retreat, you are brought back to being mindful of your inner knowing and of the reason you are on retreat.

You can also use your intention question as a check-in. Set your timer for regular intervals, and when it goes off ask yourself your intention question. See what occurs to you. You might use whatever you learn to change or add to your retreat.

Stories

This story on designing a retreat is from Frankie's first retreat.

> I didn't want to plan things. I wanted to be able to follow myself. Above all, I did not want a schedule. I visited an incredible retreat center. I got three massages, meditated in the meditation hall, and sat by the creek. I tried to stay away from chatter. What I learned wasn't profound, but the experience was. I came away realizing how rarely I wholeheartedly take time for myself. I came away realizing how much life is about choices,

like choosing to talk to other people or not. It isn't right or wrong, it is a choice. And I came away knowing the grieving for my divorce is going to take a long time.

Sherry, a mother with three young children, found having a retreat plan useful.

The idea of unstructured time scares the hell out of me. I needed a plan for my retreat, even if I didn't follow it step by step. It would be there when I got scared. I found my greatest struggle on retreat was trying to decide what to do. I was afraid I would waste my time, and it was such a precious weekend alone without Jack and the boys. Especially in the beginning, I was very jumpy and scattered. Then I got angry. I thought, "Why is this so hard for me?" I got really down on myself. But I worked with those feelings, and I did a lot of movement and body prayer to get calm. I had to keep reassuring myself that I was going to be all right. After a while, I was able to get into the experience. I couldn't believe how much calmer I felt by the end of the weekend. I made a lot of progress by being truly kind to myself.

Try using Emerging from Chaos.

See Retreat Plans: A Well-Being Retreat.

Barbra has a demanding job and also helps care for her aging mother.

When planning my day to retreat, I had to decide how I wanted to spend my day. I'm so used to taking care of everyone else, so used to being busy. I started feeling a lot of "shoulds" about how I should spend my day. I *should* plan the perfect retreat day. But then I stopped and said, "This is *my* day! I need to do what is right for me!"

I decided I wanted no real schedule and simply made a list of a few things that I was interested in doing. I spent a lot of time dealing with grief about the many changes that have taken place in my professional life and my family in the last year. Not all bad but all very big. I hadn't allowed myself to stop and feel before, so that was good.

In the end, what I did was not important. It was the chance to spend some time with me. To tune out from others and tune in to me.

Courage

Listening to your heart is not simple. Finding out who you are is not simple. It takes a lot of hard work and courage to get to know who you are and what you want.

Sue Bender, quoted in *The Feminine Face of God*

When I interviewed women for this book, I asked, "What would you most want to see in a book about retreating for women?" Interestingly, most said, "Permission." Permission to go. Permission to enjoy. Permission to descend. Permission to get wild. Permission to rage. Permission to be. Permission to move on. Permission to wallow. Permission to be ecstatic. I thought, "Yes, I am good at giving permission." But permission implies getting consent from someone. The only person's consent you need is your own, for if you place the power of going on retreat in someone else's hands, you are sunk. My encouragement, your best friend's prod out the door, or your partner's help taking care of the dog or the kids is useful; it can open the door. But only you can walk through it.

Do you hear a loud sucking noise? That's you pulling yourself out of your life. Nature abhors a vacuum. Something or someone will rush in to take your place.

Giving Yourself Support

Learning to support yourself is an essential retreat tool, the way you come to say yes to your time apart. There are many ways to give yourself support. You undoubtedly have ways of doing this already or you wouldn't continue to survive. Read over my favorite methods below, recall your own, use whatever works. The method you choose doesn't matter, as long as the way you support yourself is *with kindness* and honesty. Support never sounds like browbeating, never produces guilt, never threatens. Support can push you, excite you, even cause a healthy frisson of fear, but it never brings on heart-stopping anxiety. Here are two exercises for giving yourself support.

- When you are having doubts about retreating, whether at the very beginning of articulating your desire or in the middle of your retreat, grab a piece of paper and a pen and write down *everything* that you are saying to yourself about why you can't go, can't stay, or can't be present. Drag the doubts, the naysayers, the critics, the guilt, the shame into the light. You must write down your doubt or speak it aloud. Keeping it in your head lets the demons continue to feed on their own vitriol. Seeing it on the page or hearing it aloud allows you to see it for what it is: nothing useful. Sometimes this calms you enough to enjoy yourself. Other times, you will need the aid of a supportive voice that encourages you to retreat or loves you into staying with your retreat.

  To conjure this supportive voice, close your eyes and imagine someone you love very much—a child, your best friend, a sibling, your partner. Recall a time in which you supported this beloved one to be kind to himself or herself, to risk a new adventure, or to recover from a heartbreak. Hear yourself giving candid, sincere encouragement; really listen to your words. Then recall how your body felt when you were talking—righteous, determined, hopeful.

  Pick up your pen. Using the same sincere, encouraging voice you just recalled, holding the good feeling in your body, write why you *can* retreat, why you *can* enjoy yourself, why you *can* stick with it. *Talk to yourself the same way you would talk to someone you love.*

  Of course, what often happens when you start to talk to yourself this way is that the negative, harsh voices simply chorus louder. Write down or speak aloud their kvetching. Then respond with your encouraging voice. You will find yourself dialoguing back and forth between the encouraging voice and the critical voice. You want to avoid power struggles and shouting matches between these two selves. Your kind voice can use active listening skills with your critical voice, encouraging new information by saying, "Tell me more about how you feel," and asking for clarification: "What made you feel this way?" or "What do you need now to feel better?" This might sound like Sybil taking a class in communication skills, but, hey, it works.

If at any point you feel lost or stuck, close your eyes, relax your body by breathing deeply and slowly, then recall another time in which you loved and supported someone. Again, turn that attention to yourself.

You can use this technique anytime. It doesn't take long. It is always a tender way to clear up mind static.

• This exercise was drawn from Stephanie Dowrick's inspiring *Intimacy and Solitude Workbook.* Choose a word that expresses a quality you need to help you retreat. It might be *courage, spirit, energy, aliveness, determination, self-respect, self-worth, tenacity, clarity, perspective, insight,* or *stubbornness.* Write it in the middle of a sheet of paper. Close your eyes and hold that word in your imagination. Reflect on its meaning for you. What associations come to mind? Jot down any thoughts you have.

Close your eyes again. Go deeper into the word. Praise it in your mind. Desire it. Reach out to it. Remember times you have seen that quality in yourself, in others. Write down further associations, allowing them to radiate out from your seed word, weaving around the page.

Close your eyes again and assume a physical pose that reflects your word. Be, for a moment, this quality. Express it with your body, your posture, your energy, your breathing, your facial muscles. Be the quality for a few moments, then write down any additional thoughts while maintaining your physical pose.

End by reading over what you have written and summarizing what you learned by writing a few lines finishing the sentence "What I now see with regard to this quality is. . . ."

Ease into the Idea

If the idea of retreating gives you the shakes but you still feel a desire to try it, experiment with one of these practices. They can also act as little "warm-ups to self" when you do them in the hours or days before a retreat.

• Ask yourself first thing in the morning, before you even get out of bed, "What can I do to nurture myself today?" It may take a few days before you get answers, but ideas *will* bubble to the surface. You may want to jot them down in your journal; these are great clues to what you can do on your retreat.

- Visualize yourself on retreat. Do this in bed in the morning, at night before you slip off into sleep, in the shower, or on your lunch break. Take just a minute or two. See the place you will retreat. If you don't know what it looks like, fantasize. If you are retreating at home, see the room you will spend the most time in arranged just the way you want. Smell the air. What scents do you wish to inhale? Pine air? Roses? Bread baking? The tangy pungency of chaparral? See yourself in this wondrous setting. See yourself relishing a particular retreat activity, perhaps something you feel shy about or afraid of doing. Feel yourself relaxing and deepening into yourself. Perhaps you drink a tart lemonade, sip a steaming cup of mint tea, or mindfully eat a crisp apple. What are you wearing? What textures caress your skin? Feel the muscles in your face and neck softening. Hear the silence or exquisite music or the sharp cry of a hawk. Say to yourself, "I can do this. I can enjoy this."

  Notice what fantasies arise as you visualize. Before I went on a two-day retreat, I noticed that when I visualized myself sitting in morning meditation practice, tears were streaming down my face. I imagined that I was finally letting go of all the grief I was carrying. Then I stepped back and considered what a high expectation that was—letting go of *all* the grief. Noticing the fantasy helped me recognize the wish that lay behind it—to attend to grief I was carrying—and helped me open myself to grieving on this retreat. Making room for these thoughts deepened my experience considerably.

- Recall a moment when you felt authentically alive, very you, very centered and relaxed. It could be a moment from today, last week, ten years ago—a moment when making love, when holding your child, when working in your garden. Whatever first comes to your mind is perfect. Fully enter this moment. Recall how enthralled you felt, how comfortable you were in your own skin. Recall details: how your body felt, what you were wearing, who you were with, what your surroundings were. Take a minute or two to recall what each of your senses, including your heart, felt.

Getting Support from Others

While being able to support yourself internally is vital, often we also need outside help. Many of us need someone to care for our children, our pets, our businesses. We may need someone to bounce ideas off of or to give us emotional support. We may need someone to check in with so we feel connected and safe.

When Diana went on a mini-retreat, she wanted her husband Herb's support. "His first reaction was to roll his eyes. But when he saw how hurt I was and really wanted his support in this, he came around and made space for it. He knows I would do this whether he approved or not; I think it was a matter of *relating* how important the resignation and preparation for the retreat are to me." Diana learned two important things about asking for support: make it clear how important the support is to you, and don't ask for permission. We can't expect our partners and friends to read our minds. We have to risk being vulnerable by showing them how much we need their help. We have to be willing to give them time to adjust to what can seem like a strange or threatening idea. But if your partner can't get with the program, be certain you aren't asking for a blessing. To ask for support and be denied it is to know you can go elsewhere. To ask for a blessing is to know that if it doesn't come, you may not go. You may dry up and blow away waiting for it. Ask for baby-sitting, ask for emotional succor, perhaps ask for a reality check, but do not ask for permission.

Be conscious of whom you do ask for help. Don't sabotage yourself by asking for help from someone who will make you feel frivolous, selfish, or guilty. Your support person must be someone who is both responsible (she isn't going to encourage you to take a month off when you've been working at your job only two weeks) and imaginative (he sees past obstacles you think are insurmountable). Most of all, she or he must believe in your right to retreat. And if you think you know no one to help you, consider asking a therapist, a spiritual director, or a retreat coordinator or even calling someone at a crisis intervention line; there are options for everyone.

After you ask someone for their support, you must let the support in. I know very few women who don't have trouble receiving emotional support, whether in the form of compliments, offers of help, or emotional sustenance. Yet when we block emotional support, we reinforce the idea that we are unlovable and unworthy. Let's say you ask your partner to support you in going away for a weekend retreat, and he or she says, "Yes! Honey, you deserve this. You need this. What can I do?" What if, instead of feeling supported, you pick a fight? "You could never do it. I'll have to cook and freeze casseroles, catch up on the laundry, and leave you a printed schedule for the kids' weekend activities. By the time I get ready to go on this retreat, I'll be too exhausted. Forget it." Or what if you suddenly find yourself losing interest in going? Of course, this is all hypothetical. None of *us* would sabotage the emotional support that a partner offered or block the help that is needed to make a retreat a reality. No way, not us.

When we ask for help, we reveal ourselves as frail human beings with needs instead of invincible mythical combinations of Mother Teresa, Jane Fonda, Oprah Winfrey, and Martha Stewart. When we ask for help, we may also have to face how much we have been doing for others that they could have been doing for themselves. We may be brought face-to-face with how isolated we have become and the reality that there may be no one with whom we feel close enough to ask for help. All of this can be enough to stop us cold. It can simply feel too frightening to ask for help or to let it in. Work with your fear. Dare to ask for help. Dare to accept the offers of dog-sitting and casseroles. Dare to have your reality confirmed: "Yes, you do need a retreat. Go for it!"

See Softening Fear, below.

Support on Retreat

On certain retreats, you need to be held. You need another soul to be thinking about you, sending you good thoughts and energy. Or you may need to know someone who can contact you in case of an emergency. If you are retreating in the middle of a busy household, you may need someone outside your room fielding phone calls, keeping kids quiet, leaving meals. Or you may need someone you can contact if you need specific help (for example, your meditation teacher for help with your meditation practice) or emotional support (a close friend to talk over grief about losing your job). Or you may simply need someone close by during your retreat, reassuring you that you are connected to the world and safe.

Needing support on a retreat can puzzle some women, as in, "But I thought I was retreating to be by myself. Why would I want to have anyone near?" For others, support on a retreat can be a very welcome notion, one that makes retreating a comforting and exciting possibility instead of a lonely, daunting impossibility. The most important thing about arranging support on retreat is that if you want it, get it. If your heart whispers for a little companionship or reassurance and you don't heed that whisper, your retreat may be compromised. As I've already said, if you don't feel safe (physically and emotionally) on retreat, little will happen. You can't be guided by your inner knowing because the static of fear or worry will be too loud. When in doubt, arrange for support.

If you are going on a retreat of longer than a day or two, consider designating a check-in person. A mind game that can happen on longer retreats is that you become convinced something awful has happened at home. Your child has contracted malaria, your colleague at work has gone schizoid and is telling everyone you are embezzling millions, or you left the iron, stove, and blow dryer on and your house is engulfed in a five-alarm fire. Knowing that you have a check-in person who knows how to reach you, and that everyone important in your life knows how to reach that person in an emergency, creates an effective anxiety buster. Your check-in person interrupts you only in an emergency. (Define emergency before you leave; it is not running out of toilet paper, getting stood up by some jerk, or losing car keys.)

Another kind of support you can arrange for is asking someone to think about, pray for, or visualize or meditate on behalf of you during your retreat. You can even set aside certain times of the day for both of you to sit in meditation or pray. When someone does this for you, you feel connected and remembered, and it reinforces your sense that your retreat is valuable and worthwhile.

Having someone who is skilled in matters of the psyche or spirit available to you, either in person or by phone, is an excellent idea if you are feeling particularly anxious about retreating, if you are retreating to deal with strong, heavy subjects, or if you are practicing a spiritual discipline in which you need guidance from time to time. Choose an experienced retreat coordinator (available at retreat centers, churches, temples), a spiritual director, or a therapist as your support person. In some instances, a very balanced and loving friend can also fulfill this kind of support, but choose wisely and don't settle for a friend when you want more professional help because you don't think you are worth it.

See Retreating with Others for more options and Retreat Plans: A One-Day Retreat with a Friend.

Not that support from friends and spouses isn't valuable. When retreating in the middle of a busy home, spouses and roommates can be invaluable in keeping others away from your room or rooms, in preparing meals, perhaps even in silently meeting you for meditation once or twice a day. You might also ask a friend to be your retreat partner; the two of you retreat at the same time although alone in your own homes, with certain times set aside to talk on the phone or walk silently in nature together. Sharing your solitary experiences in this way can also enhance your retreat.

As you form your plans for retreat, listen if you need to be sustained by others. Too often we are more comfortable doing the sustaining than asking to be sustained. Asking for support and allowing yourself to need could prove to be the central teaching of your retreat.

Softening Fear

Many of us fear being alone. May Sarton captured this in *Journal of a Solitude* when she wrote, "My need to be alone is balanced against my fear of what will happen when suddenly I enter the huge empty silence if I cannot find support there. . . . It may be outwardly silent here but in the back of my mind is a clamor of human voices, too many needs, hopes, fears." On retreat, everything you ordinarily do is gone: answering phones, wiping noses, entertaining clients, carpooling, writing reports, scrubbing the bathroom tile. When you're in the middle of your crazy, repetitive life you think, "If I could just get a break." But when you finally get that break, you may feel unmoored, anxious, frightened by the open stretch, the field of possibility. Life's busyness dries us out, but it also provides a fabulous escape, allowing us to fend off disturbing questions and feelings, enabling us to keep from looking too closely at ourselves or our relationships. Some of your fear may be fear of change, of the unknown. This is a fear that I believe is hardwired into our brains; it is inescapable. So notice it, give yourself room to feel it, and then keep moving forward toward your intention. You may be afraid of feeling a bottomless rage, a floating sadness, a wild joy, an intimacy with the Divine. You may be afraid of losing your connection to others, for who are you if you aren't a wife, mother, lover, daughter, friend, success or failure, baker or writer? Mostly, I believe, fear arises because we are afraid of seeing our truth, of getting to know the bare bones of who we are and what we feel, with no busyness or relationship to distract us.

Mary Beth Holleman recounts in her essay "The Wind in My Face" in *Solo*:

> This is among the safest places to camp in Prince William sound. . . .
> I've got plenty of water and food, a dry tent, a hand-held radio. . . .
> I know I am safe. My fear of being alone is a fear of finding out what
> I'm feeling.

Alone we have no distractions to invoke. On retreat, when you start to feel sorrow about something that happened five years ago, you can't turn on the TV or start a conversation with a roommate. When you have set aside time to reflect on a decision, you are forced to look at past choices you may regret and be honest with yourself about what you truly want.

Fear is good. It is the first step toward waking up from the deadening trance of modern life. It can sharpen your senses, engage your interest, widen your vision, light a fire under your kettle, clarify your intention, and glue you to it until you come out the other side having turned fear into knowledge.

When we are alone, we may worry about being disconnected, missing something, being abandoned, never being chosen again. When you choose solitude, you are forced to remember all the times you had it and didn't want it and all the times you wanted it and couldn't get it. Memories of riding home from a bar in the back seat because your date ran into his old girlfriend and *had* to give her a ride home (but why are *you* sitting in the back seat?) may flood your mind during a meditation session. Or you may find yourself obsessing over a meeting you know is taking place while you are gone. "How many comments will be made about my absence?" Or worse, "What if no one even notices I'm gone?"

Any retreat outside your home, even an afternoon stroll in a park, brings up physical safety issues. This fear is real. Women alone are often women in danger. Women alone are women vulnerable to assault. You must provide for your safety. Take only acceptable risks. Yet be aware that fear can very effectively oppress us. It is a fine line between acting responsibly and letting fear for your physical safety turn you into a prisoner.

Here are some practices you can use when you feel fearful.

- Before you retreat, talk with your fear. It is less frightening to have this conversation while you are still ensconced in your life, although talking with your fear is a very useful practice to use on retreat as well.

  See Good Ways to Listen for a definition of spontaneous writing.

  Read over what you wrote in Intention in response to "What I fear happening on a retreat is. . . ." Sit at a table with two chairs. Become your fear. Do it with your posture, your face, your breath. (Yes, you may feel silly. No one will see you or know what you are doing, and anyway, stopping because you feel silly is as effective as stopping because you are afraid.) Now, spontaneously write as fear, answering the question "Fear, what do you want?" After you have explored that question thoroughly, move to the other chair and be yourself. What do you want to ask your fear? Do so, in writing or aloud. Physically move back and forth between chairs and roles until you feel done. If you feel stuck, use these additional questions to keep your dialogue going:

    Fear, what are you hiding?

    Fear, what gifts do you bring me?

    Fear, how can we work together on this retreat?

  After doing this, can you pinpoint one or two simple actions you can take to help you work with your fear so that you can continue? Concentrate especially on satisfying fears about your physical safety.

- Remind yourself your solitude is chosen. "I must trust that if I choose to spend time alone, the rest of the world, my world, will still be there for me when I am ready to return. I must trust that my friends will not abandon me if I choose to spend time by myself; I must trust that I will not lose control or power by being alone, apart for awhile," writes Mara Sapon-Shevin in "Reclaiming the Safety of Solitude" in *Women and Solitude*. She ends her essay with

> I can choose to be alone.
> I can be alone and still be fully connected.
> I can be alone and completely powerful.
> I can be alone with myself, not hiding from others.
> I can be alone and safe, alone and strong.

Make up your own mantra, your own poem of strength that addresses your fears. Recite it whenever you feel the need.

- If your level of anxiety about retreating feels too high or if your mood swings are very wide, from anxiety to elation, start with a mini-retreat of a few hours or a half-day.

- Remember that experiencing fear, confusion, loneliness, boredom, anger, or other uncomfortable feelings during your retreat is a normal, even unavoidable, response. Staying with your feelings is the only way to transform them into something more whole.

See Uncomfortable Beginnings, Middles, and In-Betweens and Gathering the Whole: The Feeling Spiral

Sabotage

Getting ready to retreat can sometimes feel like launching an international spy mission: people are out to get you. Your child suddenly needs you. Your dog has to go to the vet. Your mother can't be left alone. Every weekend is filled with houseguests and parties. You get a bad chest cold.

When sabotage strikes, your courage and resolve are desperately needed, along with the negotiation skills of a United Nations executive.

To go on a retreat is to invite change. Change provokes anxiety. You and the people you are in relationship with have a lot invested in things staying the way they are. When you say, "I am taking some time for myself," the alarm bells go off. Inevitably, you will encounter resistance, both from within yourself and from others.

The trickiest kind of sabotage is self-induced. Sometimes a cold is just a cold, sometimes it is a ruse you produce to trick yourself out of going, and sometimes getting a cold before a retreat is your psyche and body's way of saying, "I'm not ready to do this. Hold up."

How do you know the difference between self-sabotage that springs from fear and what appears to be self-sabotage but is instead a well-founded message of caution from your psyche? When are you are creating obstacles out of fear of being intimate with yourself, resistance to getting what you truly want, and fear of what others might think, and when do you need to slow down, alter your plans, or listen to your worries?

See Stuck in the Airport of Life.

Ask yourself. Be quiet and check in with yourself. "Why am I dragging my feet about retreating?" Look at your behavior. Does it feel self-protective, like you just can't get the energy together to plan your retreat or nothing interests you much? Perhaps you are trying to slow yourself down and need to wait a few days. When I am procrastinating, if I stop relentlessly pushing myself and simply wait, after a few days or weeks something shifts, and suddenly, easily, I am able to move forward. I work at differentiating between resistance that needs to be honored because the time is not ripe, and resistance that springs from self-loathing or fear.

Self-sabotage that does spring from fear feels suspiciously self-damaging, like when you keep "forgetting" to call the retreat center. When every day after you have shared another bitch fest lunch with colleagues, on the walk back to work, you look longingly at a tucked away cafe where you know resides the sweetest, privatest little corner window seat, just perfect for a retreat in the world.

How can you help yourself and discern when to move forward and when to change tactics? Scan this list to see which suggestions resonate.

See Courting Yourself.

- Do you feel you need more love and nurturance? Resistance grows when you hate yourself for having it. Always, always listen to your resistance. Talk to her—ask her why she is hanging around. Take her out to eat. Give her little gifts. Have faith in yourself that you will go when you are ready. Faith and self-kindness create trust.

- Look for the family messages. Are you challenging family myths by taking time alone? Did your mother retreat? Your grandmother? What would your sister, cousin, brother, father say about this venture of yours? Do you feel guilty that you are giving yourself something that other women in your family could not give themselves? What role has the work ethic played in your history? What messages about self-care and leisure time did you imbibe while growing up? What beliefs do you hold now?

- Take a mini-retreat or a retreat in the world instead, or scale back your plans.

- Use *positive* self-talk to get some energy going.

See Courage.

- Ask, "Is there something I need to alter in my plan that will make me feel better about going?" Perhaps you are challenging yourself without proper preparation. Perhaps you have consented to go with others when you really want to be alone.

- Retreat with someone else, reserve a room or cabin and put down a nonrefundable deposit, or engage in plans that are difficult to extract yourself from.

- Recognize the beliefs you hold about taking time for yourself. Are you having a hard time going because you don't think you are worth it? Do you feel it might be dangerous to declare yourself separate? Perhaps you are experiencing "an underlying discomfort with separateness and individuality that has its roots in our early family experience, where the unspoken expectation may have been that we keep a lid on our expressions of self," writes psychotherapist Harriet Lerner in her classic *The Dance of Anger.* It can help to remember that you are choosing your solitude and to make plans for connecting with people you love upon your return. This is especially true for women who live alone.

See Returning Home.

- Ask yourself, "How will I feel if I don't retreat?" If the answer is "Good" or "Relieved," you may want to put this off for a while or try a short mini-retreat or talk with someone who knows your life and personality. If the answer is "Sad," "Bereft," "I need to go," then you must work with your resistance and go.

What about when others are resisting your desire to have some time alone? Partners, children, parents, and friends can be threatened when you say, "I need some time alone." We may encounter hurt feelings: "What's wrong with our relationship? Aren't you happy? Why do you want to spend your free time alone when you could spend it with me? Don't you love me, mommy?" We may be accused of being selfish, self-centered, or spoiled, as "In my day, women never did that." Doris Grumbach wrote in *50 Days of Solitude,*

> I had told people of my intention to be alone for a time. At once I realized they looked upon this declaration as a rejection of them and their company. I felt apologetic, even ashamed, that I would have wanted such a curious thing as solitude, and then sorry that I had made a point of announcing my desire for it. I should have hidden the fact that I wished to be alone, "like a secret vice," as Anne Morrow Lindbergh described it in *Gift from the Sea.*

What can you do?

- Be ready for opposition. When you are doing mini-retreats, the cries of "I need you" will be less. The longer and larger your retreats, the more resistance or "countermoves" you will encounter. Your job is "to keep clear about [your] own position in the face of a countermove—not to prevent it from happening or to tell the other person that he or she should not be reacting this way," writes Harriet Lerner. She goes on to say that to control the reactions of people around us is impossible. "We not only want to make a change; we want the other person to like the change that we make." Doesn't that sound familiar? Realize you can be sympathetic to others' negative reactions, but you can neither control those reactions nor let them stop you.

- Clarify your position. Why are you retreating? Information can dispel anxiety. Tell your child. Tell your partner. Sometimes we create trouble by acting fishy because we don't believe what we are doing is worthwhile. When we are confident and sure, we communicate a cleaner, clearer message. If necessary, pretend you are confident, for acting confident can inspire true confidence.

- If you are feeling guilty about leaving your family, partner, or job, use that guilt to show yourself what you need to do before you leave. If I am feeling guilty about leaving my daughter for a weekend, I can examine that guilt. What part feels real and what part feels ancient and compulsive? Maybe I can skip yoga for one week to spend more time with my daughter and concentrate on being truly present when I am with her. I can wrap up a little present for my partner, Chris, to give to her while I am gone. I can affirm to myself that she will be with Chris, her father and an equal partner in raising her. Of course, there is danger in this approach, for you may overfunction, doing for others what they could do for themselves and burning out before you get away.

Use Check-In to prevent this from happening.

- Saral, a massage therapist and longtime retreatant, feels that it is important to take responsibility for taking a retreat. Before a three-month retreat, she "wrote a hundred cards for my husband, each for a different reason. 'If you miss my body,' 'If you miss my hands,' 'If you are angry with me,' etc. On each card I wrote him a little note or a quote. This way it didn't feel all about me. It's important not to blow off the people you are in relationship with." Jan left hidden notes for her nine-year-old daughter, including one wrapped around the toothpaste ("You remembered without me nagging. You're the best!"). On retreat, Alice found two fire stones, which, when struck together, make sparks. She gave these to her partner and told him they symbolized her experience. "Sometimes I literally felt like I was on fire. Other times I felt like I was flickering out."

When You Retreat, You Retreat for the World

When you retreat, you are retreating for everyone in your life. *Your retreat affects others.* Benefits are felt by the people around you. Picture the medieval anchoress in her cell. She inspired and influenced an entire city by her example. You may only set out for a drive or a walk, but your example will affect others, too. You are showing the people in your world that women can value time for themselves. Taking time away to affirm your values may lead you to make better decisions in the world or to parent better or to remember someone old and forgotten in your community. When you retreat, you refuel, and this allows you to return able to give more authentically. Away from the world, you will find that ideas on how to enrich the lives of others will occur to you spontaneously, along with the energy to implement those ideas. You are not being selfish in going on a retreat, for the definition of the word *selfish* is a "total disregard for others." When you retreat, you are showing how much you value the people you love, because when you return you will be able to give from your abundance of energy and love instead of scraping the bottom of the barrel for a few leftover dregs. You replenish the energies of others on a psychic level and can shift stuck relationships to new ground. On Buddhist retreats, the benefits of the retreat are dedicated to someone, often "for the benefit of all sentient beings." Remember that any retreat, any conscious time you take for yourself with an open heart, creates change.

Stories

This is McKenna's story of her first retreat.

> I was looking for a way to connect to that something that I describe as the center energy of the universe (or of all the universes). I believe all of nature comes from that source, and I have wanted to connect to it and be in rhythm with it in some way.

My intention was, "How could I be alone in nature as a first step in trusting nature and trusting myself?" As much as I have wanted to connect with nature, I have become increasingly and paralyzingly fearful of it. I wanted to shift out of my comfort zone and take a risk.

I started out for my retreat on a drizzling morning. I planned to spend about two hours alone on some undeveloped oceanfront acreage but when I got there and looked into its rugged terrain, a huge wave of fear came over me and I said out loud, "I *can't* go in there." I headed off to find another trail I knew of, but when I got there, I saw a small clearing, no trail, and dense forest beyond. I couldn't head into that wilderness either.

By now I felt like a failure. I was ready to go home. I persevered because I didn't want to disappoint myself. I drove to the botanical gardens (a large outside garden) and gave myself permission to take my first steps into nature there.

At the beginning of the trail, I had my opening ceremony. It was a moment when I breathed deeply and repeated to myself several times, "I am completely safe." As I walked along the trail for the first ten minutes I encountered a few people, all of whom were a great comfort to me. During the second ten minutes I encountered no one. I felt isolated and vulnerable, and a wave of fear came over me. I turned around and headed back, so I could be near people. During my forty-five minutes in nature I had moments of taking in the awesome majesty of life, this planet, this universe. I also had great moments of fear. My closing ceremony was thanking the space where I had been and the universe for protecting me. I also made a promise to come back and take another baby step "into the wild"!

Beginnings

Opening Ceremony

A retreat is moving consciously and by my own choice
into space where I can be alone with the Divine.

Marion Woodman

Your opening ceremony is how you step into retreat time. It is the activation of the archetype, the metaphorical action that marks the threshold of betwixt-and-between. It is when you turn off the electricity, light candles, lengthen your breath, smooth out your brow, let your shoulders sag, and stop concentrating on everything you should be doing. What your opening ceremony does is say, "Now." Like all meaningful ritual, it connects you with our common ancestors who, for tens of thousands of years, have performed their own versions of what you are about to create: a ceremony to help them withdraw, to stretch out, to study the landscape inside.

All ceremony ideally rises from your heart, from an authentic and clearly articulated desire to bring about a transformation. A willingness to let go and trust that you can find the best way, a suspension of your critical mind, and a clear intention are the key ingredients that bring a ceremony to life. Not coincidentally, these are also three of the elements of a satisfying retreat. However, this doesn't mean you have to stage a personal Mardi Gras. Simple is good. If you are doing mini-retreats, you might design a short ceremony you can repeat often. If you are leaving your life for a long weekend or a week, you might devote several hours or even most of a day to your ritual, letting it evolve in several stages. As one woman said to me, "Where your intention is, that's where your energy flows."

Any actions can make up an opening ceremony. Preparing to drive to your retreat location can be a ceremony. Buckle yourself in while breathing deeply, turn on soothing music, ask for a blessing from the Divine before you turn on the ignition, and drive mindfully, blessing each person you pass. If you are retreating at home, you can firmly close the door of your bedroom, lock or tape the door shut, burn incense, call in the Divine, do a few yoga asanas, and read from an inspiring book.

A Few Guidelines

Relax. You've been doing ceremony your whole life. From make-believe weddings between Barbie and Ken to Thanksgiving dinner, we are all experts at ceremony. Suspend your disbelief.

- Your ceremony will come to life as you contemplate your intention. Your intention might be "For the next twenty-four hours I intend to ask myself, How can I be more quiet inside?" So you might let silence and slowness inhabit your ceremony. If your intention is "For the next four hours I want to ask myself, How can I release my anger at my cancer?," you might think about elements of ceremony that allow release, cleansing, and dialoguing with the cancer.

See Good Ways to Listen.

- Center yourself. Walk meditatively and take in your environment with all your senses, do a series of yoga asanas, write down everything that comes into your head for ten minutes, lie on the earth and look at the sky, run, swim, canoe, do the dishes—do anything that begins to still you. One familiar centering practice is to prepare your retreat container by creating sacred space. If you are retreating at home, this is especially important. You may find the centering part of your ceremony going on for quite a while because it can take time to soothe monkey mind. Listen to yourself. Trust that the pace and content of your retreat will unfold perfectly.

See Where Will You Retreat?: Retreating at Home.

What centering practice appeals to you right now? Choose something comforting yet not too familiar. You want to shake up your perceptions even as you are calming down and turning inward.

See Good Ways to Listen.

- Find and carry out a metaphorical action that symbolizes leaving your everyday life. It can be anything: locking the front door behind you, crossing a bridge, stepping over a threshold, mailing a letter that contains all your doubts, swimming or bathing, dressing or arranging your hair in a new way, cleaning out drawers or closets, sweeping, climbing a mountain or tree or tall building, baking bread, planting seeds or bulbs. Choose an action that speaks to your interests or your imagination. Don't sweat over it—again, it doesn't have to be big or embellished or difficult. You give the action meaning by willingly suspending your disbelief. It is the difference between saying to yourself, "I'm just entering my own front door and saying a few words," and thinking, "I am crossing over into retreat time. This is no longer my home, it is my haven. When I step through this doorway, I enter altered time, outside my ordinary life."

What action floats into your head right now? Just let it come. You don't have to do it if it feels too big. But let it occur to you.

- Give voice to your yearnings. Sound has been used for eternity to open, soothe, give birth to, and harmonize the body and the mind. Research has shown that sounds or tones like the Sanskrit *om* ("Aum"), when resonated through sand or oil, arrange the substance into astonishing mandala-like patterns, patterns that echo the ancient, healing mandalas of many cultures. It is not such a leap to believe sacred sounds could also arrange healing mandalas *inside* our bodies, which are 98 percent water. Singing a childhood hymn, drumming, chanting *om* for a minute, chanting words and sounds that spontaneously arise, ringing a melodious bell, caressing a Tibetan bowl, belting it out along with your favorite opera, or listening for the silence between chords of a symphony can all open your heart.

What sounds make you feel alive? What sounds are sacred to you? What sacred sound have you always wanted to make? (It doesn't matter if you can't carry a tune.)

- Call on the Divine as you know it. Invoke your vision of Spirit to place your retreat in the hands or context of something larger than yourself. Let words pour from your heart, recite the Buddhist Loving-Kindness Meditation, see yourself as part of the web of creation, ask for a blessing *See Resources.* from the powers of the four directions, or read a spirited poem or passage from your scripture.

How have you always wanted to ask for Divine love? What words have you wanted to cry out? What image of the Divine do you wish to entreat or connect to? Now is the moment to do it.

- Make an offering. Gather flowers from your garden and give them to a stranger, put bird seed and water on your balcony, write a check to your favorite charity, plant a tree on your city block. As Loren Cruden, midwife and herbalist, writes in *The Spirit of Place,*

An offering is your spokesperson, so you want to inform it with your asking and your gratitude. You want to be sure it is representative of your best. You infuse it with love.

To whom do you want to make an offering? Spirit, your grandmother, mother, the muse of your particular art form, the earth, the place you are retreating, or perhaps your family for helping you go? How could your offering illustrate your interrelatedness to all of creation and your spirit of service to yourself and others?

- Impress all of your senses. The scent of a rose, the soothing weight of a cotton sweater, the sunny faces of cosmos and bachelor buttons, a photo of a beloved spiritual teacher, a patchouli candle burning, a fresh breeze blowing through your hair, a bowl of cool water, a succulent grape popping in your mouth—all these signal to your body that you love it, that you plan to please it and learn from it in the coming hours or days.

- Go from general to more specific, from relaxed to focused. For example, you might start your ceremony with some movement, then move into journal writing, then into meditation.

For Experienced Retreatants

Think about what worked for you on past retreats and what didn't. Don't necessarily repeat what is familiar, for one of the challenges of being a dedicated retreatant is to continue to stir things up. Another is to confront the expectations that have been built from previous luminous experiences. Your role is to create a ceremony that doesn't leave you blasé.

Stories

This is what Hannah's opening ceremony looked like for a two-day retreat at home:

> I helped my husband and child get off to his father's house for two days. As soon as their car drove away, I set a timer and allowed myself thirty minutes to clean the three rooms I was going to be in: my bedroom, bath, and living room. I did the tasks that make me feel ordered and taken care of, which included storing all the toys and shutting the doors on dirty rooms. Then I worked in the garden for as long as I

liked, concentrating on breathing in the beauty of the world, feeling the earth under my feet, and then arranging the flowers I picked.

I took a long soak with lavender oil and did lots of beauty preparations, considering that instead of making myself ready to greet a man or to be admired by others, I was making myself ready to greet and be admired by my deepest, truest self. I got into the spirit of anticipation and really decked myself out, but I was still comfortable. Then I laid out my materials for my first practice, got into my car, put on music, and drove slowly on back roads to a small bridge about two miles from my home. I left my car in a parking lot where I knew it would be safe for the weekend. I stood at the foot of that bridge, thinking about my intent. Feeling silly but daring myself to get into the spirit of it, I spoke something like this aloud: "I am leaving my everyday life behind. I am entering retreat space. My family is safe and well taken care of. I am worth this time. I can maintain my focus. My intention on this retreat is to spend forty-eight hours asking myself, Who am I and what do I need? I am ready to devote myself wholeheartedly to that question." Then I took a deep breath and, singing a childhood song, I walked slowly over the bridge. When I got to the other side, I said, "I am ready!" Then I walked home, very aware that I was now in altered space and not talking to or acknowledging anyone.

See Portrait of Your Authentic Self.

This was Brenda's opening ceremony for a mini-retreat in a park:

I came home from work early, took a quick shower, and put on my favorite sweats, warm from the dryer. I found myself moving too quickly, so I tried to breathe and count backward. I rode my bike to the park. That helped a lot. As part of my preparation, I had packed my retreat supplies several days before and visited the park to find a spot that felt good to me, so it was kind of exciting to take my bag and walk purposefully to my tree in a private corner (but close enough to people to feel safe). Then I made a circle around me from dried rosebuds, sprayed myself with rose water, and chimed my friend's Tibetan bells, which I had borrowed. I lay down with an eye pillow over my eyes. I went over my intention in my mind. I reminded myself I was going to come back here many times and I didn't have to get it right or do it all right now. I prayed for Mary, who I relate to the most, to be with me, to help me relax and be open. I lay quietly, listening to my breath and feeling the earth under me, letting my body be supported.

This is the ceremony I often did when trying to create retreat space in my office:

I gather everything I need from downstairs: water, matches, votive candles, fresh flowers. Upstairs, I straighten up or dust my desk and shrine. I light a candle under a diffuser with essential oils and another on my shrine. Then I state my intention for the day and how long I will maintain this retreat space. My intention might be "On this retreat, I intend to ask myself, How can I create an opening ceremony that helps and inspires women?" I burn sage or sweetgrass (which reminds me of rituals I have participated in at my friend's camp, Northwaters) and call in the powers of the four directions and Great Mystery, asking each direction for one of its specific qualities to help me. I do this because my strange little office is five sided, so it seems natural. Then I meditate for a few moments, focusing on being empty. If I have to leave my office, I try to maintain retreat space, which means not doing dishes or laundry, listening to messages on the answering machine, calling a friend, or consuming vast amounts of Ben & Jerry's English Toffee frozen yogurt. When I start to lose my intention, I restate it, spritz myself with lavender and geranium water, or do a few yoga stretches on the tiny deck outside my office.

See Renewing Your Spiritual Direction: Empty Vessel.

Ceremony

Find a quiet place. Center yourself by counting backward from four to one on each successive outbreath. Do this for two or three minutes or as long as you wish. Then let go of the counting and watch your mind quieting. When your attention wanders, recall your retreat intention. Listen quietly, without strain. What do you hear? When your mind wanders again, ask yourself silently, "What am I asking of this ceremony?" Listen. Ask that the perfect ceremony be revealed to you.

You may receive several specific ideas or an interesting image or nothing at all. You may want to repeat this meditation a few times; it is an excellent way to prepare to retreat.

Another way to create ceremony is to ask yourself a series of questions, perhaps journaling with each for a few minutes.

- What ceremonies or rituals have I participated in in the past that I found moving, replenishing, uplifting? What elements could I repeat for myself comfortably and authentically?

- How have I relaxed and centered myself before in ways that really worked?

- What kind of offering could I make to help me see my retreat as an act of love and service for all creation? And to help me see my interconnectedness to all?

- What poems, prose passages, or inspirational words do I love?

See Retreat Plans for more examples.

A Sample Ceremony

Here is one way to enter retreat space. It is offered as a template, a jumping-off point. You may read it and be inspired to do something completely different, or you may wish to follow it closely. Do whatever feels true to you. Be willing to switch horses midstream.

This was created for a woman retreating at home but can be adapted easily to a retreat center or outdoor area.

- Prepare.

    A large piece of paper and colored pens or paint.

    Art supplies such as beads, glitter, feathers, a photo of you.

    A piece of writing that inspires you and moves your spirit and relates to your intent.

    A Do Not Disturb sign and an answering machine.

    An offering.

    Lotion *and* a new scented soap, oil, or bath gel that you bought just for the retreat. (Save some of this new scent or product to use in future retreats or in everyday life to remind you of your retreat.)

- Write your intention in bright colors on the largest piece of paper you have. Draw around it, paste pictures or photos next to it, decorate it with flowers, glitter, doodads. Place your intention where you can see it.

- Take a few deep breaths, then read aloud the inspiring text you chose.

- Make your sacred space come alive. Unplug and hide the phone, put a message on your answering machine that informs callers you won't be returning their calls and what to do in a real emergency, cover the TV with a cloth or wheel it into the closet, put the Do Not Disturb sign on your front door, put away all signs of work and all distractions like magazines, bills, correspondence, unfinished craft projects, or food you don't want to eat. (If you have to take your ice cream and Pop-Tarts to your neighbors, do so.)

- When your retreat space feels enclosed, safe, magical, and warmed up, take a purifying bath (or swim or shower). Use a soap or bath gel that you buy specifically for this purpose or essential oils like grapefruit or neroli (which are biodegradable and can be placed on a washcloth). After a nice long soak or brisk paddle, bathe your head and say aloud, "I am washing away all my busy thoughts. My mind is clearing." Bathe your shoulders and say, "I am washing away all my tension. My body is softening." Bathe your heart and say, "I am washing away all my worries. My heart is opening." Bathe your hands and repeat, "I am washing away all my responsibilities. My hands are empty." Bathe your feet and recite, "I am washing away all exhaustion. My feet are relaxed." And finally, bathe your entire body with long strokes, saying, "I am washing away my ordinary life. There is nothing I need to do now but be here, with my most precious self." This last line can become your retreat mantra, to return to anytime you feel yourself being sucked out of retreat time and into everyday cares. If you are retreating in a city with noises all around or if you must check the phone machine for a *very* crucial phone call during your time off or if the UPS person rings your doorbell or if your child must return to get something she forgot, this is a good mantra to hold on to.

- After your bath, anoint yourself lovingly with lotion or oil, chosen especially for this retreat. Concentrate on giving attention to the parts of your body you dislike. Do something new to yourself—fix your hair differently, put on makeup or don't, go braless or don't, wear jewelry you save for important occasions, shift your habitual view of your body. Eschew the tattered sweats or yellowed bathrobe you always wear when relaxing. Wear something you have forgotten in your closet or are saving for a special occasion, sew a ceremonial robe, borrow a leotard and flowing flowered dress from a good friend, or go naked (for the truly courageous).

- Make an offering to whomever or whatever feels appropriate: to your Divinity, to the land you are retreating on, to your retreat coordinator, to your partner for helping you arrange the free time.

- This gentle half–sun salutation will get your body involved. If you are elderly or physically disabled, try this sitting down.

Stand with your feet together, big toes touching but ankles apart (you can also stand with your feet hip-width apart if this is more comfortable). Let your arms hang loosely at your sides. Close your eyes. Inhale. Exhale. Start at your scalp and move down to your toes, scanning your body. How does it feel? Does any part feel tight, dense, fearful? How about light, loose, open? Spread your toes and then root them into the floor. Draw your hips back in line with your ankles. Roll your shoulders back and down. Feel your spine lengthening as if there were a string extending from the crown of your head into the heavens. Tuck your chin slightly to further extend your spine. Breathe deeply in and out through your nose. Pause here for a few breaths. Sink into the sensation.

Bring your hands into prayer position over your heart. Recite your retreat intention out loud, with a great and open heart. Then drop your hands to your sides and, as you inhale, sweep your arms up and over your head, extending out through your shoulders, with strong legs and feet. Bring your palms together over your head and look up. Exhale and bend at the hips, swooping forward, arms out and down, head coming toward your shins. Hang here for a moment, clasping opposite elbows with your hands. Shake your head yes. Shake your head no. Relax your neck. Breathe. On an inhale, release your hands and swoop your arms out to the side and up as you lift your torso up. Once again, bring your hands over your head, palms together, and look up. On an exhale, return your hands to prayer position in front of your heart.

Repeat this several times. Each time you return to prayer position, state your intention again. Try to do so joyfully. Imagine your heart opening to the delight and possibility of your retreat. When your body feels looser and warmer, end in prayer position. Scan your body again. Imagine that your deep breaths are a prism of colored light and that you are sending this warm light to any areas that are tight or fearful. Expand your chest by rolling your shoulder blades down and toward each other.

Focus your attention on the base of your spine. Breathe into this area with a warm, full breath and chant aloud the sound *lam* three times. Take your time and use your entire exhale to make the sound. La-a-am, la-a-am, la-a-am.

Next, center your attention just below your navel. Inhale into this area and sing out three times the sound *vam*. va-a-am, va-a-am, va-a-am.

Breathe into your navel, and on your exhale vocalize *ram* three times. On an exhale, ra-a-am, ra-a-am, ra-a-am.

Concentrate your breath into your heart now. On your exhale chant *yam* three times. ya-a-am, ya-a-am, ya-a-am.

Feel your breath in your throat. Inhale deeply, and on your exhale in-tone *ham* three times. Ha-a-am, ha-a-am, ha-a-am.

Finally, breathe up and into your third eye, the area between and slightly above your eyebrows. Chant *om* three times with each exhale. Ooomm, ooomm, ooomm.

Visualize or sense a vision of the Divine as you know it: Jesus Christ, the Goddess, Mary, Buddha, Krishna, God, a brilliant fountain of light. Whatever comes to you spontaneously is perfect. Trust your feeling or image. Ask the Divine, in whatever way feels right, to help you on your retreat. Imagine streams of love flowing from the Divine over you and through you, washing away any fear, tension, worries, or fatigue that may still be present. Imagine any dark or heavy emotions washing out of the bottom of your feet. Continuing to stand tall, with your spine erect, picture your heart. See this Divine love streaming into the very core of your heart. See your intention in your heart—it may be written there in cursive script, or you may visualize a healing symbol or simply feel a good feeling. See those words or symbols or that feeling being in-fused with the incredible, unconditional love of the Divine. Realize that you don't have to do anything to receive this love. Now energize your intention by chanting a final, vibrant *om* while continuing to see or feel your intention glowing with Divine love. If you wish, you might want to ask here for specific help on your retreat.

- Feel the energy coiling and cresting in your body. This is the energy of your retreat, the energy to start your journey. Do not squander it. You are being held. You are blessed. Decide right now, in this moment, to say yes! to your retreat with all of your heart, mind, and body. Do not waste time in guilt. Do not waste time in lack of discipline or shoulds or could-haves. What do you want to do first on your retreat? What im-mediately occurs to you? Launch yourself now by jumping joyously into what you wish to do next.

Uncomfortable Beginnings, Middles, and In-Betweens

When we deliberately leave the safety of the shore of our lives,
we surrender to a mystery beyond our intent.

Ann Linnea, *Deep Water Passage*

There are always uncomfortable periods on retreats, moments when you feel bored, angry, anxious, afraid, frustrated, ridiculous, lonely, or forsaken, as in "Is this the fun part?"

The beginning of a retreat can be especially challenging. You may have experienced anticipation and excitement getting started. Now you are on retreat. What next? Suddenly, or slowly, in the middle of the afternoon or on your fourth day or whenever, you may feel let down or at a loss as to what to do next. In her story about a solo wilderness trip, E. A. Miller writes,

> The first day proved miserable. And there was nothing wrong. The pack was not too heavy, my legs felt fine, the dog was good company. But my practice of pretense had deprived me of knowing real sensations, and so I worried about the smallest things: Should I take a breath now? Should I go to the third lake today? Should I eat something? . . . Without an audience, without someone to direct my response, I was at a loss, unable to frame my own experiences.

You may feel your intention is too broad, too narrow, nonexistent, or insipid. The practices you planned, the books you brought, and the box of art supplies now seem too boring or difficult to look at. You may be swept with love for all life one minute, then with heart-thumping loneliness the next. Jamie, convinced her son was in danger, came close to getting in her car and driving 130 miles home. Dee felt so overwhelmed by her solitude, even with a friend retreating in her guest room, that she went so far as to call her ex-husband, whom she hadn't spoken to in three years. Laura Wright, a retired lay staff officer for the national Episcopal church and a writer, told the story of a shared retreat she took in 1986. She writes in *Rattle Those Dry Bones,*

> I went through the motions the first two days: praying, meditating, studying, singing. Very little was new to me except for some of the music. None of the ideas excited or challenged me. . . . By late afternoon Saturday I was tired of the whole process and ready to pack up and go home. I had had enough of those crying, laughing, bell-ringing females!

Anne Simpkins, editor of *Common Boundary* magazine, has had similar experiences on her week-long and ten-day silent meditation retreats.

> For two or three days I feel like a complete failure. What I am not understanding is all the distractions have fallen by the wayside and I'm hearing the real stuff. . . . After four or five days, I experience a complete flip and I am able to pull myself around intuitively, rather than planning.

You may struggle with unpleasant emotions during moments of transition, during meals, when you are trying to just be, at a time of the day when you would usually be with your family, and while going to sleep at night. You may feel like you need to "do" something but you aren't sure what that something is. Or you may feel what you are doing with your time is wrong, that you've made the wrong choice, that you've chosen the wrong time or place to retreat, that you don't have the "right" activities or the best materials, or that you are squandering your precious time off.

These reactions are completely normal.

See Grief: Unplanned Grief.

I have never gone on a retreat and not felt sad, lonely, afraid, confused, or that I was out of my mind for putting myself through this experience. There is always elation in the beginning—an hour or two exploring a new place or reading a new book filled with groovy practices I can't wait to try. Somewhere along the way, I begin to feel down. Lost. At a loss. I look at the schedule I made, and it all feels like a complete waste of time. I suddenly, desperately, *must* go home and hold my child. I *must* kiss my partner, Chris. Sometimes on retreat, I want to escape so badly I actually would rather be working! Anything but settling down, turning within.

Left to yourself, you are faced with yourself.

For a retreat to come alive, surrender is called for, surrender to the emotions welling up in your throat, surrender to your instinctual rhythm, surrender to the difficult discipline of being in the moment: float on your back, stare at the clouds and wait, heart open, mind hushed.

David Cooper in his spiritual classic *Silence, Simplicity, and Solitude* writes,

> Without a strong will, a person is likely to leave a retreat early. It does not take long for the initial excitement to wear off, the doubts to begin, and the wondering about what we are doing. Pain and boredom soon follow, along with any combination of anxiety, fear, anger, frustration, criticism, or other negative mind states.

I remember reading this several years ago and thinking, "This does not sound like fun. I'm not going on a retreat. Forget it." It all sounded too dry, ominous, and arduous. I wasn't up to it.

What I realize now is that I interpreted "sticking with a retreat" through the usual lens of pushing myself to excel, and I was not interested in pushing myself on retreat if it meant self-flagellation. I needed to learn to exercise my will through compassion and self-kindness, by gently encouraging myself, by being present to all the sensations and feelings without judgment. So many of us would never talk to anyone else the way we talk to ourselves. We must not let this harshness take over when difficult feelings surface on retreat. These feelings do not mean we need to push ourselves harder or that we are failing. These feelings arise when people try to be alone with themselves and think about their lives, their psyches, their purpose.

Experienced retreatants will recognize familiar signposts. "Oh, yes, this is usually when I crave chocolate so bad I smell it in the air" or "This is when I feel I have to call my son at college" or "This is about where I regret not staying with Marsha and having a baby." *These feelings signal that you are getting somewhere.* Resistance is a sign that the psychic pot is being stirred, that ghosts are being disturbed from their dusty hiding places. Think of these feelings as a giant skull-and-crossbones sign left behind by pirates to scare treasure seekers away from their secret troves. If we try to push through these feelings, we will only bruise ourselves. If we "ride the waves of the experience," as Frankie said of her first retreat, instead of trying to *control* the experience, we have a chance both to stick with an intention *and* to dissolve a layer of self-abuse. We can find through this experience a nourishing mixture of confidence and comfort.

It might help to:

• Repeat to yourself, "This is normal. I trust myself. I am safe."

- Write about what you are feeling, perhaps finishing the sentence "I am feeling. . . . "

- Work with your intention, either forming one if you haven't yet or exploring it further by writing your intention question across the top of a page, then filling five pages without stopping to rest, think, or cross out. Write and breathe, breathe and write.

- Sit still and descend into the loneliness, the longing, the doubt. Feel your feelings and yet let part of you observe you at the same time. "Isn't this interesting, I'm feeling overwhelmed and depressed. I wonder why?" This gentle process of self-inquiry is extraordinarily valuable.

- Reflect on May Sarton's words from *Mrs. Stevens Hears the Mermaids Singing:* "Loneliness is the poverty of self; solitude is the richness of self."

- Look over what you planned to do on retreat. What are you avoiding? Why?

- Have you been doing too much? Do you need to stop trying to control this experience, stop dictating what will happen when, and instead go with the flow?

- Ask yourself, "What do I really want to do that I won't allow myself to enjoy?"

- Flip through the book and see what practice or idea thrills you, scares you in a positive way. Do that one. Now.

- Do nothing. Give up all effort, all agendas. Lie or sit still and do nothing.

Almost all retreats have tough, uncomfortable, lonely moments. Be gentle with yourself, and if you can, even if only in a spirit of perversity, welcome those moments.

Stories

Laura stayed with her retreat and came to compare herself to

> a pitcher that had spent the past three days being filled up and emptied out. Filled day by day with prayer, study, songs, and laughter and poured out again in confession, tears, and silent meditation. On Thurs-

day and Friday, I had been composed of ceramic: opaque and ready to crack if dropped. By Saturday I had changed into crystal: sparkling, sheer, and primed to shatter into a million pieces at the slightest provocation. But by Sunday, the day of rebirth and resurrection, I was sterling silver. I felt solid, glowing, reflecting light and images. I knew I might be dropped and dented, I might tarnish in days to come, but I could always be polished again and returned to a radiant, open, welcoming vessel.

When you can kindly take yourself by the hand and stay with your experience, you will learn to live with fear and the depth of your retreat will increase magnificently. This doesn't mean that fear, boredom, and worries won't return on subsequent retreats or that you can't have a glorious time if everything is easy and flows perfectly. Neither is true. Just don't let the demons block your way.

For Long Retreats

You might be thinking, "What have I gotten myself into?" Suddenly, three days, a week, a month seems like an eternity. "The secret taught time and time again by masters over the centuries is the need to persist, to overrule the internal resistance, to be constant in our efforts, not to waver," believes David Cooper. It is extremely important on longer retreats to practice check-in, to have reasonable expectations, and to maintain a commitment to a schedule, even if that schedule is no schedule.

See Courage: Easing into It, What Will You Do?: Check-In, and Living Your Retreat Every Day.

For Mini-Retreats

Slow or uncomfortable moments happen during mini-retreats, too. It can be very frustrating because the limited amount of time scheduled for retreat may leave you feeling pressured to make every minute perfect. Relax. This feeling, this process, is part of your retreat. You can't rush it, you can't escape it. You can only welcome it and be kind to yourself as you experience it.

For Retreats with Others

Retreating with others is a ripe place to observe how you rely on or interact with others. If you are scheduled to be apart and discomfort sets in and suddenly you are dying to be with your partner(s), this is a good place to observe. Can you stick with your plan? Consider using what you are feeling to deepen your shared experience instead of getting busy or chatty to distance yourself from it. Call a deep listening circle. "I'm feeling really lonely and

See Retreating with Others: Deep Listening Circle.

weird. I don't want to run away from this feeling, but I don't know what to do." Use one another to produce loving discipline instead of to distract one another from feeling. One of the dangers in sharing a retreat is that you will hide in cozy friendship. While that might be easier, it also might rob you of a richer experience. And the more you use loving discipline in the rarified atmosphere of retreat, the more you can do it in daily life.

Big feelings on a shared retreat invite projection. Suddenly, your friend is driving you mad. You can't stand the way she brushes her teeth or snorts when she laughs. Many of our complexes and struggles with relationship are activated on retreat, and they can become a *huge* distraction. When you find yourself having a *strong* reaction to someone on retreat, either positive or negative, it is almost always a wake-up call to your own process, a sign pointing to something in you that you are avoiding or discounting. Kindly observe what you are saying to yourself about this person, about how marvelous or appalling she or he is. Acknowledge to yourself that though you may not understand why you feel this way, it has as much to do with you as with the other person. Dialoguing with these projections in writing is a powerful way to learn about them.

Good Ways to Listen

Within each of us, there is a silence, a silence as vast as the universe. We are afraid of it. And we long for it. And when we experience that silence, we remember who we are. Creatures of the stars, created from the birth of galaxies, created from the cooling of this planet, created from dust and gas, created from the elements, created from time and space, created from silence. Silence is the source of all that exists, the unfathomable stillness where vibration began, the first oscillation, the first word, from which life emerged. Silence is our deepest nature, our home, our common ground, our peace. Silence reveals, silence heals. Silence is where God dwells. We yearn to be there. We yearn to share it.

Gunilla Norris, *Sharing Silence*

Think of the suggestions in this chapter as the primary colors of retreating, the fundamentals of contacting your authenticity, of hearing your true self. You can paint a masterpiece using only these colors, you can mix them together to create new and ever more astonishing shades, or you can use them as part of a multimedia collage. You'll want to include a bit of them on just about every retreat. They can be used alone, with another practice, and as transitions between home and retreat time or between retreat practices.

Prepare

See the basic list in What Will You Do?

Being

Maureen Murdock's definition of *being* in *The Heroine's Journey* perfectly describes the heart of a woman's retreat, the sometimes arduous but greatly rewarding process of self-acceptance. "Being requires accepting oneself, staying within oneself and not doing to prove oneself." To be is to live, for a moment, as a spiritual virgin, one-in-yourself, existing in a true relationship with yourself. When you are being, you are free of the need to do, to move, to plan, to improve, to prove, to accomplish, to strive, to push, or to criticize. Being is where you contact your authenticity, not with your rational, verbal brain but with your body, your intuitive feeling nature, your instinctual self.

Being is most often associated with meditation, with Ram Dass's declaration "Be Here Now," with following your breath or repeating a mantra to enable you to remain in the present moment. While I believe strongly in the need for and power of meditation, *being present* is different from just *being*. Being is about existing in a nondoing state, listening for guidance from our authentic self, scanning our body's subtle tightenings and expansions for information, and breathing with—sitting alongside—who we are in that moment without moving to criticize or improve. Meditation techniques can calm and center us so we can hear our authenticity apart from our din of worries and obsessions, but inherent in meditation is doing, the doing of calming the mind. Being is about accepting whatever is there.

In the end, being is almost impossible to describe. It is not a destination; it is never a goal to check off. The edges of being are outlined with self-trust, feeling soft, open, accepting. Yet it is a discipline. When you start to feel an emotion, you don't jump up to go for a walk or get a handful of crackers to munch. You breathe and sit and feel.

It is easy to forget how to be. We may lose this ability early or late in childhood. What Carol Gilligan and Lyn Brown are describing in their research on adolescent girls losing their sense of self is, among other things, girls losing their ability to be.

The longer you do, the harder it becomes to simply be. A friend and I were playing with our children when one of us leaped up for the fifty-seventh time within three minutes. "I can see why mothers never bother to sit down at all," I said, meaning it feels easier to keep going, to do the dishes instead of stopping and checking in with yourself, to rush to return phone calls instead of really talking to a friend, to start another load of laundry rather than sinking down for a rest in the humid spring grass. Over time, to keep going is less frustrating and less scary than stopping to be. In addition, people in many cultures look askance at just being. You are being lazy, you are wasting time, you aren't productive, what's the end result, how will you get ahead? The reasons you should not retreat are the reasons you should not be. Combine the two (being *on* retreat) and you could be in for an anxiety-guilt cocktail with a critical-voice chaser.

See Courage and Living Your Retreat Every Day.

Being is not a state you stalk but one you invite. Everything about a retreat invites being, once you get past anxiety and guilt. Being is the blood and air of your retreat, the feeling place you want to reside in. There are millions of ways to foster being—walking, meditating, breathing deeply, talking to your authentic self—but in the end, being sneaks up on you. You set up a conducive environment or you do something that helps quiet your mind or you relax your body, and you wait. You don't try to define it or study it or grasp it. You just hold the tension of wanting to leap up and, for God's sake, get something accomplished. You observe how your body feels. You give up expectations. You hang out.

Being comes in snatches, wavering states of at-one-ment interspersed with white-knuckled fear or control or worry or mindlessness. With practice, being does become easier. There is no perfect state to attain, no one to compare yourself to, no master degree in being that is rewarded. In that way, it is much like meditation practices. You just do it.

You can foster being by collecting some of the following ingredients.

Environment

Certain places encourage being more than others. It is easier to be on a porch looking over the ocean than in a taxi stuck in a traffic jam in downtown Manhattan. Yet wherever you are, you *can* find or create a good being place.

You already know what kinds of places, sounds, textures, lighting, and temperature help you relax and center. For me, it is bed. For Diane, it is the bath. For Jodie, a creek. For you, perhaps the crook of a tree, the ocean, or curling up in a blanket watching a sunset. Name places that trigger being for you. Recall what you enjoyed as a child, what smells, places, situations absorbed you. If the smell of lavender does it, keep lavender oil on hand. If a whiff of suntan lotion and the beat of the ocean do it, but it is the dead of winter in Indiana, get a heat lamp and coconut oil and a tape of the surf, draw a warm bath, and see what happens.

I Am Enough

One of the most wonderful beliefs more and more women are embracing is "I am perfect in my imperfection." There is a joyous acceptance of the limitations of self and life. By letting go of endless self-improvement schemes (even if just for a few moments)—of thinking that if you weighed this or owned that, then everything would be all right—you let go of the need to ceaselessly do. You invite being into your retreat.

Find a comfy spot. As you inhale deeply and slowly, repeat silently, "I am not all things," and as you exhale slowly and fully, repeat "I am enough." When other thoughts barge into your mind, bring yourself back to the words. Use the words *I am enough* like a stream of water to wash away frenzy, comparison, the need to go anywhere. When you are ready, let go of the mantra and float. When you tighten back up with thoughts of "I should be getting ready for my hike" or "After this meditation I should get ready to go back" or "What exactly am I supposed to be feeling?," return to your breath and the words. You will dance in and out of feeling like you are enough. Fine. Unlike certain types of meditation, the point is not to empty your mind but to simply pause and feel. No judgment, no goal, just keep returning to the words when you feel the need.

Here are some more centering phrases, inspired by Buddhist monk and teacher Thich Nhat Hanh.

- "Breathing in, I am at peace; breathing out, I let go."

- "Breathing in my rich dark center, breathing out false, hurrying me."

- "Breathing in, I trust; breathing out, I grin."

- On an inhale, "I am the wind"; on an exhale, "I am the rain"; next inhale, "I am the earth"; exhale, "I am the tree."

- On an inhale, "I am in my center"; on an exhale, "All is well."

Wrap Being Around

Float being in the midst of another activity. Choose an activity that does not frustrate you, does not demand much attention, and does not feel like work. Bird-watching, quilting, knitting a sweater, beading, shelling peas, making tortillas or cookies or bread, building a sand castle, gardening (if it doesn't feel like work or an improvement project), tracing an image, weaving flower garlands, arranging flowers, walking barefoot outside, watching the moonrise or the sunset, stroking a cat, getting on a bus with destination unknown, centering clay on a potter's wheel, floating on a still lake in warm sunshine—the list is (mercifully) endless. Immerse yourself in something enjoyable with no purpose, no goal, no stopping point, no clock ticking, and see if being comes calling.

When You Can't Empty Your Mind

What do you do when you want to be but you can't get there? You feel too hyped up, too frantic, too jumpy, too too.

Check your caffeine and sugar consumption. The java and sugar Jones are not conducive to being. Drink a lot of water, eat a little protein, and cut down on your coffee or doughnut intake when you know you will be retreating.

Do something physical. Combine exercise with the meditation "I am enough" or counting your footsteps as you walk or listening to classical music on headphones. (I used to love to ride my bike fast very early in the morning with Beethoven's Fifth pounding on my headphones. It left no room for chattering monkey mind.)

See The Smell of Your Own Sweat, below.

See Resources: Audios.

Breathe. Being is intimate with breath.

Ask yourself, "What am I avoiding feeling?" or "What am I feeling right now?"

The Smell of Your Own Sweat

I often begin a retreat slightly frantic. If I've had to drive, I may feel bloated with highway haze. I almost always feel greedy for the coming experience, hyped up; I can't wait to relax and feel good, which of course makes relaxing impossible. So I begin my retreats with movement. A little yoga, a slow walk, and dancing what I am feeling are my favorite ways to make the transition.

Inhabiting your body joyfully and mindfully can be a challenge for most women. It is sometimes easier to pretend you are a large head and everything below your neck doesn't exist. But inhabiting your body, viscerally realizing that you are spirit incarnate, is a most important task, intimately linked to becoming at one with yourself. To most of us, inhabiting the body is our Achilles' heel. We are okay as long as the scale says a certain number. We are okay as long as we get to the gym a certain number of times per week. We are okay as long as we don't have to stand naked in front of a department store mirror under fluorescent lights. We are okay as long as we can float somewhere above our bodies, a little detached, separated from our bodily processes.

But we are missing so much by perpetuating this mind-spirit-body split. One of the most healing things you can do on retreat is to connect with your body, with the sweet, grounding smell of your own sweat, the reassuring movement of your muscles. This opens the gateway for a body-centered stillness, the organic experience of "I am not a spiritual being saddled with a body, I am spirit in a body with a mind, and all are valuable." Allowing yourself to be in your body without judgment or ridicule can open the feminine heart and still the rapacious critical mind like little else.

Choosing Movement

Ask yourself:

- What physical movement would best serve my intention?

- Would movement help me reach an altered state? What movement or exercise appeals to me?

- Do I need physical help releasing emotions?

There are countless ways to use movement on a retreat. You can do a movement discipline that you have been studying, like yoga or Sufi dancing. You can take a class or an entire retreat in a new form of movement. You can put on music that beckons you to turn inward while moving, listening to what your body wants to do. You can walk in nature, swim, bike, roller-blade, canoe, run, scull, do ballet or gymnastics, jump on a trampoline—you name it. The important distinction is that you move *exactly the way you want* and that you do it within the context of your retreat.

You won't be doing what you want if you feel compelled to do aerobics because a day without exercise is a day you will eat only 300 calories. You will be allowing a punitive should to enter your retreat.

What connects movement with your retreat is being mindful while moving. Bring your attention to your intention, again and again, while moving. Imagine you are dancing your retreat question. Be open to any ideas, images, or feelings that surface as you meld movement and your retreat question. By doing this, you open a passage for nonverbal, body-based wisdom to enliven your retreat. Muscle holds memory, muscle holds wisdom. Liberate memory and wisdom by being conscious while moving.

Moving with Others

Meditative movement has the oldest association with retreats. Hatha yoga, tai chi chuan, walking meditation, some martial arts, some forms of dancing, the Japanese tea ceremony, a rousing tennis game, or a round of golf can find a place on retreat. It is all in how you approach and make use of your experience. It is challenging to consider interacting with others or even competing on a retreat. Competition is about as far from a traditional retreat activity as you can get. But I think of my good friend Zahra, who finds her spiritual sustenance in playing tennis with friends. There is room on retreat for these activities, if they feed you.

If you do meet with others on your retreat, say for a game of tennis, you need to extend your retreat container. If you spend time chatting, explaining your retreat, or even deflecting a compliment, your retreat will be diminished or destroyed. If you feel you must be polite or if it will be stressful to get to where you play (dealing with traffic, parking, and so forth), you might want to forgo this. To extend your container, you may wish to talk to your team-mates before your retreat about what you will be doing. "I am taking three days for a retreat over Labor Day weekend to rest and think. I want to play tennis each day with you, but I want to meet and play in as much silence as possible. Would that be okay?" Or you might say, "I'm taking a day off and I want to play racquetball. I might be sort of quiet, so don't worry and don't try to joke me into talking. I just want to show up, play hard, and be comfortable being quiet." These kinds of requests can challenge friendships and open up all kinds of discussion. Sometimes friends you play sports with know you only in a limited way. Bringing up the subject of a retreat can bring new areas of your life into the relationship. Think about this—can you trust this person to support you in this way? Perhaps instead of sharing your intent, you can extend your retreat container by repeating a mantra or meditation poem silently to yourself. The meditations listed under I Am Enough and repetition of words like *love, peace, well-being, trust, centered, calm, serenity,* and *courage* are effective choices.

Movement to Let Off Steam

Sometimes on retreat the emotional pressure can become so intense that you feel you must get away from yourself. Movement is a healthy way to deal with these feelings (usually better than eating or watching TV). Try to choose consciously by saying to yourself something like, "I need to tune out for a while. I'm going for a run." Then, immediately after your moving distraction, write, paint, or reflect for ten minutes on how you feel.

Movement as Prayer

See Reviving Your Spiritual Direction: Imaging the Divine.

Body prayer is prayer using your body. The definition of *prayer* is, of course, up to you. I use body prayer to move me closer to the Divine, to get me out of my head, to help me express gratitude, and to give form to happiness and grief when these emotions threaten to spin me into behavior I do not like.

Here are a few examples of body prayer. These work very well as transitions between retreat activities and as warm-ups to spontaneous writing, painting, and other sedentary activities.

- I learned this from Unitarian minister Sara Campbell: Begin with your hands in a prayer position in front of your chest. Bow. Return to prayer position. Keeping your palms together, raise them over your head, then open your arms into a gesture of receiving. Bring your hands back together and clap. Then bring your hands down, and with your hands in prayer position, bow again. Repeat until you feel finished.

- This is adapted from Celeste Snowber Schroeder's book *Embodied Prayer*. Experiment with body positions where you can rock back and forth. Try lying on the floor holding your knees, rocking forward and back. Or lie on your side and rock your shoulders back and forth. Or sit in a rocking chair. Once you have established a comforting rocking rhythm, meditate on one of these lines:

  > Under the Beloved's wings I take refuge.

  > God (or your image that conjures up a protecting Divine presence) encircles me in Love.

  > I am embraced by the Divine.

  > I am safe in the arms of the Goddess (or your image that conjures up a healing Divine feminine presence).

  > I am utterly safe and known by the Divine.

- Imagine yourself held. Imagine yourself being rocked. Visualize your image of the Divine loving you with the greatest love imaginable and then some. Feel this love in your body as you rock. Feel this healing, protective presence.

- Use your whole body to express a word or phrase that symbolizes what you are experiencing in your life or on this retreat. Select a word from the list below or make up your own. Put on some music or pick up a drum, take a few deep breaths, and repeat the word or phrase to yourself and aloud a few times. What thoughts come to mind? Enlarge on them through movement instead of through words. Using the music and your body, explore your thoughts and feelings by moving your hands, feet, legs, arms, head, shoulders, waist, hips, every part of you. Get out of your verbal mind and discover wisdom through movement. For example, Carol chose *acceptance* as her word. She was retreating to understand her daughter's coming out as a lesbian. Carol began by playing some sweet, lullaby-like music and moving to express her memories of motherhood. Then she moved into some journal writing, listing all the things she needed to accept about her daughter, from the loss of the traditional wedding she had secretly dreamed of orchestrating to telling her own mother. Then she picked up a rattle and began to chant the word *acceptance*. "I felt silly and sure hoped no one heard me, but chanting was the only way I could stop thinking and start expressing myself in movement instead of words. I sort of moved through my list, acting out with my body how I could feel more accepting. I finally moved beyond words and into that nonthinking, feeling place. It felt great to stop chewing over this in my mind and ask my body to help me express and understand." Carol returned to this practice several times during her retreat. Persist and be willing to suspend your disbelief, and you will be moved to rich places (pun intended).

Surrender to a Higher Power

The Dance of Life

The Struggle to Know

Coming Home

Being in My Center

Opening to Mystery

Breaking Open to Love

Burning with Life

Trapped in Quicksand

Letting Go of _____

Leaping Through the Fire of _____

Pushed and Pulled by _____

Clinging to _____

Spiraling Through

Pausing in the Stillness

Swimming in Grief

Safety

See Retreating with Others.

For many women, hiking in nature is an excellent choice of movement but one that can feel too scary when done alone. I take my 110-pound dog along for protection (you can borrow a dog). Other women hike with a friend, arranging ahead of time to meet and hike silently, with a hug at the beginning and end. Being silent with a friend is often a very challenging and extremely fruitful retreat practice.

Divine Landscape

Creek, oak, ocean, mountaintop, arroyo, mesa, cloud, earth, valley, vista, sea, rock, tree: home. The natural world refreshes like nothing else. The immensity of nature puts your own struggles into perspective, helping you to feel both insignificant and vital, a blink in the eye of God and a universe in your own right. "I listened to the chorus of constant surf and the birds and thought, 'It's okay to be tiny and not take myself seriously,'" said Diane of a retreat she enjoyed in a friend's miniature cabin overlooking the Pacific.

Being in nature is most conducive to being yourself. The longer (or the more actively present) you are there, the more pretensions, useless behaviors, and worries are peeled away. In the face of all that immensity and simplicity, in the face of the sure cycle of life and death, the size of your thighs or the self-hatred you feel for having an affair just isn't as important. The truth about how you need to be and what you need to do is revealed like an agate ground smooth by a river.

- Spend at least two days and one night living as closely as you dare with nature. Wake with the sun, sleep with the dark, eat when you are hungry, invite nature as your companion, and listen to what she has to say.

- Lie on the ground and listen to the earth beneath you. Ask her, "Earth, how would you handle my intention?"

- Listen to water. Sit in the rain. Immerse yourself in a large body of water. What does it tell you about yourself?

- Sculpt your dilemma, your life, your emotions, in sand.

- Sit with your back against a tree for an hour and ask her advice.

- Sleep overnight in your own backyard and see how your perspective shifts.

- Plant something, and as you do, contemplate the life in the plant or seeds, the alchemy of dirt, seed, water, and sun. How does it relate to your life, your retreat?

- Go for a night walk alone or with a friend, Be silent and hike in the dark, keeping your flashlight off as much as possible. Listen in the darkness. Listen to your heart. Listen to your fears. Listen to the Divine. Experience all your senses sharpening. Stop along the way and sit in silence.

- Find a poem or short prose piece about nature that you love. Read it aloud outside. Sit and see what happens. If you become restless, read it again, even slower this time.

- Stand at the edge of a cliff or other precipice in nature (a tall building will work in a pinch). Relate the feeling of standing there to a life experience you have had or to your intention. After a time, if possible, go to the bottom of this cliff or building and look up at where you've been. What does the change in altitude feel like in your body? Can you relate it to what is shifting in you on your retreat?

- Find an aspect of yourself that is represented in nature. An arching pine tree riddled with holes from woodpeckers, a pile of rocks that proudly expose their age in their strata, or a meandering, peaceful brook could be symbols of your different qualities, moods, or beliefs. Sit with your symbol. Dialogue with it in writing, through painting, or by sculpting in the dirt.

Nature as Mirror

This retreat practice was modeled on a retreat in *Jubilee Time,* by Marie Harris. It can be part of a long retreat, or each session can constitute a mini-retreat. If you do a mini-retreat, allow an extra few minutes for your opening and closing ceremonies, and relate these to nature.

Choose a time three or four times during the course of one retreat to be in nature. Early morning, afternoon, early evening, and perhaps night work well, but whenever you can be sure to get away will work fine. Choose how long each session will be—from five minutes to several hours. Choose a place to be. Your porch, a rooftop, a backyard, a park, any place out-of-doors where you can feel and see the natural world will do.

Set a timer or alarm to remind you to retreat at these precise times.

At the chosen time, go to your place and sit. Reflect on your retreat question. Pose it to the crow, the breeze, the peony. Watch for answers reflected there. Be in nature and listen for insights, but don't straitjacket them into logical, cause-and-effect sense. If you like, write, draw, or photograph what you feel, sense, see.

This exercise can be repeated over several consecutive days on a long retreat.

Soothe

The poet Mary Oliver implores, "You only have to love the soft animal of your body, love what it loves." A woman's retreat beseeches you to inhabit and venerate your body, gratify your senses, indulge in healthy self-nurturing with glee. One of the themes underlying a woman's retreat is soothing yourself, self-nurturing at its most basic and delicious. Massage, a lavender-and-grapefruit-oil bath, an afternoon nap, lemon tea and raisin toast: comfort has to be a part of your retreat, especially if you are tackling a difficult issue or if you are retreating because you are hurt, bruised, or wearied.

Choosing things to soothe yourself is usually easier than allowing yourself to enjoy the soothing you select. Perhaps more than any other retreat practice, taking time to enjoy yourself, to luxuriate, to take pleasure in filling your own physical desires can seem reckless, dangerous, immoral, not worthy of your precious time off. But if you had listened to that voice, the same one that demands that you exercise five hours each day, never let your dirty laundry pile up, and write a thank-you note before you've unwrapped the gift, you never would have considered retreating in the first place. Brava for choosing retreat! Now keep going: dare to utterly enjoy yourself!

What would it be like to give yourself exactly what your body needs? What would it be like to eat a cherry so slowly it dissolves on your tongue? Or to drink tea as an offering of love to your throat? To create a still life with lilies in your mother's antique vase, a favorite photograph of you, three lemons and a red apple, all draped with a silk scarf simply for the spiritual pleasure of creating beauty? To pause long enough to truly choose what you want to do, to ask your authentic self, "What do you need to be soothed, to feel good?" To ask your body—even each individual sense—what it needs. To do so is to embrace yourself with a lover's touch. It may take quite a while and many gentle attempts at self-soothing; it may even feel impossible at times; but as you keep asking, "What do I truly enjoy?" and "How can I love the soft animal of my body?" you invite love into your life.

Shadow Comfort

Soothing yourself can become tricky, however, when shadow comfort or addictive behaviors get tangled up in your plans. For example, what soothes me best is eating. Sometimes food is just the ticket, and I can eat in a way that is conscious and nurturing. But often I eat to stay busy and distracted, and I eat things that make me feel bad. How can I make better self-care choices while on retreat? By listening to what my body really needs and by daring to give it to her *and enjoy it while I do*. When we wholeheartedly treat ourselves well, leaving no room for guilt, we can short-circuit the need for shadow comfort. The need to smoke, overeat, or watch mindless TV comes from a place of deprivation, neediness, and boredom. If we can honor ourselves by enjoying our soothing, savoring it, smacking our lips, being extravagant in our enjoyment, we may find ourselves making better choices.

I'm not suggesting it is easy to change addictive behavior. I know what it is like to live with an addictive personality, to be driven to behavior that is self-defeating, even self-destructive, although it may masquerade as self-nurturing behavior. However, the rarefied air of a retreat does provide a break from the compulsive nature of addictions. Because you are not in ordinary space and time and are freed from stress by the retreat archetype, it is easier to not pick up the cigarette, to eat with care, to not shop. Yet it is important to avoid the expectation that your behavior will change permanently. We all know it is never that easy.

I hope it is clear that I am *not* advocating playing the ascetic. Healthy self-nurturing does not involve denying yourself all familiar comforts. If you do so, you will feel virtuous and pure during your retreat, but soon afterward the needs and habits you've been repressing will spring up and cuff you on the shoulder. (I've made it through this type of a retreat, but soon after I'm devouring a bag of something dark and sweet.) Instead, provide for your needs by kindly indulging yourself in ways that *affirm you and support you in your retreat process*. Plan ahead of time what comforts you must have. Then you will not have to leave your retreat to drive to the store for a package of double-chocolate brownie mix or make a kamikaze shopping assault on the mall. When you give thought to your comfort needs ahead of time and build-in ways to indulge yourself, even if that means a tiny dose of shadow comfort, you'll feel safe enough to stay in the retreat container and be more able to integrate your insights and energy into your ordinary life.

Ask yourself:

- What are my favorite ways to comfort myself?

- Which of these have a place on this retreat?

And a good question to use on retreat when you need soothing:

- What would comfort me right now in a healthy, life-affirming way?

Some favorite soothers:

- Massage. Have someone come to your home, or find a massage therapist who works in a tranquil, pleasing place.

- Body and room mists. I use sprays on my face a lot during my retreats, especially during retreats in the world.

- Soothing drinks. Cool water with lemon or hot water with lemon and a little honey.

- Favorite books. Reread one from childhood; spend unlimited time browsing in a bookstore, unlimited time reading something totally for enjoyment, or unlimited time in a library.

- The sound and feel of water. Sit by a fountain or creek; float in warm water naked; listen to rain on the roof; walk in the rain.

- The comfort of your bed. Make up your bed with clean, scented sheets and go to bed in the middle of the day; eat in bed; read in bed; write in bed.

- Flowers. Pick and arrange flowers; buy an armful of flowers at a farmers' or wholesale market.

- Candlelight. Light a tray of scented votive candles; float candles in water.

- Music. Browse in a music store; listen to a piece of music while doing nothing else.

But avoid these: haircuts, facials, manicures, or body wraps. Anything that feels like maintenance or like something you do to please others doesn't have a place on retreat (facing myself in a salon mirror is *not* soothing). In general, avoid beauty salons on retreat; they tend to awaken feelings of inadequacy.

Spontaneous Writing

Spontaneous writing is an excellent way to elbow your way past resistance, boredom, and lack of direction and get into the VIP party room where the really interesting stuff is happening. In spontaneous writing you choose a subject or a question and write about it for as long as you like without stopping. I find using a watch or timer gives me a structure to work with, but if that feels too rushed to you, then decide at the start how many pages you will fill up without stopping—three to five will push you without depressing you.

When I have that feeling of running around in circles unable to concentrate on anything, I stop, grab my journal, and write across the top of the page, "I am stuck because" or "I don't want to" or "I am feeling." Then I write without stopping for ten minutes. First I write about what a slug I am, then I write about what a waste of time doing anything remotely spiritual is for a slug like me, then I graduate to writing about how sluglike I feel, and then, if I keep going, often a small miracle happens and I start glimpsing something besides being a slug, something beyond my self-loathing. I almost always learn what I need to know and where I need to go next. At the very least, I feel less sluglike when I'm finished.

Other people prefer to simply write, keeping the hand moving, seeing what subjects emerge. See what works for you.

Whatever method you choose, write without editing, without stopping, without reading back over what you have written, without giving in to the voices that say, "This is stupid, I'm not coming up with anything new, how much longer do I have to go, I hate writing, blah, blah, blah." Just spill what is inside you onto the page as quickly as you can. Avoid thinking. Stay in the moment, even if that moment is nothing but you whining. Don't imagine you know what is going to come reeling out of your pen. Complain, rant, bitch—but keep your hand moving.

Experiment with writing with your nondominant hand, with clustering, with writing around and upside down on the page, with combining movement and writing or sound and writing or meditation and writing.

See What Will You Do? for an explanation of clustering.

Use spontaneous writing whenever you feel bored, stuck, tired, afraid, worried, excited, close to a discovery, or in need of contact with someone else. Use it to calm down before a retreat. Use it as a mini-retreat every morning.

Some sentence starters:

> I am feeling . . .
>
> I see that . . .
>
> I am avoiding . . .
>
> I am ready to accept . . .
>
> I remember . . .

If I got really quiet, I would see that . . .

I believe . . .

I'm afraid . . .

I am . . .

I love and appreciate . . .

I hate . . .

I acknowledge myself for . . .

I feel gratitude for . . .

Spontaneous Drawing

It has been said by Freud and other people with beards that the psyche communicates in symbols, that when we think in pictures we are given direct access to the preverbal, emotional state, which when tapped into can deliver up pure psychic gold.

In spontaneous drawing, the less formal training you have in art and the less you get caught up in how the images look, the better. This is often *very* hard to do. We live in a very visually sophisticated society. We learn to compare ourselves to others at a very early age. Many of us had art teachers from hell. In spontaneous drawing, you are not making art. You are communicating with the forgotten, shy, enigmatic parts of yourself, the nascent rumblings of your truth. There is no need to plan, no right way to create, no rules to adhere to.

You can use spontaneous drawing without a subject in mind or to explore a specific question or issue.

Get your paper and art materials. Arrange them where you can work comfortably and in good light. Close your eyes and take a few deep breaths. Open your eyes and select a color. Notice what color your hand wants to move toward. Notice how your hand, your arm, wants to move across the paper. Follow your inklings of images. Put them on the paper. Don't stop yourself because you see only a blob or because what you see in your mind's eye is beyond your ability to render. Stay open. Try.

Create without caring about the result. Ask yourself, "What would I draw if I didn't have to worry about how it looked?" and "What would I draw if I didn't have to worry about hurting anyone? What would I draw if I weren't afraid?" If you wish, do lots of drawing quickly. It helps to work with materials that are inexpensive so you aren't worried about cost. Tempera paints are ideal.

If you are stuck, pick up a color, any color, and move it across the page. Scribble and breathe and forget about being profound or producing something that makes sense. Offer up your resistance, control, and desire for a certain outcome. Ask yourself, "What do I least want to draw right now?"

The more you practice spontaneous drawing, the easier it will become to enjoy the process and to bring forth something you can learn from—not necessarily on an intellectual or literal basis, but always on an emotional one.

After you are finished drawing, dialogue with the image or journal about the creative process.

Stories

Kristina is a mother and an actress; she had recently moved from a city to a small town and had just stopped smoking.

> My intention on this retreat is, "How can I begin to contain my energy in a more mindful, tolerant, and graceful manner? How can I breathe more?" I am looking for a way out of my habits and patterns that no longer serve me or my goals now that I am living in this new place.
>
> I woke up and the first thing I thought was, "Find your natural rhythm again." I stretched and did some sun salutations as I looked out to the ocean. Every time I started thinking, "I ought to . . ." I took a deep breath and said, almost spontaneously, "Containment."
>
> I free-associated with the word and image of *containment*, using clustering and drawing. At first, I got stuck because the quality of containment almost has a negative association for me, something I would *never* imagine of myself. Then I realized there is strength and economy of movement in the quality of containment. I did more movement to music and ended up with one hand covering the top of my head and one hand over my heart with my head bowed. I determined I could do the few errands I felt I had to do to get ready for the holidays with mindfulness and in silence.
>
> I drove to town in silence (instead of listening to music like I usually do). I was slow and methodical in everything I did. I found myself breathing deeper and tuning in to my body. Tension lessened. I got a

few funny looks from shop owners when I pointed to my mouth and shook my head after they asked, "How do you want to pay for this?" or "Can I help you?" But in general, my foray into the world was very pleasant and relaxed. When monkey mind kicked into gear, I reminded myself, "Keep yourself contained" and "Save it for what matters."

At home, I ate some soup I had made very slowly, savoring each bite. I had been craving fruit and ate that slowly with great enjoyment. I was suddenly aware that I almost never eat fruit—I had the embarrassing revelation that I always give it to my son instead of eating it myself. Oh horrors, might I be filling my own cravings through him? Or am I so busy making sure he gets a balanced meal that I only eat to satisfy my hunger and never hear my own nutritional longings? I felt ashamed and sad and also angry at myself.

I was tired and I went into my son's tent, crawled into a sleeping bag, and meditated for a full forty-five minutes. I wept a little. I missed my old friend, the cigarette. Not that I craved one, but I felt a void. The prospect of going inside myself for silence and inspiration—instead of to that thing (the cigarette) that physically sets me outside and separate from those that need me—was scary territory. I became quiet and emptied of all concerns.

I worked in clay and felt myself come alive again, doing what I love. I made a person with five hands and inside that person was another person, looking out from a womb/cave, smiling and still. I took a long, silent walk on the beach. A meditation walk. I asked the possibility of this mindfulness/containment to come into my body and build a nest. Very clearly I saw that this is an absolute necessity for the next version of my life, an inner adjustment to this move.

For my closing, I made a nest of rocks and shells as an altarpiece to signify and symbolize this new gift/change in my life.

I celebrated myself with a lavender bath, a fire, and a glass of wine. Doing nothing, nothing but being.

For Long Retreats

Include a little of everything. Punctuate your retreat with a practice like Divine Landscape: Nature as Mirror. Or use body prayer or a walk combined with the meditation Being: I Am Enough as a transition activity. Do an exercise from Soothe if you start to feel sad or lost.

For Mini-Retreats

When you are feeling the need for retreat but aren't sure what to do, simply set aside a half hour to do one activity from this chapter. Write, draw, be, or move. Remember to do an opening and closing ceremony.

For Retreats in the World

Being, movement, spontaneous writing, and even spontaneous drawing can all be done with other people around or on the spur of the moment. Carry your journal and pen, colored pencils, and an eight-by-twelve sketchbook with you in a bag or in your car so you can take advantage of moments alone.

For Retreats with Others

When your retreat includes other people, you can deepen your practices together by starting a group retreat with a movement class or hiring a massage therapist to come to your retreat location or doing spontaneous writing or drawing in the same room (without commenting at any time on one another's work) or visiting remote places in nature together.

Contemplations

*I beg you . . . to have patience with everything unresolved in your heart
and try to love the questions themselves as if they were locked rooms
or books written in a very foreign language. Don't search for the answers, which could not be given you now, because you would not be able
to live them. And the point is, to live everything. Live the questions now.
Perhaps then, someday far in the future, you will gradually, without
even noticing it, live your way into the answer.*

Rainer Maria Rilke, *Letters to a Young Poet,*
translated by Stephen Mitchell

I have long pondered this passage on loving the questions. For many years I
hated every word of it. I actually once screamed at Rilke, "But I want the answers!" (He didn't answer.) I am a black-and-white person, someone who
hates ambiguity outside of movie theaters and novels, someone who jumps to
conclusions, makes assumptions, expects either the best or the worst and rarely
considers the in-between. Yet as I gain a glimpse of maturity and as I care for
my child, love for the shade of gray has grown in me.

When studying retreat traditions, I was struck by the role that contemplation
played in these retreats, especially in the Benedictine tradition of *lectio:* reading and listening to the word. It is done by quieting body and mind, then se-
lecting a short text and reading it slowly, listening to it with "the ears of your
heart," as oblate and writer Macrina Wiederkehr describes it.

See Resources. Contemplation is pondering, musing, looking at with continued attention.
There are many ways to contemplate and an endless number of things to
focus attention upon. I have composed a partial list of books, videos, tapes,
and even images to contemplate, and below is a list of ways to work with the
words, sounds, or images you choose.

In addition to looking at Resources, you might wish to try the Bible. I found
reading the psalms and changing *God* to *Great Mystery* or *She* opened up an

amazing storehouse of metaphors. You might also search your bookshelves for a story, poem, or passage that has lingered in your imagination since you first read it. Or visit a great independent bookstore during or before your retreat. Stand in the middle of the store, silently repeat your retreat intention, and then follow your intuition to a section, reach for a book, and let it fall open to a page.

But where does the bit about loving the questions come in? In addition to pondering stories, poems, and reprints of great art, contemplating ecstatic, hearty, and untamed questions is extraordinarily useful. I have come to love good questions (well, *love* is too generous; how about *tolerate?*), to view them as a beguiling trail to internal alertness.

Ways to Work with Questions and Other Material

- Active imagination. Allow a story to develop from the question, or let a story you read become alive. Instead of observing, as you would do in a visualization, participate in the story. Talk, move about, create something, pray, sing, do whatever actions unfold. Avoid controlling the story; let it unfold. Use the story or question to listen to yourself, to see what that self says to you through action and symbolism. Whatever occurs to you is perfect. Record your adventures.

- Movement. Dance, express, expand with your body your reactions to and feelings about the chosen piece or question.

- Spontaneous writing or painting. Without thinking, planning, or conjecturing outcome, interact with the work you choose.

  See Good Ways to Listen.

- Sound. Sing a song you know or make one up, make sound without logical meaning, drum a drum, play a bugle, compose music as your path.

- Sculpt your reactions in clay, papier-mâché, or Play-Doh, on the earth herself, or in a shallow tray filled with clean sand, small rocks, twigs, moss, and any miniature things you might have about.

- Compose a prayer in response. Pray it with all your heart.

- Write a responsive reading. One part is read by a leader, the other is read by a group. Recite it by yourself, when retreating with others, or with your family or friends when you return home.

- Create a collage of images by way of a reply. Cut them from old magazines, use photos, trace from books, and draw some yourself.

- Make a greeting card and send it to someone who you hope will understand and share your experience.

- Make a ceremonial doll that reflects your wonderment.

- Draw on your face or body with body paints or makeup how your body feels reading or seeing the work or question.

- Write a poem consisting of the images you read or saw as you contemplated. Weave your reactions in.

- Design a shrine to create a spiritual home for your musings.

- Cook a meal by making or finding recipes that emotionally feed the hunger stirred by your thoughts.

- Imagine a quilt design in response. Sketch it out.

- Walk or run, and as you do, create a chant or song that matches your rhythm and is inspired by what you are working on.

- Sit quietly and breathe the story, question, or image into your body.

Questions

Look through the questions below. Choose one that makes your skin crawl, your heart pound, your skin break out in goose bumps, one that bores you to tears or makes your eyes cross in bewilderment. An extreme reaction indicates that the question may be for you. Take the question and prospect with it, using one of the methods listed above. Remember Rilke's maddening admonition: love the questions. As I see it, that means don't jump for *the* answer, for a conclusion, or for a plan of action. Hang out in the gray zone. Accept that there may be no answer or that you may not be ready to hear it. Play it, sketch it, unravel it, flip it over and look at the underside, pour light on it, dip it in paint, bathe it in tears.

- What is my calling in life? Am I living it? Have I rejected it? Do I truly wish to find it?

- How can I bring the gift of myself to the world?

- What do I seek?

- What did my face look like before I was born?

- What and whom do I call beloved? Why?

- What would I die for?

- What do I still trust as I did when I was a child?

- The snake sheds her skin, the moon sheds its shadow. What have I shed to be reborn? When has my hope been restored?

- When am I too busy to breathe?

- If I made a confession or a catalog of my greatest secrets and shames, what would I list? What images would I see?

- What is my greatest accomplishment? What am I most proud of in my life?

- What and whom do I hate?

- Who and what have I forsaken? Do I know why?

- If I met my authentic self on the street, what would she look like? What would we talk about? What gift would she give me?

- What do I imagine it is like to be born? What do I imagine it is like to die?

- What does it feel like to be completely and unconditionally loved? What does it feel like to love someone or something in that way?

- If I could die and come back, having experienced the interconnectedness and sanctity of all life and having seen that spark alive in each person, how would my life change?

- How can I live gratitude?

- What color, shape, and texture is hope? Love? Faith? Waiting? Sisterhood? Inspiration? Courage? Freedom?

- What is my relationship to truth?

- How do I live with integrity?

- What do I value most in this life? How do I reflect these values back to the cosmos and to those I love each day?

- How do I practice compassion?

- Where does my power come from? How do I use my power? When do I use it?

- What am I when I am empty?

- What do I trust?

- What am I obedient to?

- If my ears were open to the song of the universe, what would I hear?

- What is the metaphor of my life?

- What is the mystery of my life? How must I dance with this mystery?

- How have I killed the song of my life? How can I bring it to life?

- How can I be content with whatever I have, wherever I am, whatever I am doing?

- How must I live if I believe I am enough?

- What would happen if I responded to pain and mistakes with self-kindness and vulnerability instead of self-hatred and recriminations?

- What would my life look like if I had a poet's heart? A sculptor's hands? A composer's ear? A master cook's palate?

- What will it take for me to change? Am I in enough pain? Do I honestly wish to change anything about myself or my life?

- What is home? Where am I at home?

- What would it take for me to celebrate and welcome death?

- What would living in the silence beyond sound look like? Feel like? Sound like? Taste like?

- How does the place, the land where I live, have spiritual relevance to me? How does it rise up, anoint, and love me? How do I anoint and love it?

- If I could bring something or someone to life again, who or what would I choose? How would I do it?

- How have I experienced the Divine moving within me?

- I am walking a labyrinth, with high walls and too many twists and turns to find my way out. I am about to turn the corner to face the center. What will I find here? What would I find tomorrow? Next month? In ten years?

- If all of life is a meditation, what am I spending most of my time meditating on?

Intention Chart

	INTRODUCTION	HOW TO USE THIS BOOK	A WOMAN'S RETREAT	A RETREAT OUTLINE	THE CALL TO RETREAT	INTENTION	FOR HOW LONG WILL YOU RETREAT?	WHERE WILL YOU RETREAT?: YOUR PHYSICAL AND EMOTIONAL CONTAINERS	WHAT WILL YOU DO?	COURAGE	OPENING CEREMONY	UNCOMFORTABLE BEGINNINGS, MIDDLES, AND IN-BETWEENS	GOOD WAYS TO LISTEN	CONTEMPLATIONS	GATHERING THE WHOLE
Can I allow myself to relax and be?	1		11	31	33	41	48		74				113	136	147
How can I listen to and honor my own inner wisdom?	1		12	31	32	41	48	69	71	81	98		113	133	147
How can I live my own life, inhabit my own center?	1		12		33	41	50	69	75		98		113	134	147
How can I love and respect myself more?	1				32	39		67	75	93	98		124		147
How can I trust nature and trust myself?			13		33	41		62	73	86	98	107	122		147
What is my relationship with the Divine right now?						41	48		73	82	98		119	134	
How can I feel the love of the Divine?			14		36	39	49	62	75	81	98		113 119	133	150
How can I revive my faith in a benevolent universe?			14	29	36	41	50	62	75	93	98		120	134	
What do I need to do for my spiritual growth?	4		13	29		41		59	71		98	107	113 119	133	147
How can I bring the fullness of me into my work life?					34	41	56	64	75		98		124	137	149
Is this the right _____ (place, relationship, job) for me right now?						41	50		75	85	98		123		147

Intention Chart

EMERGING FROM CHAOS INTO BALANCE	GETTING JUICY	THE STATE OF BEING	COURTING YOURSELF	FEEDING THE ARTIST	PORTRAIT OF YOUR AUTHENTICITY	ONE WHO CHOOSES	MARKING A PASSAGE	GRIEVING	REVIVING YOUR SPIRITUAL DIRECTION	STUCK IN THE AIRPORT OF LIFE	RETURNING HOME	CLOSING CEREMONY	LIVING YOUR RETREAT EVERY DAY	RETREATING WITH OTHERS	
158	161		173					212	229	241	253	259			Can I allow myself to relax and be?
	161	165	173	179	188		203	215	229	242	258	259	268	279	How can I listen to and honor my own inner wisdom?
	161	165	175	183	188		207		223		251	259	268		How can I live my own life, inhabit my own center?
	161	165	172		188				231	241	253	259	266	279	How can I love and respect myself more?
156			175	184				215	231	246		259	268		How can I trust nature and trust myself?
	161	168		183		196	205		224			259	268		What is my relationship with the Divine right now?
	161		174					220	229 231	246		259	267	279	How can I feel the love of the Divine?
		169		183		194		215	234	246	256	259	267	273	How can I revive my faith in a benevolent universe?
156	161	168	172		188			220	223			259	268	279	What do I need to do for my spiritual growth?
158	161	166	175	184		194		219	231	242	251	259	267	273	How can I bring the fullness of me into my work life?
166	161	167	174		188	194	203		231	240 242	254	259		273	Is this the right _____ (place, relationship, job) for me right now?

Intention Chart

	INTRODUCTION	HOW TO USE THIS BOOK	A WOMAN'S RETREAT	A RETREAT OUTLINE	THE CALL TO RETREAT	INTENTION	FOR HOW LONG WILL YOU RETREAT?	WHERE WILL YOU RETREAT?: YOUR PHYSICAL AND EMOTIONAL CONTAINERS	WHAT WILL YOU DO?	COURAGE	OPENING CEREMONY	UNCOMFORTABLE BEGINNINGS, MIDDLES, AND IN-BETWEENS	GOOD WAYS TO LISTEN	CONTEMPLATIONS	GATHERING THE WHOLE
Should I commit to this relationship through marriage?			20		36	41	58	63	71 73	86	98	107	123	133	147
How can I make time for myself in my life?	1		12 26	31	35	39	52	65	71	80	102		117	135	142
How can I stop feeling so frantic and out of control?			15	31	33	39	52	62 63	71	80	102	107	129		147
What can I do to make peace with my body?			23		36	41	53	67	74	86	104		117 124	135 138	150
How can I be a mother and an artist too?			19	29	35	40 45	52	63	75	80	98		128		
How can I recharge my creativity?	1		13	29		41	57		73		98		126	133	147
How can I create more lightness and joy in my life?			23	31		41			74		98		113	133	149
Why is this chronic illness in my life?			23	31		41	53	67	75	83	104		117	133	150
How can I accept and let go of _____ (person, relationship, job, health)?					36	41		60	73	81	98	107	124		
How can I begin to accept my and others' imperfections?	3					39	53		75		98		115		149

Intention Chart

EMERGING FROM CHAOS INTO BALANCE	GETTING JUICY	THE STATE OF BEING	COURTING YOURSELF	FEEDING THE ARTIST	PORTRAIT OF YOUR AUTHENTICITY	ONE WHO CHOOSES	MARKING A PASSAGE	GRIEVING	REVIVING YOUR SPIRITUAL DIRECTION	STUCK IN THE AIRPORT OF LIFE	RETURNING HOME	CLOSING CEREMONY	LIVING YOUR RETREAT EVERY DAY	RETREATING WITH OTHERS	
	161	165	174		191	194	203			242	254	259	268		Should I commit to this relationship through marriage?
		165	173		192			215	229	238	251	259	268		How can I make time for myself in my life?
155			175		188			210	229	241	252	259	270		How can I stop feeling so frantic and out of control?
156	161	167	175	184	188	197	203	215	232	246	253	259	269		What can I do to make peace with my body?
	161	168 / 169	172	184		194		215	224	244	254	259	268	304	How can I be a mother and an artist too?
	161	168	172	179	188			215	224 / 232	244		259	268	281 / 283	How can I recharge my creativity?
158	161		173	184			203	215	231	244	253	259	270	273	How can I create more lightness and joy in my life?
156	161		175		188		203	215 / 221	231	242 / 246		259	268		Why is this chronic illness in my life?
		165	176		191	194	203	217	231	237	256	259			How can I accept and let go of _____ (person, relationship, job, health)?
	161		172	186			203	217	227 / 231	241		259	268	273	How can I begin to accept my and others' imperfections?

Intention Chart

	INTRODUCTION	HOW TO USE THIS BOOK	A WOMAN'S RETREAT	A RETREAT OUTLINE	THE CALL TO RETREAT	INTENTION	FOR HOW LONG WILL YOU RETREAT?	WHERE WILL YOU RETREAT?: YOUR PHYSICAL AND EMOTIONAL CONTAINERS	WHAT WILL YOU DO?	COURAGE	OPENING CEREMONY	UNCOMFORTABLE BEGINNINGS, MIDDLES, AND IN-BETWEENS	GOOD WAYS TO LISTEN	CONTEMPLATIONS	GATHERING THE WHOLE
What is the best way to lift this sadness I feel?	2		19	31	35	41		60	71		98	107	113		147
Why can't I get on with my life?			15	31	33	41	48	60	73	89	98	107	126	133	147
How can I change the direction in which I am going?				31		41	50	60	75	80, 83	98		117, 125	136	147
How can I create courage to follow through on the changes I want to make?	2	13			33	41	52	63	71	80	98	107	126		147
What is appropriate for me in the next third of my life?		13		34	38	51		74			98		126	133	147
How can I celebrate the recent changes/good fortune in my life?				29		41		60	74	83	98		124, 125		
How can I be comfortable living alone?			22	31	35	42	53	65, 69		80	98	107	113		147
How can I create structure in my life that will help me to love and respect myself?	2		15	31	35	41		63, 65	71	83, 86	103	107	115, 125	133	
Does my life really matter?	3		14		35	41			75	85	98		113	133	

Intention Chart

EMERGING FROM CHAOS INTO BALANCE	GETTING JUICY	THE STATE OF BEING	COURTING YOURSELF	FEEDING THE ARTIST	PORTRAIT OF YOUR AUTHENTICITY	ONE WHO CHOOSES	MARKING A PASSAGE	GRIEVING	REVIVING YOUR SPIRITUAL DIRECTION	STUCK IN THE AIRPORT OF LIFE	RETURNING HOME	CLOSING CEREMONY	LIVING YOUR RETREAT EVERY DAY	RETREATING WITH OTHERS	
156	161		174	184			203	210	231	240	252	259	266	273	What is the best way to lift this sadness I feel?
155	161		175		194		203	215	227	237		259	266	273	Why can't I get on with my life?
158	161				188	194	203		224	241		259	266	273	How can I change the direction in which I am going?
158	161			184		194	206		224	244	256	259	270	273	How can I create courage to follow through on the changes I want to make?
	161	165	175		188	194	203		227	241		259			What is appropriate for me in the next third of my life?
158	161		174	180	188		203		231			259		273 282	How can I celebrate the recent changes/good fortune in my life?
158	161		172	184	188		203	215		241	253	259	267	273	How can I be comfortable living alone?
155			173	185			203		229	242	252	259	268	273	How can I create structure in my life that will help me to love and respect myself?
	161	165			188			220	227	241		259	267		Does my life really matter?

Practices

Gathering the Whole

For I am the first and the last.
I am the honored one and the scorned one.
I am the whore and the holy one.
I am the wife and the virgin.
I am the mother and the daughter
. . . .
I am the silence that is incomprehensible
and the idea whose remembrance is frequent.
I am the voice whose sound is manifold
and the word whose appearance is multiple.
I am the utterance of my name.

The Thunder, Perfect Mind,
from *The Nag Hammadi Library*

Do you often think to yourself, "If I could just find some time to sit still, to gather all of me into one still point, then I could get a grip on my life; then I could feel or create or have a libido again"? Do you wish you could have a few moments to practice self-acceptance, to say hello to the aspects of yourself that are homely, repellent, catty, judgmental, lewd, lonely, or sacred and to be with them, even hug them, or at least acknowledge their existence?

Mary Wheat confesses in her essay "In the Middle," in *Rattle Those Dry Bones,*

> How do I achieve wholeness, integration, and reconciliation of my
> thousand different selves? My journey moves inward, deep into myself,
> into soul, the glue that binds body and mind together. . . . I must learn
> to recognize the strangers within, to greet and welcome selves I do not
> love, to feed and water each part of myself. Yet my interior hospitality is
> often shallow; I am shy and frightened of so many of my selves. I learn
> that nourishing each part of myself is hard work, counterintuitive to
> my comforting image of nurture.

The time to provide that interior hospitality has arrived. You need no longer resemble a pack of playing cards scattered in a game of Fifty-Two Pick-Up.

The following meditation on gathering the whole can be used in several ways. You can record it before your retreat with music in the background. You can

---

read a bit, close your eyes, visualize for a few moments, then come back and read a little more. You can read it several times, relax, and replay it in your imagination, loosely following the narrative. You may wish to do this meditation in writing or with spontaneous painting.

Prepare

See Resources.

Meditative music.

A plate or tray or large sheet of paper.

Your journal and pen and drawing materials.

Objects and images that represent your various selves.

Put on some meditative music that soothes you and helps you go into your center.

Curl up somewhere comforting in your retreat space. If it is summer, you might sit outside in a patch of tension-melting sunshine. If it is winter, you could wrap yourself in a soft blanket and sit by a fire or a tray of candles. If you have a rocking chair handy, use it. Don't limit yourself by being even slightly uncomfortable. Take all the time you need.

Rock yourself. Close your eyes. Say to yourself, "I invite all the parts of me, forgotten, loved, hurried, ignored, and disliked, to gather together. All are welcome." This is your intention. Do you mean it? Rock and ask yourself if you really want to slow down and bring all your selves together. If you wish, change the intention to reflect what you really desire and are willing to do, and repeat that intention aloud.

When you are ready, say softly to yourself, "Sh-sh-shh" or "Hush" or some other motherly, calming sound. Gently, lovingly, shush away all busy thoughts. You are making room for your selves by becoming still inside. Keep shushing and rocking until you feel calm and quiet. Don't beat yourself up if it feels like it takes forever or if you can't do it. Don't worry. There is all the time in the world.

When you are as still as the moment before sunrise, allow an image of a round table to arise in your mind's eye. What is the table made out of? What does the surface feel like? (You don't have to see it clearly; you can sense it, feel it, see shadows.) There are chairs around this table. What do the chairs look like? Straight backs? Soft, oversized, leather? Or is each one different?

Take a moment to feel the shape and texture of a chair. Notice how empty the chairs are. They are waiting.

If you are willing and want to, invite the part of yourself that you call the responsible self, the self you are most familiar with, to come sit at this table. Ask her to sit down, take a moment out of her busy day. Give her a chance to talk. Is she carrying anything? Let her tell you what role she plays in your life. Ask her how she feels about that role.

When you have spent enough time with this part of yourself, you may wish to ask the part of yourself you love the best to come and sit at your table. Be open to whoever arrives. Touch her if you can. Tell her all the things you love about her. If she is not the aspect that you are most familiar with, ask her why.

When you are ready, ask the part of you that judges others to come to the table. How does she enter the room? How does she carry her body? Ask her what her role in your life is. Ask her how she has been judged. Listen with an open heart to whatever she has to say. See if you have a gift to give her.

It is time to ask the part of you that is still a child to come sit for a while. What age is the child who appears? Does more than one child wish to come to your table? Give her a gift, something you always wanted. Treat her as you would a child you adore but perhaps don't feel completely comfortable with. Give her time to warm up to you. Ask her what she needs in order to feel nurtured. She may not be able to respond clearly, and you may have to guess, but do ask. Reassure her that you will take care of her on this retreat.

Ask the part of your self that pushes to get things done to come to your table and sit awhile. You may or may not be familiar with her. Invite her to sit down and have a well-deserved rest. Ask her what she needs to help her know when to push and when to let go. You might want to massage her neck or feet or to meditate with her. Let her be critical and push you away if she needs to, but persist in your welcoming.

See if there is a do-nothing, laid-back, or lazy self that could make her way to your table. You must breathe and wait for her to appear. And you must silence the pusher and judge for this one to appear. What does this self have to say? What gift is she willing to give you? What does she need?

When you are ready, ask the part of you that is critical of you and the other selves to come on in. Look closely at her. What or whom does her face resemble? How does she carry her body? How does it feel to sit near her? Ask her what she needs to be nurtured. Ask her what she needs to feel loved. Ask her what she fears happening if she stops criticizing. Welcome her and love her the best you can.

Is there a warrior inside you, a spirit that defends, demands, stands up for you and others? Invite her to the table. She might have helped you come on this retreat, so you might want to thank her. How do the others feel around her? Is she hard or easy for you to see and speak to? Remember to ask her what she needs to be nurtured.

How about the pleaser, the nice girl, the lady? Surely she doesn't want to miss a party. What is she wearing? What does she do when faced with all these parts of yourself? Or have you already met her as your responsible self? She may be part of your responsible self but also one in her own. How does it feel to be with her? Comfortable, familiar, irritating? Be sure to ask her what she needs. Sit with her until she can tell you. Be patient. Remember, she is part of you, too.

Who is lagging behind? Who is hurt, hiding, almost extinct? Draw the vulnerable child or another hidden self into your room. Kind words, an averted look, or remembering to rock your body may help this one to appear. Do not block her entrance by chastising yourself for ignoring her until now. Embrace her with an open heart. Ask her what she needs to be nurtured. She may not have words. She may speak in images or feeling bursts. Offer her your understanding. Sit with her in stillness for a while.

Could you entice your highest self, your spiritual nature, to your table? Can you feel her light? Does her shape or even her appearance surprise you? How do you feel sitting near her? Do the others react in any way? Ask her what she needs to be renewed. Ask her what messages she carries from other realms.

Where is your physical self? The aspect of you that has a vulva and a sex drive, that has fantasies, desires, moist places? Does she dance into the room, shaking her hips? Or does she slide shyly into her chair, legs crossed? When was the last time you listened to her needs? What does she want on this retreat?

Can you call in your most loathed part to sit awhile? She is an aspect of yourself you despise. She is the most secret, most hidden you, the part that if someone else saw, you are positive they would have nothing to do with you ever again. Let whoever comes be okay. Stop judging for a moment. Can you find anything to appreciate or like about this part of you? Try to hold to your intention to welcome all. Try to see her beauty and usefulness and to offer love. What role does she play in your life? What warmth can you offer her? What gift can she give you? Why is she part of you? What does she need?

Open your heart and imagination more. Whom do you wish to summon? Whom are you afraid to see? Who has a message for you? Allow anyone and everyone who wishes to join you, and without whom you would not be you, to come to your table. All are equal. All are welcome. Name them as they arrive. Rock and shush and invite. Take your time. Someone shy but very important may be waiting in the wings to come sit but only if she sees that you mean it, that you are slowing down, honoring all, making room, reserving judgment.

Allow your various selves to communicate with one another and with you. What will cultivate wholeness and acceptance? Again, the images and the words may not be clear. Let the answer flow through you. There is no need to control or force. Watching and welcoming are your touchstones if you start to feel lost or if you feel you are pushing the experience.

Shush. Rock. Hold the tension of gathering the whole. Listen.

Step back and see the whole. Open your arms and gather them all in. Ask if everyone will hold hands. See the circle. Say a prayer to the Divine asking that all these selves stay with you, that they help you on your retreat. Ask for a blessing for each self, a specific gift of help, guidance, or love. Thank everyone for showing up.

Come back slowly and with soft eyes. Write or draw your insights into your congregation of self.

Making a Mandala

Investigate your retreat environment for objects or images that represent each of the selves that came to your table, and draw, paint, or collage a symbol for each self. Your pleaser girlie self might be a tube of lipstick. Your warrior self might be a picture of a woman protesting nuclear weapons.

See Portrait of Your Authenticity: Prepare for how to do a symbol scan.

Draw a large circle or use a tray to represent the table. Make it large enough to hold all the representations of selves you might find or make. Arrange your symbols around the plate or paper in whatever order feels good, making a representation of your whole.

Place in the middle of your mandala an image, words, a poem, or a combination of these things that represents for you wholeness, balance, the Divine.

Meditate on your round table, your mandala, your medicine wheel. Ask the center for guidance on how to bring all of you into accord. Journal for a few minutes about this experience, these images. What can you do to maintain this wholeness when you return to ordinary life?

Leave your mandala where you can see it throughout your retreat. Keep it intact and in a place of reverence where it will not be disturbed or ridiculed.

You might want to build a shrine around it or include it on your shrine. Invite additional insights through meditation and journaling with it.

Stories

This was part of Sandy's one-day retreat.

> I was interested in meeting my authentic self. In my visualization, she came to the table quickly. I was very upset to see she was not perfect. She is human with rough edges and jagged places. It was so hard to accept her and sit there with her because of this. She is really pissed off at me because I've rejected her for so many years for her faults.
>
> We grabbed hold of each other's wrists. I was clear I was never going to let go no matter what the struggle. I was open enough in the beginning to see some of the things she likes—walking, the beach, to be alone. But I kept coming back to "She's not perfect." I was so afraid I would find out things I didn't like about her, I kept shutting down. She told me she wasn't interested in revealing her good parts because she wanted me to embrace the whole. I was clear I was committed to doing that, but I still kept shutting down. It was a struggle but also very profound to sit there with her.

Susan did the visualization as part of her retreat.

> My table was large with many people/parts from various stages of my life present. Lots of little children were at the table. One was especially cute and made me laugh aloud. There was a teenage self and lots of older selves there.
>
> The strangest self was the critical self. It came in the form of a cockatoo—white with a dark beak. Its criticism was in the form of pecking. I tried to get this creature in a human form, but that just wasn't to be. Everyone else was female and looked like me at some period in my life. There was one exception. My higher self came in the form of pure, brilliant white light.
>
> This whole group was a lively bunch. They sat around together and it felt very comfortable, and whole, somehow. I think the overall sense was one of a peaceful gathering, even with the mean-spirit part present. The brilliant light seemed to be the predominant energy. It was like a huge umbrella, except it was on everything and everyone at the same time.

For Long Retreats

Do this exercise at the beginning of your retreat and then repeat it at the end, noting new insights or seeing if your visualization changes. Consider using the mandala-making portion as an ongoing practice for your entire retreat, keeping an eye out for symbolic objects to add to it and going back from time to time to work with the symbols.

For Mini-Retreats

Take five minutes to visualize the round table with only one chair. Invite the self you most need to be with to come sit for a while. Spend a few moments being together. You may talk or exchange gifts or not.

See Retreat Plans: A One-Day Well-Being Retreat.

For Retreats in the World

Read the visualization, then venture out in the world to look for images and tokens that represent your selves. Gather these to compose a mandala later. Or make a mandala in the forest or on the beach, using found and created symbols. Watching such a mandala be washed away by the sea or visiting it later, after wind and rain have changed it, can be a powerful meditation on the transience of life.

For Retreats with Others

Take turns reading the meditation to one another, or have one woman read it, then separate to work on your mandalas. You can also tape the meditation, listen to it together, then paint, write, or dance your perceptions at the same time. Or each woman does the practice alone, then all can come together to explain your mandalas to one another and to add symbols to one another's to represent additional selves or qualities you recognize in your friends.

For a group that has been working together for a while, try making living mandalas using people to represent different selves. In centered, sacred space, have someone read (or record and play back) the meditation, then each woman takes a turn directing a mini-play of her various selves. She picks a woman to describe one self, places her in the circle, and instructs her on how to play that character, talking, gesturing, acting out whatever behavior she feels fits. When her mandala is complete, the woman whose mandala it is stands in the center and listens to what each woman would like to say to her. She finishes by asking all her selves to hold hands and chant, "We have gathered together. We have slowed down. Everyone is welcome. We can hold the center." Repeat this until each woman who wants to has created her circle of selves. End the entire practice with a song or a big hug.

A practical point: you need a group of at least eight to do this but no more than twelve. You must limit the amount of time each woman takes to set up and direct her mandala. No less than fifteen minutes is needed, but you could take up to an hour. With a group of ten, this exercise could easily take three hours or a whole day.

Emerging from Chaos into Balance

All will be well
and all will be well
and all manners of things will be well.

Julian of Norwich

Complicated, busy, painful, troubled periods in life happen more often than we would like. Sometimes I am able to react calmly, sailing through pandemonium, dealing well with grief. Others times, I'm lost. Submerged. Frantic. I feel like a horse wearing blinders. I can't see what I need to do, what needs to change. I feel hog-tied by confusion, unsure of my choices, and I respond by moving faster and faster, which only makes things worse. I want to climb out of my life, stand on top of it, and survey the whole big, sprawling mess. I'm having minor accidents, snapping at store clerks, driving rudely, missing appointments, forgetting birthdays, feeling like I'm making matters worse. At times like these, I know I'm lost in chaos.

If you are retreating to get a grip on your life, to stop lurching around with a perpetual frown creasing your forehead, this is a good practice to do. It works especially well at the beginning of a retreat.

Prepare

Six sheets of paper or your journal.

A pencil or pen.

Drawing materials.

The Feeling Spiral

When your life resembles one long *ER* episode, only no cute doctor ever appears to rescue you, it can be hard to stay current with concrete things like mortgages and birthdays, let alone feelings. The only problem is, these stressful times can become extra depress-ful times because you are carrying last week's, last month's, last year's feelings on your back. When an old feeling gets triggered by a present situation or when you simply haven't had a breather to catch up with yourself, your present reaction can be more painful, more volatile. Your ability to see clearly what is in front of you becomes clouded. You become more and more frantic because you haven't had time to feel. Tracing these feelings back to the origin helps you untangle your responses, and while the chaotic feelings may surface again, your perceptions and reactions get lighter and clearer with practice.

Read through the following list. Copy into your journal each emotion you've felt recently or each word that you feel a strong "hit" from. Do this quickly.

Angry, Awesome, Creative, Confused, Delighted, Dull, Irritable, Hurried, Scared, Resentful, Fascinated, False, Elated, Frantic, Good, Graced, Gloomy, Irreverent, Irresistible, Happy, Uptight, Self-protective, Glad, Shameful, Guilty, Humiliated, Anxious, Easygoing, Uneasy, Mean, Exuberant, Unstable, Old, Dispassionate, Serious, Dried out, Funny, Intelligent, Mysterious, Powerless, Empowered, Puzzled, Feminine, Extraordinary, Inspired, Maternal, Original, Glorious, Violent, Whimsical, Worried, Uncompromising, Rigid, Relentless, Quiet, Spirited, Truthful, Terrified, Tense, Trusting, Stifled, Stubborn, Picking fights, Empathetic, Zealous, Letting go, Inventive, Serene, Overflowing, Neglected, Unfeeling, Lively, Majestic, Loathsome, Queenlike, Vulnerable, Masculine, Unreachable, Incompetent, Inconsequential, Sensuous, Clear, Heartless, Jealous, Beautiful, Radiant, Gray, Devoted, Petty, Abused, Juicy, Needy, Receptive, Raw, Shaky, Powerful, Kind, Sad, Enthusiastic, Closed off, Busy, Wrung out, Capable, Sexy, Playful, Generous, Stingy, Envious, Feeble, Bored, Depressed, Exhausted, Out-of-the-loop, Calm, Stuck, Mighty, Helpless, Luminous, Holy, Critical, Criticized, Judgmental, Ardent, Spry, Know-it-all, Insufferable, Blank, Friendly, Bossy, Intense, Seductive, Satisfied, Caring, Invaded, Invasive, Suspicious, Graceful, Reverent, Frustrated, Fulfilled, Grateful, Bitchy, Fertile, Flexible, Forgiving, Outgoing, Inwardly focused, Faithful, Faithless, Emotional, Too big for your britches, Without a voice, Without boundaries, Need to curl up with a blanket and be read stories to.

Take each emotion you circled and trace it back to the original core. For example, you may have circled *Guilt*. Ask yourself, "When did I last feel guilty?" Perhaps you remember rushing to exercise class, behind in your work, your child wailing, "Mommy, don't go." Ask yourself, "Where did this guilt come from?" Perhaps what comes to mind is feeling like you're never doing enough. Keep tracing it back by asking again, "Where did that feeling come from?" Maybe the slimy finger of shame glides over your heart, perhaps you glimpse images of times you failed at something. Again, "Where did that feeling come from?" A queasy feeling of fear stirs in you, loosely tied to a primal image of not being accepted. You have hit one of the basic five, the irreducible emotions of *anger, joy, fear, love*, and *hurt*. Every emotion comes down to one of these at its heart. Guilt may spring from fear, resentment from anger, creativity from love. You know you have contacted ground zero when you ask, "Where did this feeling come from?" and one of the basic five echoes back at you. You know you have hit the truth when you *feel it in your body*. Fear and anger are often felt as a clutching in your stomach, a pain in your neck, a band of tightness around your head, or clenched fists or jaw. Joy and love might express themselves as an ache in your throat, an opening around your heart, or a lightness in your whole being. Hurt can be a burning, tears in your eyes, or wanting to curl up and be hugged.

What does it feel like to be in this basic feeling? To ride the sensation? Sometimes it helps to write about how you are feeling, to trace the memories and associations that might arise. Or you might find this to be a nonverbal process, one that begs to be drawn or to be expressed in movement. Painting, drawing, sculpting clay, and walking are all helpful ways to "stay with" and deepen your experience. Or sitting or lying still and breathing deeply might be best.

See Good Ways to Listen and Contemplations: Ways to Work with Questions.

When you feel that you've ridden this emotion out, choose another one that you circled and work through it. You will find each time you trace your feeling that it gets both easier to find where the feeling started and harder because with each attempt you feel more. That's good. Track the origin of your chaos a couple more times. Tracing several feelings back to their sources is enough to reveal what core feelings are active in your life right now and allows you to coax them into the open for a good airing.

This is an exercise that can be repeated whenever you are experiencing a hard time and your reaction is confusion, anxiety, and increasingly faster movement. Each time you descend the spiral, you learn more about what triggers you, what ancient associations from your genes, from your childhood, or from your adult choices influence you. It is never an easy descent, but it amazingly opens up space for you to begin to view your life more calmly, unburdened by a refrigerator stuffed with stale emotions.

You may want to take a rest here. This is a good place to take a break or end if you are doing a mini-retreat.

Standing on Top of Your Life

Spread out six pieces of paper if you have room. If you are on a retreat in the world, do one list at a time in your journal.

You're going to make four lists. Your first list will be everything you can think of in response to "What I hate about my life right now is. . . ." Be as scrupulously honest with yourself as you dare. No one is going to read it but you. Write quickly. Keep going until everything is out on paper.

Next list everything you can think of in response to "What is missing in my life right now is. . . ." Name your longings, your wistfulness, your regrets. Don't write down something because you feel you should.

Next list "What I love about my life right now is. . . ." Be specific. Remember little things like a certain kind of tea you relish or the way your bed supports you when you collapse into it at night, and big ones like your best friend, your children, your health.

When you feel you have recorded everything, pretend you are your closest friend. What would he or she add? *Do you agree?* If you do, add it. If not, record it on another piece of paper with that person's initials next to it. If you have a partner or lover, pretend you are that person and see if his or her perspective adds any new ideas. Do you accept them? If so, add them. If not, note them with initials on the other piece of paper. What about your mom? Your dad? (As you know, they don't have to be living to have an opinion.) Your sister? Your cat? Are there either any other opinions that you need to get out of the way or any people whose viewpoints might be helpful?

See Opening Ceremony: A Few Guidelines and Good Ways to Listen: I Am Enough.

Get out another sheet of paper. Close your eyes. Inhale slowly and deeply. On your exhale, let out a big sigh. Spend a few moments centering yourself.

See in your mind's eye your image of the Divine. Let an image spontaneously appear to you. Don't edit, don't refuse. No need to hurry, no need to force. Just let an image materialize. Feel streams of warmth and light flowing to you from this image, washing away negativity, doubt, worry, chaos, frantic rushing. Let yourself be bathed. Let yourself be supported by this love. (You may be saying, "What visualization hooey crap." Perhaps, but it feels good. Even the intellectual, stuck-up part of me knows that what my mind imagines, my body echoes by producing corresponding reactions. So think of this as a healing session. You don't have to really believe anything.)

When you are ready, perhaps your image of the Divine gently asks you, "Where are you in your life right now?" Whatever images, symbols, feelings, or sensations arise are perfect. Don't refuse. Thank whoever has appeared, and, coming back with soft eyes, with no need to hurry or worry about outcome, render your vision of where you are in your life on paper, using color, shape, symbols, and images. What it looks like is *not* important. (Repeat after me, What it looks like is not important.) It is *bypassing the words* to get to the more intuitive, dreamlike state of images and symbols that is important.

Work on this as long as you like. If you need to do more than one drawing, fine. Post it someplace where you can see it, and take a break. Pick some berries, plant some tomatoes, read about a woman on retreat, eat brie and fresh bread by a lake—anything that nourishes you. This is another good stopping point if you are doing a mini-retreat, but don't skip the self-nurturing. Leave time for a warm bath or a stroll, if only for ten minutes.

Come back and read over your lists of emotions. At the end of each list, write a few lines of feedback, a response to what you wrote. You might start your feedback with "I see" or "I now feel" or "I learned."

Sit quietly in front of your drawing for a few moments. Look at it with the eyes of a total stranger. What insights or connections might this stranger see? Write a bit of feedback about your drawing. "What I see" is a good place to start.

Place your drawing next to your lists. Either spread them out on the floor or tack them on a wall. Make a fourth list in response to the question "How can I experience more balance and peace in my life?" Write quickly. Write everything. If you feel stuck, skim the first three lists and your drawing. If you feel panicky, know you are not making a commitment to do anything (you might not be ready to take action for days, weeks, months, years), but that doesn't mean you can't *acknowledge* what you *might* need.

Contemplate your drawing and your lists for the rest of your retreat. If you are going back to your regular life now, post them where you can see them. They are little road maps to help you see through the chaos. Hopefully, you feel a little clearer, lighter, more hopeful, and less anxious now.

For Long Retreats

If at any time you are feeling jumpy or anxious or that you aren't "getting enough" from your retreat, do the feeling spiral. Do it several times. Meditate on your lists. What associations, ideas, visions come to mind? You might find the lists suggesting another retreat activity—anything from making a collage on how to experience more peace and balance to dancing out the frustration and rage of your "What I hate about my life right now . . ." list.

For Mini-Retreats

See Retreat Plans: A One-Hour Getting Current Retreat. The feeling spiral can be safely done in an hour or a bit less. Just be sure to contain it between opening and closing ceremonies. Standing on Top of Your Life can be done quickly as a brief check-in with yourself. Do only the question "How can I experience more balance and peace in my life?"

For Retreats in the World

Standing on Top of Your Life lends itself to being done on a cliff overlooking the ocean or at a table in a café. Unless you are comfortable with strangers offering you tissues, the feeling spiral is best done in privacy.

For Retreats with Others

You could do the visualization together, either having someone record it beforehand on a tape or having someone read it while everyone else relaxes and listens.

Another group activity is to display your lists in a circle, including the piece of paper with others' voices on it that you did not include in your own list. Silently, each woman walks around the circle reading the others' lists and adding her comments on the extra sheet of paper, with her initials. Then everyone reads the comments and sits together in a circle to discuss them.

Or do a brainstorming session on how to bring to life one or two of the ideas you each listed in "To experience more balance and peace in my life. . . ." When brainstorming, anything goes. Everyone speaks her ideas. Nothing is censored. No one comments on someone else's ideas, either positively or negatively. Use a tape recorder or have someone record the ideas. After the wildness has run its course for one woman, switch to another. Then after everyone has had a turn, take a break. Then go back to the first woman and do what Barbara Sher calls a barn raising: think of people you know, skills you have, and other practical ways you can help her take *concrete* steps toward realizing one of the brainstorming ideas she likes.

Getting Juicy

You are living juicy! Ride into your life on a creative cycle, full of juice, abundance and ecstatic wonderment. You are a star.

SARK, *Living Juicy*

How would you feel about reclaiming the energy that modern life drains from you, reanimating your feminine fire, turning up the sound on your instinctual nature? Give a hoot and a holler, work up a lather. You may be saying, "But I'm so tired. I just want to go to bed. I just need to not think for a while. Reading that novel I bought sounds much better." Trust me, this is what this exercise is for, to overcome the ennui, the limits, the dryness that comes from living too much, too long, without time for yourself, until you feel like you are choking under a cloak of chalky dust. Do this one exercise and then see if you want to spend the rest of your time reading and napping. If you do, great. But try this first.

This exercise is a good one to do if you are feeling stuck when working with another practice in this book or when you are feeling tired, nervous, depressed, or anxious. It works well at the beginning of your retreat, too.

Prepare

Propulsive, intense dance music and slower, more meditative movement music.

Your journal and a pen.

A drum or rattle.

Imagine yourself as a bonsai tree, pruned and forced to grow in a tiny dish, squeezed so that you are only an eighth of your potential glory. This is what happens to most of us. We are hobbled by our beliefs, society's constraints on what being a woman *should* entail, and the often harsh requirements of survival. But today, right now, in this moment, you can choose to leave that tiny dish. With a crack in your knees and a groan torn from your chest, you can yank your roots free and spread your toes in the earth.

Start right now, right here. If the weather permits, walk outside (if not, do this facing a window). Plant your feet apart. Curl your toes into the soil. Fling your arms wide open. Arch your back and neck, puff your chest out, pull your shoulder blades together, and imagine your heart opening to the sun. Breathe. Stay here for a moment. Contemplate the question "What will it take for me to be fully alive?" Listen for the feelings this question stirs up.

Relax your back, neck, and arms. Align your spine. Open your eyes.

Take a deep breath and let out a sound. Do it again, louder.

What are you holding on to? Let it out with a final "Ahh."

Grab your drum or rattle or put on music and thump along with it. Feeling awkward? Never done this before? *No one* need know what you do on this retreat. You can tell them you did your nails for three days or read Sartre. This is *your* time. Dare. Breathe, close your eyes, and feel the music. There is no right way to do this. The point is to get out of your head.

Experiment with tempos. Drum or move through any fatigue, any doubt, any voices that might be saying how bad you are at this, how stupid it is. Drum or dance energy up from the base of your spine.

Keep playing until you begin to feel you *must* make sounds to accompany your drumming or the music. Don't open your mouth until you can't resist. Belt out your song of soul juice. Give a voice to being fully alive.

Sense the energy of life moving through you. Allow yourself to open. Push yourself past your usual stopping point, where you give in to boredom, limits, smallness, self-criticism.

At your own pace and at an organic stopping point, put down your drum or turn off the music and check in with your body. How does it feel? Do you feel energy running up your spine? Do you feel silly? Tired? No judgment, no expectations. Lovingly check in. Want to quit all this nonsense and lie in the sun? Before you do, try finishing this last part.

Put on some slightly slower music that still inspires movement. Listen for a moment without moving.

Shake your feet. Lift and spread your toes, feeling each one separate and flex.

Roll your hips in a few wide, slow circles. Sensuous. Bend your knees a bit. Now rotate your hips in the opposite direction.

Shake out your hands. Snap your wrists and fingers.

Tense your shoulders by bringing them up to your ears. Squeeze tight, then let out a big sigh as you release. Repeat a few times.

Visualize the music melding with the place in your body where your most powerful life energy is stored: your laughter, your wisdom, what makes you *you*. It might be your throat, the base of your spine, your solar plexus, your womb. Spontaneously pick a spot. Feel the music shaping that energy, magnifying it, pulsing it throughout your body. It may feel like a bolt shooting up your spine or a soft glow expanding.

Allow the music and your energy to move you. Instead of controlling your movement, let the movement flow through you. Let the music and your energy soften and warm any rigid, bored, lonely, tired places in your body. Let the music and energy breathe you, lift you, spin you. The music/energy makes the effort, you don't.

Forget "dancing," forget trying to *do* anything.

Feel yourself coming alive. Don't let the voice of inertia stop you. Let this new energy carry you longer and further and deeper than ever before.

Gyrate, pirouette, leap, grind: fully alive.

Ask the music/energy, "If I were fully alive, how would I move?" Let her answer through movement. If you could, for just one moment, relax the inner critic, the layers of sadness and tiredness that may have settled on your vital soul, what would you do? Dance being fully alive.

Keep going until you can feel your chi, your life energy, setting you on fire (even if it is just a little warmth in your hands and feet).

When you feel you have danced your very essence into heat, pick up your journal and, *without thinking,* write everything you can think of to complete this sentence: "To be fully alive, I could. . . ." Feel the energy in your body from drumming and dancing. Stay in this fluid, hot, juicy state. Write standing up while you continue to sway or move your feet. Allow words to rush forth unrestricted. Write a poem or a list, write down what you sang or chanted. "To be fully alive, I could. . . ."

Finish with three slow "Ahhs" or other sounds from deep in your belly.

End by grounding yourself, perhaps by lying on the ground. Breathe and check your balance. "How do I feel? What do I want to do next? What do I yearn for?" Follow your instincts.

For Long Retreats

Do this practice a number of times. Experiment with listening to yourself through your physical body. See if it gets easier the deeper you move into retreat time.

For Mini-Retreats

This exercise makes a great mini-retreat in itself. Try doing it in the morning, before work, before a Friday night date, or before you attend a kids' party. You can do it in only ten or fifteen minutes.

For Retreats in the World

Listen to music on a personal stereo with headphones while walking. Swing your arms and legs energetically. After a few minutes, finish this sentence: "To be fully alive, I could. . . ."

For Retreats with Others

You can drum and dance together, using one another's energy to magnify your own. However, in most groups the issue becomes one of inhibition and of trying to drum in sync. It usually takes several tries or an experienced drummer. Try working off one another's sounds, drumming, and dancing. Don't fight feeling gawky, unmusical, or nervous. Acknowledge these feelings in yourself, yet keep going. Making the transition into dancing or journaling can be a little tricky. Avoid worrying about what others need, and stay focused on your own process. It is fine if one woman keeps dancing ten minutes after everyone else is finished, as long as the group has discussed this ahead of time. Don't try to end together. Have a place others can go off to write, rest, or eat and allow the dancing to continue.

The State of Being

With stammering lips and insufficient sounds,
I strive and struggle to deliver right
the music of my nature. . . .

Elizabeth Barrett Browning

The president gives state of the union addresses. Children have quarterly reviews with their teachers about how they are doing. Bosses dispense yearly performance reviews. But where is the routine assessment of what matters most, the state of your soul? Where is the time for simple reflection?

Now is the time to report on how your inner life is informing your daily decisions, not from a logical place but from an intuitive place. This is the time to ask, "How am I doing?" and to wait for the answer from within.

Try to do this practice all in one sitting. Be aware that boredom or an inability to focus is often a sign that you simply are out of practice focusing on yourself. Persist by using kindness and your sense of humor. If you get stuck or feel uninspired, try using a different medium. For example, if you are using spontaneous drawing but after a few tries you feel bored, switch to movement.

Prepare

Choose one or more ways to explore the questions given here. You might write in your journal on one question, dance another, do a visualization with another, then make a collage. Or meditate on all the questions and then write

See Contemplations and Good Ways to Listen.

a list or story. Gather whatever materials you may need for your chosen medium of exploration:

Drum.

See Resources. Music to dance to.

Drawing supplies.

Clay.

One or two things to entertain your senses with—a bite of something luscious, a whiff of a favorite perfume.

Have your supplies all ready to go.

Center and calm yourself in whatever way you choose.

Close your eyes. Imagine yourself in your environment, your habitat, your home. (If you are retreating at home and no one else is around, walk around your environment first, then sit down and close your eyes.) Resist viewing your rooms in any categorical or logical fashion. See what associations come up when your mind drifts with the words *shelter, sanctuary, hearth, refuge, the ones I live with, design, sound, smell, comfort, safe*. Place your hand on your belly. When you have contemplated home for a few minutes, using your medium of choice (journaling, painting, sculpting), explore these questions:

- What parts of me need more from my environment?

- What might *more* look like?

- What parts of me need less from my environment?

- What might *less* look like?

Take a few deep breaths. Close your eyes. Focus on your work. Turn the notions of *profession, calling, project, life's work, responsibility, purpose, business* around in your heart. Forget going through a typical day at work. Float instead in whatever sensations and images arise. If you feel yourself becoming depressed, judgmental, or anxious, take several deep breaths and then observe that feeling. You are not that feeling, but what can it teach you? When you wish, ask yourself:

- What parts of me need more from my work?

- What might *more* look like?

- What parts of me need less from my work?

- What might *less* look like?

- What do I need to give to my work?

- What do I need to give less of?

Once again, unravel, analyze, explore these questions in whatever medium you wish. If you feel stuck, try a new medium. If you always do journal writing, try movement or talking into a tape recorder.

Stretch, breathe, get comfortable, and close your eyes. If you like, put your hand on your heart or hug yourself. What comes to mind when you reflect on *love*? On *attachment, intimacy, commitment, relationship, joining, surrender*? What faces float to mind? What scenes? What joys? What longings?

- What parts of me need more from love?

- What might *more* look like?

- What parts of me need less from love?

- What might *less* look like?

- What can I give to love?

Work with these questions.

Close your eyes and breathe deeply. Scan your body. How do you feel in your envelope of flesh? Concentrate on images of your sexuality. What does your sexuality look like, taste like, sound like? Do you know her? Do you like her? What is the state of *your libido, your passion, desire, vulnerability, orgasm, fantasy, tenderness, physical closeness?* Try exploring these questions with your body, using movement:

- What parts of me need more from sex?

- What might *more* look like?

- What parts of me need less from sex?

- What might *less* look like?

Close your eyes and assess the relationships in your life. Spend a few minutes with each of the important people in your life—your mate, children, mother, father, friends, enemies, work mates, roommates, family, clergy, women's group, and reading circle. Forget order of importance and see who comes to mind. Write about your feelings. Ask yourself as each person comes to visit:

- What parts of me need more from this person?

- What might *more* look like?

- What parts of me need less?

- What might *less* look like?

- What can I give in this relationship?

- Where am I giving too much?

Close your eyes and allow an image of your creative life to come before you. (Don't skip this section because you think you have no creative life. Living a creative life means living in a way that reflects the unique you.) Contemplate the words *create, invent, choose, alive, surprise, imagination, challenge, seeing something familiar for the first time, reaching, reframing, dreaming.*

- What parts of me need more from my creativity?

- What might *more* look like?

- What parts of me need less from my creativity?

- What might *less* look like?

- What can I give to my creative life?

What do you wish to create with these questions that would bring verve to this realm? What medium could you explore? Finally, close your eyes one last time. If you like, ask for a blessing or say a prayer. Now focus on your spiritual life. What images, feelings, scenes arise? Expand past the obvious (church, spiritual group, walking in nature). Where does *holy, remarkable, illuminated, turning it over, wisdom, faith, nurturance, awe, bliss, circle, centered, inner truth, God, Goddess, Divine, Beloved, transformation, redemption* take you? Place your hands on your body where the Divine resides.

- What parts of me need more from spirit?

- What might *more* look like?

- What parts of me need less from spirit?

- What might *less* look like?

- What can I give spirit?

- What medium will help me learn more from these questions?

You may feel tired, overwhelmed, and depressed or exhilarated, thrilled, and ready to move to Paris, become a diva, and drink only expensive champagne. However you feel in this moment, now is *not* the time to act. It is the time to affirm your trust and faith in yourself. Create a brief ritual of promise. I like to light a candle and pray. Some people like to draw up simple contracts with themselves, setting a date by which they will do a certain thing. All that matters is that you make a solemn promise to yourself to honor the insights and promptings that have just emerged, *when the time is right.* A favorite prayer of mine for this moment is

> Dear Great One,
> May I have faith in myself and your energy.
> May I remember my truth, my spark of life, my gift.
> When I am lost in the pit of despair and can't even make a collect call
>   for help,
> May I trust that I will find my way back to my truth,
> to these insights that I have found today.
> Help me to co-create the best life for myself and for all those I love.
> So may it be.
> And so it is.

Stories

Diane is a mother of two young children, a writer, and the co-owner of a computer imaging company.

> It was a rainy Saturday morning and I was trapped inside a small house with two restless children. My newspaper was soggy, crusty dishes were in piles everywhere, and my period was due at any moment. Trapped in the netherworld of parenting without so much as a drop of milk for my coffee.
>
> By 10:30 A.M. I had already screamed at everyone, cried twice, and considered an alternative lifestyle. None of these activities improved my situation, so I turned to the only thing that really helps me in these times: a good soak. There is an indoor pool near my house that is heated to 90 degrees. I packed up my family for an amniotic Band-Aid.
>
> While my husband and kids were playing in the shallow end, I slipped off to the deep end and floated around on a kickboard. Noticing how tense I was, I put the board under my back and, face up, enjoyed the sensation of effortless, pointless movement.
>
> I closed my eyes and let my feet and ears dangle under the water, shutting out sound and sensation. I was in retreat. I consciously began to check in with each part of my body as I floated around. I could hear my children, but the water softened and muted their voices.

I spent a few minutes floating, softening tension, and reviewing my life.

I glided toward the shallow end and noticed that the nearer I got to my family, the more I had to make little adjustments in my balance to stay afloat. Their activity caused little ripples that unsteadied me unless I corrected myself on my kickboard. A few times I let myself be toppled over, and then, face down, I'd concentrate on relaxing every muscle in my body, beginning with my extremities and moving toward my center. Then I'd stick my head out for air, fill my lungs, and reposition the board below me again.

This went on for some time, until I headed back to the deep end. I contemplated this little exercise and how it related to what was working and not working in my daily life. Eyes closed, I thought about how each day my children and I reenact this same scene; their lives send ripples into mine, and I try to adjust and balance myself to avoid being thrown over completely. Sometimes I do flip, and go facedown into a dead man's float, like this morning. When that happens, I know I must consciously remind myself to soften, and take time to take care of my needs. Literally and figuratively, I recognized that I must have my own support in place so that I can respond to the waves my children make.

I slowly lifted my head out of the water, and the sound of my children's voices sounded musical and joyous to me. I opened my eyes and looked at them, and they appeared to me as perfectly formed parcels of trust and love. A wave of tenderness washed over me as I joined them in the shallow end.

For Long Retreats

See Contemplations.
Include areas of your life that I have missed. Get creative with the mediums you use. Try ones that require more preparation or time, such as making a mask, doll, or earth shrine.

For Mini-Retreats

See Retreat Plans: A One-Hour Getting Current Retreat.
Close the door of your office or sink into the couch while dinner cooks, before the kids get home. Pick one or two areas to ask yourself about, the ones that feel most out of balance. Do that part of the practice as meditation or visualization or through journal writing. The questions many women use for this kind of check-in are

- What part of me needs more from my work?

- What part of me needs less?

- What part of me needs more from love?
- What part of me needs less?

- What part of me needs more from this person or relationship?
- What part of me needs less?

For Retreats in the World

This is an especially good practice to do while hiking, canoeing, running, working in an art studio, or looking out from a tall building or after doing service work at a hospice or retirement home.

For Retreats with Others

After doing the practice on your own, come into a deep listening circle. Each woman asks for feedback from the others on one or two areas of her life. One way to ask for feedback is "What does my work life look like to you? What do you think I need more or less of?" If you are retreating with people who know only certain sides of one another, you may have to limit your questions to those areas. For example, a group of eight women who met regularly to support one another in their creative pursuits retreated together. They used this practice to give feedback to each woman on four areas of her creative life: work (getting projects finished, trying to sell, getting paid on time), risk taking, feeding the creative spirit, and developing technique. As always, it is imperative to use the circle guidelines with great care and loving-kindness.

See Retreating with Others: Deep Listening Circle.

Courting Yourself

*You must become aware of the richness in you and come
to believe in it and know it is there. . . . Once you become
aware of it and have faith in it, you will be all right.*

Brenda Ueland, *If You Want to Write*

Two definitions of *courting* are "to try to gain the love or affection of, especially to seek to marry" and "to seek someone's love; to woo." I would add "to prove your commitment to someone and to gain someone's trust."

What do you need to do to prove your love to yourself? What would you like to do? While courting yourself can surely be a daily action, a retreat is a powerful time to focus on this because you are taken away from your habitual ways of perceiving yourself. You are in the perfect space to court at-one-ment, the realization that you are the lover and the beloved, that you are whole and complete in yourself. You can shower yourself with the kind of thoughtfulness you want from a lover. You can affirm that you possess the same commitment to your relationship to yourself as you do to a beloved partner, that you will be there through sickness and health, in good times and in bad. That you actually want to spend time in your own company.

Prepare

Your journal and a pen.

Reclaiming Your Desires

Use one, two, or all of the questions below to discover how you might like to court yourself.

- Recall all the ways you have pleasured, pampered, and loved other people in your life: lovers, children, friends, sisters. Perhaps you've made favorite meals, rubbed feet, bought thoughtful gifts, typed papers, made costumes, reassured, dressed up for. . . . What do you do for others?

  Loving actions I do for others . . .

  Loving thoughts I have for others . . .

  Loving things I say about others . . .

- Spend a moment or two thinking about your relationship with yourself. Run through the same categories.

  Loving actions I do for me . . .

  Loving thoughts I have for myself . . .

  Loving things I say about myself . . .

- Imagine how you would want your ideal lover to court you. What would he or she do? If you are in a relationship, especially a long-term one, what do you find yourself wishing your partner would do for you? Think about all the times you have found yourself saying, "I wish someone would _____ for me."

- Imagine how you would like your ideal lover to perceive you. What qualities would you most like to be appreciated for, loved for, known for in your relationship?

- Ask yourself, If I were trying to convince myself that I loved myself, I would. . . .

- Ask yourself, If I were courting the most essential, authentic me, what courting actions or behaviors would I *avoid?*

Suggestions for Wooing Yourself

The only rule about courting yourself is that you enjoy it and that it increases your self-esteem. Shadow comfort and addictions have no place in courting.

See Good Ways to Listen: Shadow Comfort.

You don't want to court your false self, the self that is so good at pleasing others or the self that doesn't believe in you. You want to do things that make you say, "Oh, yes, that really pleases *me*."

One snag that arises when courting yourself is the feeling that to do so you must be worthy, you must be special, beautiful, talented, one of the chosen. For those of us who suffered through high school with pimples and flat chests, it can seem impossible to believe we could be desired. But whatever our limitations and whatever our pasts, our humanity—our basic aliveness— means that we are good enough for self-love, self-respect, self-kindness. You don't have to do or be anything to deserve this.

Writes Frank Andrews in *The Art and Practice of Loving,*

> In self-love there is no object being loved, and no object doing the loving; there is the experience of loving. That is what self-love means. All loving is self-love. The experience of a yes directed toward a beloved affirms at the same time the life in which it occurs.

Here are some self-courting traditions you might enjoy:

- Experiment with loving that doesn't diminish you but increases your love for yourself. Love your cat, and feel the good feelings of being someone who is capable of love. Write a letter to a good friend, and as you do, recall the mutual regard you feel for each other when you are together. This practice is not done in the spirit of "Look how great I am because I can love" or "I am worthwhile because someone loves me." Instead, gently acknowledge the spirit of the Tibetan word *Namasté,* which translates roughly as "The god in me bows to the god in you." To love is to be love and to be worthy of love.

- Write a love letter *to yourself* using John Gray and Barbara DeAngelis's technique. Address the letter to yourself, for example: "Dear Jennifer." Begin the letter with criticisms you have about your relationship with yourself, the ways you are falling short in your self-care. Then write about what you are afraid of in your relationship with yourself. Move into listing what you desire in this relationship, what you are pining for. End with an expression of true love to yourself. Just write a few sentences for each area—criticism, fear, wants, and love—from you to you. Do not end your letter until you genuinely feel and express love for yourself, even if that means taking a break and doing something else for awhile. Mail your letter to yourself. Open it days, weeks, or months from now or on a retreat one year from the day you wrote it. Or give it to a friend and ask her or him to mail it to you next time she or he notices you are feeling down.

- Complete these sentences: "I feel _____. I need _____. I want _____." This exercise comes from Kay Hagan's *Internal Affairs*. An example: "I feel tired. I need to rest. I want to take a nap with my cat." Or "I am feeling excited. I need to do something with this energy. I feel the urge to eat, but what I really want to do is paint."

- Imagine love beaming from your hands. Visualize this love however you wish, but see it with your mind's eye. Direct this love to whatever part of you needs attention—a part of your body, an aspect of your psyche. Nothing is too insignificant or too horrific for this love to ease.

- This courting tradition is from *The Intimacy and Solitude Workbook* by Stephanie Dowrick. Make a list of what you can trust about yourself. Start with the basics. Include everything you can think of—nothing is too ridiculous. Include only the things you are sure of, even if they are negative or sad. Don't include what you trust about others; you can add that at a later date. Forget order of importance. Here's my partial list:

  I trust I love my daughter.

  I trust I will wear clothes when I go out of the house.

  I trust I love Chris.

  I trust I will feed my dog, Atticus, and take care of him when he is sick.

  I trust I try very hard to be a loyal and caring friend.

  I trust I will wake up in the morning.

  I trust I can walk.

  I trust myself to deal with loss.

  I trust I can read.

  What do you trust about yourself? Work on this list over the course of several retreats (this is a great retreat-in-the-world activity). Read it aloud. If you wish, you can also make a separate list about what you trust about others.

Stories

Saral told me her story of courting herself during a three-month retreat she took to heal herself of childhood abuse:

I had heard of a ritual in which a woman married herself, and I wanted to do that. But I was unable to commit to myself, so I had to court myself first. Before I left on retreat, I bought a ring because my wedding ring reminded me of my commitment to my husband. I had realized when deciding to take my retreat that I had always committed to others first. I found I could wear the ring only on top of my wedding ring. I wasn't ready yet. Then on the day I left, without noticing, I switched the positions of the rings. When I got out of the car, after driving for three days, I noticed the switch and I remember saying, "How perfect," because this retreat was the first time I put myself first. It was the perfect symbol.

Marylee discovered she loved the idea of courting herself:

I set this retreat intention: "How can I recharge and honor myself?" I could only take one day away because of a big project at work. When I was doing the exercise "Imagine how I would want my ideal lover to court me," I discovered surprise was a big element. But how could I surprise myself?

I decided to write down on cards the courting actions I wanted, to put them in a box, and to draw them out as I went along. Some of the things I wrote were eating lobster and drinking champagne on the beach at sunset, rubbing scented lotion on my body, getting compliments (I wrote down some affirmations and put those in another box to pull out when I needed a compliment), reviewing personal goals and my level of commitment, meditating, eating frozen bananas with chocolate sauce, and window-shopping in this funky, youthful part of town. Of course, I had to do the arrangements myself, which I thought would take the surprise out of it, but I kept reminding myself it was for me, for my beloved.

I am a skeptic. I didn't expect to feel any different, but I did. I felt kinder toward myself and hungry for more time with me. I loved the box idea because it made me feel I was being taken care of. Next time, I want to do a retreat at a spa.

Margie is recently divorced, and she hated the idea of courting herself:

It seemed like a cheap replacement for the real thing. What I wanted from my ideal lover was to feel I was beautiful and that he would never leave me. I couldn't figure how I was going to be beautiful for myself. Getting dressed up and taking myself out to dinner to eat alone made me want to shoot myself. I asked myself, "What makes me feel beautiful besides someone telling me?" I made a list: I feel beautiful when I'm clean from a shower, when I'm fishing alone on the lake, when I'm sore from exercising, when I get a manicure and a pedicure, when my apartment is clean, when I go to sleep in a pretty nightgown, when I take time to make my surroundings pretty, when I take time to make myself a nice meal instead of a Lean Cuisine, when I'm alone and don't look in any mirrors. As I was doing this, I realized that I didn't trust my view of my beauty unless there was someone else (preferably a man) to tell me I was beautiful. And that somehow this was tied into my not trusting that I would always be there for myself. I realized through doing this what I wanted from a man he could never give me—to be there forever—but I could give it to myself. In fact, I'm the only one who could ever give this to me.

I set up my retreat weekend (Friday to Sunday midmorning) to be about reassuring myself and believing I was beautiful. My intention didn't become clear until the first evening when I realized the question I was asking myself was "How can I live my life and feel worthwhile without someone else telling me I am?" I did things like look up the word *beautiful* in the dictionary. I covered all my mirrors with scarves. I arranged flowers for myself, and as I did, I thought, "This is for me because I like me." I made myself a perfect omelet, which took three tries. I felt strange at times, but I kept at it. The best part was working on my attitude, on telling myself as I did each little thing that I was doing it because I found myself worthwhile and likable. That was powerful and very difficult.

For Long Retreats

Almost every retreat can benefit from elements of courting yourself. This is an especially useful chapter to turn to when you are feeling lonely during your retreat. I interviewed several women who dedicated many a retreat to courting themselves. As one said, "How can I treat my partner with respect and love when I don't treat myself that way?" Another woman said, "It was too embarrassing to treat myself nicely with anyone else around. But after doing it in solitude for about a year, it spread to the rest of my life."

For Mini-Retreats

Organize a mini-retreat around a theme: courting your body, courting your attitude, courting your spirit, courting your home, courting your rhythms,

See Retreat Plans: A One-Day Well-Being Retreat and A Half-Day Trust Retreat.

doing for yourself what you do for others. Use the questions from Reclaiming Your Desires to determine what you can do for yourself.

For Retreats in the World

A great spur-of-the-moment courting retreat is to make a trust list. Another is to get a massage.

For Retreats with Others

See Retreating with Others: Affirmation Circle and Retreating with Others: Soliloquy Circle.

You could take turns performing self-marriage ceremonies for one another. Sitting in a circle giving one another neck and back massages, washing one another's hair (this works best outdoors when it is warm), and massaging one another's hands or feet while taking in what you are receiving are all good group courting exercises. So is an affirmation circle. Also try a soliloquy circle, doing timed talking on the subjects "Courting Myself," "Loving Myself," "Shame," and "Guilt."

Feeding the Artist

It is above all by the imagination that we
achieve perception and compassion and hope.

Ursula K. Le Guin

If there is one cosmic law I know the consequences of ignoring, it is this one: you cannot create from an empty well. Your creative center, the place where the artist resides, must be fed. She must go spelunking in crystal caves, gorge herself on gory fairy tales, sip 1908 vintage port and curse like a sailor, sleep in a three-hundred-year-old white pine tree, exult like one-hundred-and-three-year-old potter Beatrice Wood, and imbibe succulent art and fresh perspective for breakfast, lunch, and dinner.

Taking time on retreat or creating a retreat solely to feed your artist, to pamper your muse, sends a powerful message to yourself: "I am a creative person. I see life creatively. I am worth being recharged."

Prepare

Gather art experiences that delight, stir, excite, and recharge you. Photographs of Camille Claudel's sculptures, a recording of a Cajun concert, tickets to a Wendy Wasserstein play, directions to a maze garden, a guidebook of nearby architectural sites, a video of Picasso at work—anything that is feasible and animates you.

Your journal and a pen.

See Resources. Meditative music.

An offering to your muse.

The energy to be outrageous.

Perhaps drawing materials, dance music, drum or rattle, or clay.

Immerse Yourself

If you ever took a good art class (by *art* I mean writing, film, pottery, weaving, jewelry making, most creative pursuits), you probably have experienced being immersed in your art form. When I was at film school, I would often see two films during the day and another at night. Somewhere in the midst of all that sitting in the dark watching, the deluge would begin. Ideas. An image for a short film, a bit of dialogue for a screenplay, a character's name. But more important, I would feel creative tension building, the urge to do something, until I could contain it no longer and would have to create.

This practice is about total immersion in the creative minds of others. This means viewing, touching, reading, hearing, swimming in someone else's mind besides your own. Do not work at any creative endeavor when doing this. Fill yourself up so you can work after your retreat. Pull together a range of arts to gorge yourself on, then work out the mix of what you will do when. If you love movies, watch videos or go see movies you don't usually consider, perhaps foreign films or documentaries. But also visit three art galleries in a row, eat an arty lunch of French onion soup, tart apples, and wine, then check out a huge pile of art books from the library and some Native American mythology, visit a sculpture garden on the way home, and when you get there curl up with all your books for feasting and musing.

This practice takes a bit of preparation. You will need to assemble a surfeit of art, choosing what will make you swoon and what will irritate you as a grain of sand irritates an oyster, and how you will partake of it in a way that fits your intention and the style of retreat. As always, start with a few questions:

- What part of my creativity do I wish to feed?

- What artistic mediums excite and inspire me?

- What artistic mediums haven't I been exposed to? What makes me nervous? What stretches me, puzzles me, disturbs me?

- What artistic mediums fit with my intention and the style of retreat I'm planning?

Don't be upset if you don't have many answers. Many creative people don't put much thought into what recharges the grace of creation. We don't want to look too closely at what works, superstitious that if we do, it might stop. We duck our heads and just get on with it, hoping all will be well, then later wonder why we have run out of energy or worthwhile ideas.

Artist retreats fit well into all four styles of retreat. Retreats in the world are especially common, because to feed your muse you may find yourself strolling through a historic courtyard, attending a museum show, or visiting a public garden. What is important is to have your emotional container in place.

See Where Will You Retreat?: Your Emotional and Physical Containers.

Searching for what you will immerse yourself in can become a wonderful mini-retreat. Carve out an hour for yourself, breathe deeply, and before you start, remember your intention, your holy question, and let it guide you.

Obviously, where you live and what style retreat you have in mind will shape what you immerse yourself in. If there are no art galleries for five hundred miles, if *poetry* is a dirty word, and the library is closed from lack of funds, you are going to have to search harder for an art form to luxuriate in. But almost everywhere there is a video store. Perhaps they have a hidden section (not near the action-adventure aisle) where you might find videos of art, documentaries, or classic films. Perhaps there is a bookstore or library in a nearby town, with shelves of glistening fiction and poetry, children's books, and journals by artists-at-work. There is always some kind of architecture and history to discover, a local artist to meet and perhaps watch work, people to watch at a park, the shapes of rocks and trees to study. If you live in a city, the challenge becomes not finding what you want to gulp but choosing carefully from among the riches. Again, your intention acts as an effective filter.

Avoid the intellectual. If you love reading literary criticism or history, avoid it on this retreat. If you tend to be intellectually snobby, read comics, watch a little TV, change your perspective. Also, you *do not* want to approach this as study, as learning more about your medium. For example, if you are a poet, don't study poetry. Read it differently than you usually do, quicker or slower, or read poets you poo-poo as beneath you or think too lofty for you to grasp.

When you start to get creatively excited, when ideas begin to surface, do not work. Do not sculpt, paint, or take a photograph. You want to be filling up and *holding in* the beauty, the passion, the terrible truth of others' work. When you start to feel like you *have* to work, that means your tank is filling up. This is one time you do want to top it off. Hold on to your ideas. Build the pressure. If you must make notes, make very brief notes.

If you can, wrap this retreat around a night or a nap, so that you can incubate a dream. Before you go to sleep, ask for a dream. Be ready to catch the fertile dreams that bubble to the surface by keeping a pen and notebook handy.

For All You Nonartists

I'll bet almost everyone reading this section is thinking, "I can't do this practice because I'm not an artist. This is only for people who have talent, who can do more than paint by numbers." To this nasty voice, I can say only that if you continue to treat yourself this way, you will never live. No matter who you are or what you do, if this is what you yearn to do, *do it*. There simply isn't enough time in life to play it small.

A Partial List of Mediums to Get You Percolating

See Resources.

Books: Journals by artists, biographies of courageous women, novels about the immensity of life, crisp short stories, incandescent poetry, historical tales.

Films: Classic videos, interviews with visionaries, documentaries about women, your favorite films of all time.

Theater: Community, on video, Broadway, off-Broadway, reading plays aloud, radio dramas, NPR.

Visual Art: Murals on a street corner, Picasso fragments of faces, visual history of art, children's drawings on a library wall, formations of stones, the turret on the downtown bank, display windows, quilts, hats, costumes.

Sculpture: Museums, sculpture gardens, bowls in your home, sand on the beach, woodworks, landscapes, plant shapes, trees.

Dance: Modern, ballet, Sufi, on TV, on video, in a theater.

Storytelling: At the library, on tape, at a storytelling workshop or festival.

Music: Bach fugues, Telemann symphonies, gospel music, trance dance music, Tibetan bells, Thelonious Monk, the Beatles.

Calling the Muse

In Greek mythology, the Muses were the daughters of Zeus and Mnemosyne, the Goddess of memory who knew everything that had happened since the beginning of time. The Muses were patrons of the creative arts. As archetypes, muses represent the inner source of exquisite energy that artists dream of having flow through them when producing (hopefully effortlessly) a creative work.

Developing a relationship with your muse is another way of recharging your creative center. This practice is about familiarizing yourself with and then kneeling down to the part of you, or the part of the Divine, that inspires your creativity.

Center yourself however you choose. When you are ready, bring your muse into your mind's eye. What does she or he look like? Spend a few moments sensing details. What is she wearing? What does she smell like? What is she surrounded by? Notice the details. Perhaps she takes your hand. Does the muse have anything to say? Does the muse demand anything from you?

See Good Ways to Listen: I Am Enough and Opening Ceremony.

Draw, write, sculpt, sing, dance what you saw, sensed, or felt about your muse. Work through worries about whether you have any ability or whether this is a real encounter and the feeling that you have nothing to say. Develop a relationship to this side of you. It may be a struggle. It may take a few tries. That's okay.

Create an invocation for your muse. It could be a chant, a prayer, a poem, a dance, or a drawing. You may want to dialogue with your muse, asking her what will help her flow through you. This is an invocation you can carry back with you, to use before you create.

End by making an offering to the muse. How can you show her you honor her? Build a shrine in your backyard, bury your litany of doubts about your artistic abilities, mail the check for that series of drawing classes, or teach a child how to play the piano. This offering must speak to your intention to honor the ineffable grace of the muse. "To imagine the muse is to bring spirit into form. Every activity of the creative process requires that we bring spirit into form, that we create a vessel—ourselves or a work of art—that can hold spirit," writes Deena Metzger in *Writing for Your Life*. This practice was inspired by her writing about the muse.

Be Outrageous

Routine parches the artist. Sameness breeds cookie-cutter creativity. Devote all or part of your retreat to being outrageous, the definition of which in this context is "extremely unusual or unconventional; extraordinary and beyond all reason; and extravagant or immoderate."

Kind of daring, isn't it? How far can you go? Does being outrageous fit your intention? How will it work on a retreat? What is your point in being outrageous? What will it serve? Sometimes the only way to learn is by doing and seeing how it feels. Does it feed you or just terrorize you? If you feel fear, of whom are you afraid? Or perhaps being outrageous reawakens a playful joy, a moment of weightlessness, free from propriety at last!

What will you do? Paint your body blue? Sunbathe naked? Eat ice cream with your hands? Sleep on a different side of the bed? Eat seaweed for lunch? Bake cookies and eat as many as you want for dinner? Stay up all night and read erotic fiction? Leave a gift for a friend and never tell her who it is from? Write a letter to a friend who hurt your feelings (whether yesterday or ten years ago), telling her why you are hurt? Experiment in an artistic discipline you absolutely know you can't do and not care how it comes out? Walk in the desert and scream? Start a project that you don't think you'll live long enough to finish? Wear a cape? Live in silence for a week? Be alone with nothing to do for two days? Sleep naked?

See Good Ways to Listen: Shadow Comfort. What does your artist need you to shake up? What will wake you up? Sometimes even subtle shifts feed your creative center. Note: for those of us with addictive personalities, this is not an invitation to drink a gallon of vodka and invite a boat full of Russian sailors over or to take a new credit card out for a romp. Moderation can still be present. This is *healthy* outrageousness.

Stories

Here is Deena Metzger's story of how she came to take a year off to retreat and write. It is from her extraordinary book *Writing for Your Life.*

> A year after we imagined a year off, my dear friend Barbara Myerhoff died. Alerted to the suddenness of death, I regretted how consistently I had subordinated the inclinations of the imagination to more practical

concerns, and I determined to take time to redefine and recommit myself. Despite difficulties, I quickly arranged to take an extended leave from my work. For the first time in my life, I had time to write, and the writer within, who had always had second-class status, became a full citizen with a newfound ability to determine the course of her life. Priorities and considerations that had been determined previously by the roles of mother, breadwinner, and teacher were reconsidered and renegotiated.

Before the retreat, I did not know that I could maintain two absolute commitments; afterward, this seemed possible.

For Retreats in the World

You may often find yourself in public on this type of retreat, doing all or part of your retreat in an art gallery or movie theater or while looking at architecture. Planning takes on a more important role: to avoid disappointment (a closed museum) or stress (getting caught in rush hour). Give some thought to where you will go when. Get directions, call to see if places are open, choose off times to visit. Also, designate a way to maintain your retreat container. This protects you from the enervating influences of things like rude clerks, smelly bathrooms, and crowded buses, which can rob you of your intentionality and the depth of your sacred time.

See Where Will You Retreat?: Creating Emotional Support.

For Long Retreats

Although these practices were not written with a working retreat in mind, on a longer retreat in which you wish to jump-start a project, one way to approach it is to spend the first two or three days immersing yourself in outrageous, playful, liberating behavior, art of all kinds, and the invoking of your muse. All the while you feel the tension of wanting to work arising, but you hold, hold it until you absolutely cannot hold it anymore. At that point you allow yourself to entertain in your mind's eye (or ear) only—not on paper, canvas, piano, or cloth yet—what you will do. Again, hold the tension until the painting you want to paint, the piece of music you want to compose, the mathematical equation you are trying to unravel becomes clear in your mind. It will not appear all at once, complete. What does appear may not be the beginning. It will be part of what you are searching for. Hold that until it gets too big for your mind and until you are sure you will lose it. Only then make notes: write, play, paint, compute to capture it. When you have recorded your idea, go back to some art immersion or muse calling or other play, and

See Retreat Plans: A Two-Day Artist Retreat.

build up some more tension. Tell yourself you cannot work until the next part of your work is clear in your head, like a movie, soundtrack, or giant billboard. Then record that part. Continue this way throughout your retreat.

If you try this process, an inner voice may say discouraging things: "You'll forget something important." If you feel an idea slipping away, stop wherever you are, take a deep breath, let go of your grasping fear, and relax. The voice will also say, "This is too much playing, this isn't productive. You could be getting so much more work done." Perhaps true, but probably not. Either way, working is not the point. The point is, you are on retreat. This is not your usual world. This way of working requires radical trust in your own imagination, in your worth as an artist. Do you deserve to be fed?

For Mini-Retreats

See Retreat Plans: A Half-Hour Jump-Starting Your Creativity Retreat.

Calling the muse works well as a mini-retreat, as does doing something outrageous. If you have only an hour or two, be sure to give yourself an art experience that really curls your toes with delight and newness. To feel a real recharging, you may need to do several mini-retreats close together. The more time you can grab in a row, the more you will experience the spell of this practice.

For Retreats with Others

You can support one another on this quest by planning your immersion, enjoying all or part of it together, and *not* discussing it afterward except in terms of feelings. This is not the time for intellectual art dissection. Instead, talk about how the poem made you feel. What images came to mind? What memories? How does your body feel? Also, if nascent ideas begin to come to you, do not share them with your friends. Nothing will fritter away the inspiration faster.

A friend can be helpful on this retreat in two additional ways. First, if you choose to go out into the world for your art, you can act as containers for each other, maintaining a silent and inward attitude. This is often easier to do with someone than alone. Second, you can read aloud to each other, especially poetry or plays. This helps these mediums to come alive.

When doing an artist retreat with a friend, beware of catering to her tastes or she to yours. If she wants to watch twelve Audrey Hepburn movies in a row and you want to watch only one and then see some Kabuki or leaf through a bunch of Ansel Adams photography books, then please, separate.

If you are working with a larger group that shares the same interests—for example, a group of potters—you might be able to gain access to an experience that an individual couldn't, like watching a master potter work or being alone in a pottery exhibit at a museum after hours. After sharing your art immersion, gather in a circle. Place a candle in the center of the circle, darken the room, and invite each person to call out feeling and sensory words she felt when viewing the art. As each person speaks, a web of beauty is spun overhead, deepening and expanding the experience for all.

Another way a group can be supportive is to help you move from the feasting stage into the working stage. For example, if you are part of an ongoing writers' group, each of you might retreat alone on a particular weekend, doing whatever you wish to feed your artist, then come together as a group, not to share your ideas but to voice your commitment to what you will do next with your work. "I will write one short story based on my thoughts in the next two weeks." "I will honor my need to feed my artist by doing this retreat again this weekend and not working until I can't bear the pressure."

Portrait of Your Authenticity

*Come into my lap and sit in the center of your soul. Drink the living
waters of memory and give birth to yourself. What you unearth will
stun you. You will paint the walls of this cave in thanksgiving.*

Meinrad Craighead, *The Litany of the Great River*

Who is the authentic you? What values, beliefs, actions, thoughts, and relationships fit you? What is most essentially you? How can you gain or regain a "luminous, virtually religious sense of [your] inner life radiating into and nourishing the outer, wider world"? This is how essayist Michael Ventura describes it in "A Dance for Your Life in the Marriage Zone," in *Shadow Dancing in the U.S.A.*

Making a portrait of your authenticity entails reclaiming muted parts of yourself and then creating a symbolic visual representation of what you discover. Part of this work is sifting through what belongs to you and what belongs to others—culture, parents, spouses, friends. Part of this work is trusting that taking time to name and depict the essential you is precious work—but that is the challenge of the entire retreat process. Locating your authenticity can be a radical act, a declaration: "This is me, and this is what I like, value, need, respect." But to name your authenticity is not to pinpoint a static state but rather to note that a particular collection of selves, behaviors, and beliefs feels true in this moment, and to be aware that your collection of selves will change and grow as your life unfolds.

The following exercise is a long one. You will need to take breaks and weave in other practices or activities. Try to work on your portrait for an hour at a time.

Prepare

An outline of your body on a larger-than-life-sized piece of white butcher paper. Have someone draw an outline of your body in pencil on the paper *before* your retreat. Think about what posture or silhouette would most capture the authentic you. Move around on the paper until you feel you have captured that feeling. If drawing an outline of your body makes you too unhappy, then draw just your head, hands, and feet, leaving the middle blank. Leave room on the outside and on the top and bottom of your outline.

Art materials such as watercolors, tempera paints, felt markers, pastels, crayons.

A pile of magazines and catalogs. Visit used bookstores, ask friends, ask your dentist.

Masking tape.

Scissors.

Brushes and water containers if you are using paints.

Glue or rubber cement.

If you like, before your retreat, take a few minutes to do a symbol gathering scan. Go through sewing baskets, junk drawers, and your attic while meditating on the question "If my authenticity were an object, what would she be?" Do not hesitate to grab anything and everything that speaks to you or simply seems interesting. Keep repeating the question to yourself and listen visually for answers. Try doing this in a junk, bead, or stationery store (you can combine it with searching for a birthday gift for your sister-in-law or favors for your child's birthday party). A charm, a scrap from your old Brownie uniform, an image from a greeting card, an old earring, a poem—all are examples of physical things that could embody your question.

Creating Your Portrait

Tape the outline of your body to a wall. Spread out your materials. It is important to begin this practice in a calm, centered state. You will have difficulty

---

See Good Ways to Listen: I Am Enough.

naming what is authentic to you if you are not in touch with an authentic body state. Spend some time becoming centered.

When you feel at rest, read over the questions you will find below. With the questions, your outline, and art materials in front of you, respond *visually* to the questions. As you mull over a set of questions, you may feel led to draw on a part of your outline or to paste a found symbol on it, or you may leaf through the magazines you collected and cut out images that fit. You may also add words, bits of poetry or song, or quotes, but work with these after you have spent time with images. Use the questions to enter a feeling, imaging state. It is easy when doing this kind of chronological exercise to feel bored, as in "I can't remember anything; this is stupid." Stop thinking and try *looking*. Read the questions a few times as you look; wait and hold; then move into creating.

If you find yourself getting caught up in "This is ugly" or "I'm no good at art," then do the dialoguing exercise in Courage: Giving Yourself Support. Stretching, dancing, or taking deep breaths and letting out big "Ahhs" can be useful, too.

When, as you work with the questions below, you remember things that don't feel authentic—that don't fit but that feel important—paste or draw those on the outside of your outline.

- Imagine yourself as a child around the age of three to five. What was your favorite toy? What was your greatest fear? What were you afraid of being caught doing? What did you receive praise for? Where did you feel safe and comforted? What part of your body corresponds to this age?

- Imagine yourself as a preadolescent girl, perhaps eight years old. What did you do when you were alone? Did you have a favorite hiding place? What were you passionate about: trees, horses, soccer, dolls? Who was your best friend? How did you feel when you were with her? Were there any places or people with whom you felt uncomfortable or with whom you had to hide a part of yourself to fit in or get approval? If so, locate these on the outside of your body outline.

- Recall when you were thirteen. How did you feel in your body? What gave you pleasure: riding your bike fast, lying on the ground in the autumn, dancing alone in your room, kissing? When did you feel uncomfortable in your body—gawky, looked at, judged? How did your body feel around boys? Around other girls? Around teachers? Around ministers or rabbis, healers, priests, or nuns? Around your parents?

- Think back to your late teens and early twenties. What choices were you making at this time—perhaps to go to school, get married, take a particular job? Choose one or two big choices. Looking back, what decisions sprang from what you wanted and needed to do? What sprang from desire to fit in or fear or not knowing what you wanted? What was your favorite way to comfort yourself at this age? What was happening with your body sexually? What did you most resent about becoming an adult?

- Scan forward in your life, using the questions below, until you reach the present. Don't belabor this; allow impressions, memories, ideas, symbols to surface in their own time, in their own way. Your milestones will occur to you naturally and *visually* if you allow them to.

  What was my favorite way to spend my alone time?

  With whom did I feel most like me?

  What did I do (if anything) that I now regret doing because it feels false to me or was mostly about pleasing others?

  How much time did I spend doing what I found meaningful?

  How did I feel in my body? How did I view myself physically?

- Be in your present age and life.

  I feel most like me when I . . .

  What I like most about myself is . . .

  What I most value in my life right now is . . .

  I never find to time to _____ anymore.

  When I am alone, I like to . . .

  My authentic self looks like . . .

  My authentic relationships look like . . .

  What I would like to change in my life to live more authentically is . . . (Put the images and words from this last question on the outside of your outline.)

Reflecting

Take time away from your portrait. Then come back and spend a few minutes meditating on it. If you were going to name this woman, what would you name her? Writing in second person, describe this woman. What do you see? What is she going to do next? What does she need to survive and thrive? Pretend you don't know her and see what occurs to you. For example, "You have tangled seaweed hair and strong legs covered with mountains and a river running from your heart. Your arms are crossed across your chest—you're not taking any more nonsense."

Keep this portrait where you see it often. Meditate on it once a year on a birthday retreat.

For Long Retreats

You might want to begin this practice early in your retreat and use it as a thread throughout your retreat, doing other things and then returning to work on it.

For Mini-Retreats

This practice works well on mini-retreats. Try to set aside at least an hour and a half for each session and, if possible, space your retreats close together to keep your interest alive.

For Retreats in the World

Take yourself to a visually fertile place like a junk shop, costume shop, museum bookstore, or scenic bluff, and read over one or two questions from an age that interests you. Then look around for images and objects that capture your eye. How do these images or things relate to your questions? For example, in contemplating "What does my authentic self look like?," you might choose a imposing mountain or a rusted but still-working lamp. Make notes of what you choose and, if you wish, dialogue with your choices later, but for right now remain visual and intuitive. Don't think about making sense.

For Retreats with Others

Display all your portraits in one place. Spend a few minutes studying each. Sit in a deep listening circle. Each woman responds to a portrait, finishing with the woman who created it speaking last. She describes what the process of working on it was like, what she sees in the finished image, and what, if any, changes she envisions for her life. Repeat for each woman.

If you do work on your portraits together in the same room, center together before beginning work and then work in silence with no comments on one another's work. No comments about artistic ability or whose portrait is best are allowed at any time on the retreat.

For Experienced Retreatants

If you've worked with this practice recently, instead of using the questions, use your intention question and make a mini-portrait of just your head or of a part of your body you wish to heal or come into a better relationship with. Collect images, center yourself, then contemplate your intention question while looking at what you've collected. Reply and explore your question visually, drawing in your own images, perhaps adding words.

One Who Chooses

All you need is deep within you waiting to unfold
and reveal itself. All you have to do is be still and take
time to seek what is within, and you will surely find it.

Eileen Cady, cofounder of Findhorn

A painting hangs over our fireplace. The image is a boat on a fast-flowing river. Just ahead, hidden in deep shadows, is a fork, a divergence into two streams. Every time I look at the painting, the feeling of not knowing what is ahead, yet not being able to stop—of being carried along on the current—jars me. It is such a visual metaphor for life: there is rarely enough information, rarely enough time. So much is decided by the seat of your pants.

But today could be different. You've gotten off the boat and have withdrawn from the stream of life to consider all the possibilities open to you. You've done what women who run white water do. You're scouting ahead, studying the river to see where the rocks are, where the canoe-eating holes may lie. But even as you scan the water from the shore, you know from the twitch in your stomach that there are no guarantees. You can be as experienced as a Colorado River guide, planning your route through the churning waters with great care, and still capsize. And this is the reality you must be willing to welcome or at least open the door to. There is Divine guidance available, you do have knowledge inside of you, and shit still happens. There are no guarantees that the decision you make will work out the way you want. It may work out better. It may simply turn out differently. It may feel, ten years from now, like a huge disaster and, ten years after that, like an amazing blessing. All are possibilities. We are never sure, perhaps until the day we die, whether choosing each fork brought a blessing or a curse. You cannot truly move forward without acknowledging this lack of certainty.

The process of making a decision is often one we try to do while in nature, and it is rarely one we can put into words. Karen Warren writes in "November Sojourn" in *Solo,*

> Most times I want to pause to take stock of my life from a perspective that only comes when I'm alone in the woods. One year, spurred on by my partner, I went out with the very specific reason of figuring out if I wanted a child in my life. Here was the adventuring woman, who five years earlier had disdained the permanency of a credit card and a car loan, now trying to decide to have a child. I choked so hard it took another year and another November sojourn before I had the courage to broach the subject again.

My friend Randi recalls sitting on a boulder overlooking the river outside Austin, trying to decide if getting married was the right choice. "I wish I had had a set of instructions, a way to deliberate."

You may find that simply taking the time, taking long walks, letting yourself mull and weigh, opens the door for you. You may find that doing one or two parts of this practice is enough and then your own process takes over. Or you may find yourself needing more structure, especially if you are exhausted or in a panic. This is why I devised and road-tested this practice.

Prepare

> Information about your choices. For example, if you are trying to decide whether to adopt a child, gather facts about costs, possibility, the amount of time you might have to wait, and so forth. If you are thinking about getting married, bring along pictures of the two of you together, letters he or she has written you and letters you have written, and perhaps a gift or ring given to you. If you are contemplating a career change, put together a list comparing your current job with the job you are considering.

> A few touchstone objects. These remind you of your strength, your ability to persevere, your connection to other women, your connection to the Divine as you know it. A piece of rose quartz, a picture of Susan B. Anthony, and a necklace your grandmother made you could be touchstones.

Your journal and a pen.

Drawing materials or clay.

Candle.

Timer.

Tarot deck, Bible, I Ching, or other divination system (optional: borrow one from a friend).

Clothing you can exercise in.

See Resources. Inspiring words.

Part 1

It is much easier to consider your options, to locate your desires, and to give yourself space to honor how difficult your decision may be if you are coming from a place of self-trust. Choose to believe in yourself and your ability to gain access to your inner knowledge.

The first thing you may wish to do is create a focusing point, a meditation spot, a "question shrine." Arrange the touchstones you brought with you that help you feel mighty and effectual; wait to add the things that are associated with your decision, your question. Have your writing materials close by.

Imagine a loving presence, someone or something that is so wise, so accepting of you, so plugged in to the Universal Wisdom that nothing can shake her. This may be your vision of the Divine, a guide you have worked with in the past, or a sweet notion of goodness and comfort. Don't force the image to come. Visualize or sense this presence near you. When she or he or it feels real, vibrant, comforting, loving, and truly there, imagine her speaking to you about encouragement, courage, ability, and trust.

Close your eyes and breathe long and deep. Settle into silence for a few moments. There is nothing to consider, nowhere to go, nothing to do.

If you feel too agitated to sit quietly, walk slowly in a large circle around your space a few times.

When you are ready, write across the top of a piece of paper the question facing you. Write it big and bold. Try to frame your question as a *could*. For example:

• What could my life be like if I took the job?

- What could my life be like if I had a child?

- What could my life be like if I separated from my partner?

- What could my life be like if I bought a house?

- What could my life be like if I had an abortion?

- What could my life be like if I went to law school?

- What could my life be like if I . . .

Add your question to your shrine. Around it place the objects you brought that relate to your question: pictures, letters, postcards, keepsakes. Study your creation for a few moments.

Notice: How does your body feel? Your shoulders? Your belly? Your neck? Simply observe.

Whenever it feels right (it could be two minutes or twenty, depending on your clock), do a physical activity that is solitary and repetitive and that will push you physically, at least a little. Dancing, yoga, walking uphill (a mountain, foothill, incline, whatever is available and possible for your body), walking by an ocean or a large lake or lively river, snowshoeing or cross-country skiing in a quiet area, canoeing, and swimming laps (in a quiet pool or, better yet, a warm, calm body of water) are all ideal choices. If you don't move your body much or if you are doing this at home in the middle of a city or if you don't have much time, dancing is a good choice.

Don't give in to the voice that says, "I'm too tired to walk" or "This is stupid. There is no question what I must choose." Confusion and the desire to sleep or eat or give up are just tricks we use to try to protect ourselves from facing life. (Chocolate, too, is a trick—a very good one, to be sure, but still a trick.) It's normal to feel anxiety about making a choice. It's normal to want to check out. I struggle with checking out every day of my life. Most of us do. And if you absolutely have to, okay, take a break. Go read under a tree for a while or pull the covers over your head and eat two bowls of breakfast cereal. The question will still be here, as will the desire that led you to this moment in the first place. You can always come back.

Feel the question in your body as you move. Where does it physically reside in this moment? Can you move that part of your body? Sense with the intelligence of your body where energy needs to flow. You may find yourself wanting to run or to swing your hips or to hunch over and crawl. Do it. Move the question with you. Repeat it aloud a few times as you move.

While you are moving, on an inhale repeat, "I am breathing in trust and clarity." On your next exhale repeat aloud, "I am breathing out doubt and confusion." Concentrate on the words; don't just mouth them, believe them. Your mind will wander. Bring it back to your inhale of trust and clarity, your exhale of doubt and confusion. Keep going long enough to feel the words shift your energy. It may take ten minutes, or it may be two hours. Keep bringing yourself back to your breath as you sweat and move, inhale and exhale, trust and clarify.

When you are finished, find a still place, take a few deep breaths, and check in with yourself. How do you feel? What words capture the change, if any? *Open, energetic, calm, tired, trusting, decisive, anxious?* Briefly, name your sensations.

As soon as you can, get your writing materials and write this statement across the top of a blank page of paper:

- If I could do anything in my life right now, I would choose to . . .

Get to spontaneous writing quickly, "leaking" as little energy as possible. Avoid unnecessary conversations, busyness, or frantic thinking. Set a timer (if you have one handy) for three minutes, or fill three pages without stopping. If you get stuck, write the words *if only* over and over again. If negative thoughts like "I could never do that" or "What's the point, it's too late" come up, write those down, too.

See Good Ways to Listen: Soothe. When you are finished, put your journal away without reading what you wrote, and take a break. If you are on a longer retreat, now might be a good time to do a ritual bath and have a self-affirming meal, to baby yourself a bit. If you must return to daily life, remember to do some kind of closing ceremony, no matter how brief.

Part 2

Center yourself. Sit in front of your focusing point, your question shrine. Light your candle. Take your journal and write across the top of a fresh sheet of paper:

- What *should* my life be like?

Set your timer for three minutes, or fill three pages. Keep your hand moving; let the question write you. If you get stuck, write the word *should* over and over.

Spend a few minutes investigating where each of these shoulds came from. To whom or what can you attribute each thought or belief? This process helps you tease out the beliefs that are masquerading as yours and helps you examine whether these are beliefs you want to keep. Separate what you think you *should* do from what you truly *want* to do. Display your shoulds on your shrine.

Reread what you wrote in response to "If I could do anything. . . ." If any new insights or ideas emerge, no matter how far-fetched, write these on a new page or in the margin. Select the three or four ideas that make you breathe with excitement or make your heart race. Write these possibilities as questions, using the same phrasing you did before. For example:

- What could my life be like if I entered a convent?

- What could my life be like if I had another baby?

- What could my life be like if I changed careers and became a yoga teacher?

- What could my life be like if I bought an espresso machine?

- What could my life be like if I went back to school?

- What could my life be like if I just accepted this situation?

Add these to your shrine. Study this gathering of words and objects as you breathe. What do you see? Any interesting new associations or ideas? Can you connect any of the questions to the list of shoulds? Breathe into any ideas that arise. Don't rush to do anything. Wait and breathe. You are not tight and panicking, not disdainful and judging, but reverent, conscious, relaxed, accepting.

If nothing new comes to you, don't worry. There are many stages to this exploration; if new thoughts are not stimulated now, just doing the exercise will help unlock them later.

Take a break and ease out of your head. You could walk slowly in nature silently repeating "I trust myself" and observing how animals and plants trust themselves as they play, hunt, and grow. Or you might choose to read a book about a woman who made courageous choices while you curl up by a fire or under a quilt. This gives your conscious mind a break while feeding your unconscious vibrant fire. Another self-soothing activity is to begin an ego book, a collection of glowing letters from those who love you, photos of happy times, awards or ribbons from that contest you won in fifth grade, a pressed flower from another retreat, or anything that reminds you of your wonderful attributes.

See Resources.

Part 3

Settle in front of your shrine and light your candle. Place your drawing materials nearby. Reread everything you have written during this exploration. Take your time.

Get into a comfortable position where you sit relaxed with your spine straight. Arrange a chair to support your back or a cushion under your butt. Still your mind by counting backward from four to one on successive exhales. Settle into your center.

Repeat the following out loud:

> I, _____ (add your name), gather my wisdom around me.
>
> I am able to sit with myself and my question.
>
> I believe I can gain access to my inner knowledge, my still, quiet voice. I believe in my ability to listen to this voice.
>
> I, _____ (add your name), trust myself. I trust my own perceptions, my hunches, my way of knowing.

Breathe and sit and wait. If your mind gets insane or you get anxious, repeat with each inhale, "What is possible?" With each exhale, relax into trusting your own process. If you don't like sitting still, walk around your shrine very slowly, maintaining deep, slow breathing and asking, "What is possible?"

If something begins to occur to you, don't rush. Wait. Hush. Hold the image, the feeling, the inkling, and breathe into it. Don't try to push an answer. Hold the energy. Let it grow.

When you feel ripe, whether a course of action has occurred to you or not, come quietly out of your meditation, take up your drawing materials and let an image emerge, or do more spontaneous writing, sculpture, or movement—whatever fits.

Put your drawing, notes, or sculpture on your shrine. Observe it for a few moments. See if additional insights present themselves.

You might like to draw a tarot card at this point if you feel you need extra guidance or to test your decision. Shuffle the cards until you feel ready to fan them out face down. Choose the card you are drawn to. What is the first thing that comes to mind when you see the card? Now place it next to your drawing. Any similarities? Don't read a guidebook that tells you what the card is supposed to mean unless you absolutely have to. Trust your imagination to tell you what the symbol means.

Another way is to open a great book at random, let your finger run down the page until you feel like stopping, then read what you land upon. How does that fit with what is unfolding for you? Does it shed any new light? Meditate, play with, ponder the words.

See Resources for title suggestions.

Now write, with as much detail as possible, your answer to the question

- What will my life be like when I . . . ?

Use your imagination to spin out a tale of what is going to happen next. Create the best possible scenario. If you've decided to go to law school, create a world in which you study well for the LSATs, you get into the school of your choice, you find the grants and loans you need. Bring in some of your dreaming from "If I could do anything I would. . . ." Allow yourself to see the very best emerging. Write about others' reactions to your decision; imagine them being helpful or supportive.

Reward yourself for getting through this process. How can you celebrate yourself? If you feel raw from examining your life or from the magnitude of your decision, you might consciously choose to check out for an hour or two, to take a nap or watch a video. Or perhaps you need to write in your journal or talk to someone about how good you feel about pushing yourself to examine your issue. Perhaps you need to breathe and simply stay with how you are feeling. Often I feel so good after I've stuck with this process, I want to do something that makes me feel bad (eat or tense up and lose myself in busyness) because I am uncomfortable feeling proud of myself. It helps me to take a walk (you can see from this book I take a lot of walks) and say to myself, "It is okay to feel good. Nothing bad is going to happen if I'm proud of myself."

See Resources.

But I Still Don't Know What to Do!

Perhaps it isn't time to make a decision yet. That time may come in five minutes, five hours, or five months, but perhaps it isn't the season yet. What does it feel like to live with not knowing? Does it feel right? Does it feel right but scary? Or does it feel like you are avoiding making a decision? By not choosing, you are still making a choice. Change is the law of the universe.

Get comfortable again, breathe, and ask yourself:

- How am I benefiting from not deciding?

- How else could I get the same payoff in a healthier way?

- What is my greatest fear around this decision?

What if there is a time component to your decision, a dragon breathing down your neck—like "Should I take the transfer or get married?" What if the luxury of waiting is not yours? First, do a reality check to be sure that this is so. Could you buy more time from your boss or your lover or whoever needs a decision now? Is there any feasible, sane way to wait? Again, only wait if it feels right. If you are not sure, it is time to do some more sitting or walking and asking, "What do I need to know?" You may want to repeat part of this ritual *after* taking a break. If you are trying to do this in the midst of your life, you may need to take a longer retreat outside your home. You may want to change this ritual by adding some parts of your own. You may need to seek more outside information and then come back to your quiet, still center.

For Long Retreats

See Good Ways to Listen: Shadow Comfort for a definition of healthy self-nuturing.

This practice is best suited for a long retreat. Do each section separately, giving yourself breathing room in between. Include lots of healthy self-nurturing.

For Mini-Retreats

If you are doing this on a mini-retreat, do one section per retreat. Try to do the retreats on consecutive days or every other day. Keep your question shrine where you can see it between retreats. Be sure to have an opening and closing ceremony each time.

For Retreats in the World

Not recommended except out in nature in solitude.

For Retreats with Others

Also not recommended except when using a friend or retreat coordinator to reflect back your decision.

Marking a Passage

Life is a bridge. Cross over it,
but build no house on it.

Indian proverb,
retold by Bruce Chatwin,
The Songlines

Turning fifty, celebrating an anniversary of your sobriety, living through the breakup of a relationship, experiencing the birth of your child or grandchild, losing a job, getting married, entering menopause, finishing a dissertation, recovering from an illness—your life is regularly enlivened and pummeled by change. Life's passages can mystify you, damage you, or overwhelm you. When you take the time to acknowledge and reflect on them, they can also bestow wisdom and expand your vision of who you are and what you are capable of.

To mark a passage is to acknowledge that a change has occurred, that you are not the same person you were before. There has been a break, a shift, a lurch, or a flourish. A retreat furnishes the crucial element of reflection by which change is transmuted into wisdom. Here is an opportunity to acknowledge the *reality* of your hurt, your excitement, or your fear. Within the safe container of a retreat, you can listen to your instincts and allow those instincts to show you how to chronicle this shift in your life, how to take the beauty or the pain and turn it into something illuminating and meaningful.

You may wish to travel as part of your retreat, to read over years of old journals, to sort through photographs, to clean closets and plan a giant yard sale, to climb a mountain, to dive under the ocean, to construct a teepee in your backyard and live it for a month. As part of this expression, you might wish to weave in elements of the following practice.

Prepare

An object that symbolizes the passage you want to mark—your baby's tiny undershirt, a copy of your divorce papers, a photograph of the house you just bought, your sobriety pin, a baby picture of you. If you don't have access to or can't find an appropriate object, draw one or make one out of clay. If you can't think of a symbol or don't have time to do this now, wait to do this until you are on your retreat.

Your journal and a pen.

Reflecting on Your Passage

Celebrating, mourning, or wrestling with a life passage is an extraordinarily personal act. No woman's ceremony will resemble that of another; each will be unique. As when creating your opening and closing ceremonies, here, too, the same guidelines apply: you know exactly what to do if you listen and follow your instincts. What brings this practice to life is believing you have the authority and ability to mark your passage. Allow yourself to take your needs and actions seriously and yet keep a spirit of play active.

Begin by reflecting on the person you were before this shift occurred. Ask yourself:

- How would I describe myself before?

See Good Ways to Listen and Contemplations.

Using whatever method or medium you like, describe your life before this change.

When the passage you are marking is a loud and clear one (the birth of a child, the death of a spouse, moving across the country), it is easy and perhaps painful to see the changes that have taken place and may still be happening. If the passage you are marking isn't dramatic or distinct (a birthday or a marriage after living together), it may feel harder to distinguish the changes. If this is the case, look for details of how your life has shifted. Ask yourself other questions:

- What brought me here?

- What do I want to acknowledge?

- What is changing in my life that I have not been willing to see?

Be aware that sometimes you start this process only to see that you are too close to your passage to mark it yet. Trust that and let it go for the time being.

Dialogue with the symbol you chose before, or create one now. If no symbol seems appropriate, then dialogue with yourself to find one.

See Courage: Giving Yourself Support.

In whatever way you wish, work with these questions:

- How have I been changed by this passage?

- Is there a gift to be claimed?

Then, using spontaneous writing or drawing, explore the question

- What do I want the next part of my life to look like?

One way to enhance this process is to draw a circle in the middle of a piece of unlined paper, then close your eyes and relax, repeating the question a few times in your mind. Then visualize an image of the Divine as you know it illuminating your question. Ask the Divine for its help in showing you what is best for you in this new phase of your life. When an idea, symbol, or image comes to you, focus on it while imagining it bathed in brilliant light. Then gently come back to the circle on your paper, and fill it with a combination of images and words you felt or saw.

Do something with your body that embodies this change. In some countries not so long ago, women in mourning shaved their heads and wore black for a year. I'm not suggesting anything quite so dramatic. A more familiar example is for women to change their hairstyles or dye their hair when going through a relationship breakup. It is couched as a way of cheering yourself up, but it signals to you and everyone who sees you that something is different. What would bring this change into your body in a way that feels positive, accepting, growth promoting, kind? You may choose an action to perform on retreat, or you may decide on something you can do in the next few days. For example, if you are marking a big birthday, you might try downhill skiing or taking a dance workshop. If you've become a mother, perhaps you will buy some new clothes that allow you to be comfortable and that hide stains well. Decorating yourself with rub-on tattoos, painting your body with body paints or makeup, walking in a different way—whatever brings your passage home.

Stories

This is Ann's story:

I had breast cancer, and although I had been in remission for almost a year, I still felt like I was "sick." I wanted to do a rite of passage to acknowledge the me that was well, the me that got sick, and the me that was well but forever changed. I specifically wanted a way to live with the fear of a recurrence.

I took two days and one night for a retreat on a friend's land about two hours from my home. As part of my opening ceremony, before I left home I sat my family down to tell them what I was doing and to announce that the woman who came back home would not be the woman they had worried about and had taken care of. I gave them each a framed picture of me doing something physical and looking healthy and a pin that said, "I am the son of a healthy mom" and "I am the husband of a healthy wife."

On the drive there I listened to rock 'n' roll, something I had not felt like doing since getting ill. It had seemed too young and hopeful.

I arrived at my spot and spent lots of time setting up my tent and getting comfortable. Then I went for a long hike and focused on how good it felt to move. Back at my camp, I sat down and meditated for quite a while on the question "How would I describe myself before?" Images of nursing my son, of wearing a bathing suit, of being comfortable changing in the gym dressing room, of making love came first, then feelings of trusting my body, of taking it for granted, of never thinking this could happen to me. I realized, too, that I hadn't been as in my body as I am now. I wrote about my impressions and then spent some time physically getting out the rage that emerged (for the umpteenth time) by chopping wood.

Then I looked at my symbol of the change, which was my prosthesis. Before I had seen my prosthesis as another way I had to change myself to be attractive. But as I dialogued with it, I found I appreciated it when I wanted to "pass" but that I no longer felt I needed to wear it every day.

Then I meditated on the questions "How have I been changed by this passage? Is there a gift to be claimed?" I hated the idea of a gift and resisted it mightily. But as I let my mind drift with the questions, I couldn't deny that the me I am now is more resilient. I am more able to decide what is important to me and less likely to do something I don't want to do. I actually feel more in my body. It was painful to see good things coming from the cancer, but they became real to me in that moment. I started to cry.

I changed the last question to "How can the new me deal with my fear of recurrence?" When I asked God to help me, I saw myself handing God this bucket oozing with black, tarry stuff, which seemed to symbolize my fear and the physical cancer. I resisted surrounding that image with light, but when I finally did it, the bucket changed into a bucket full of brilliant-colored fish that swam all around me. When I came out of meditation and drew the fish, I found myself thinking about the story in the Bible where Jesus turns water into wine and loaves into fish (at least that's the way I remembered it), and I realized that every time I felt the fear of becoming sick again, I had to do something to transform that fear into something nourishing. The words *transfiguration* and *transformation* kept banging around in my head. I knew that I had answered what I wanted the next part of my life to look like—I wanted it to be about finding the courage to transform my fear into love. I had no idea how I would do it, but I felt very eager to try.

I made the new me real by using face paints to paint a fish over my breast and to read Deena Metzger's poem "Tree" out loud to the trees.

On the way home I stopped and bought fish for dinner.

This is Jan's story.

For my thirty-seventh birthday I made the usual plan with my partner for going out to dinner. It was supposed to be a no-big-deal birthday, but this longing to be alone and think kept growing in me. So at the last minute I took off alone for the weekend to a bed-and-breakfast. I got some flack, but I felt I had to go.

See Retreat Plans: A One-Day Birthday Retreat.

What made this passage real to me was deciding to trust that I felt I was on the cusp of changing even if the outward signs didn't say so. When I journaled about how I would describe myself before, all I could think was, "Before what?" I was going back to work on Monday, back to Sharon; everything was the same. But when I tried the question "What is changing in my life that I have not been willing to see?," I drew blood. I decided to do spontaneous writing for twenty minutes (which felt very long and painful), and what emerged was that I maybe wanted a child. Now, for a thirty-seven-year-old lesbian who never has come out to her parents or her co-workers, that is not an easy thing to admit.

After a break in which I jogged until I was exhausted and then took a long shower, I thought about a symbol. What was it? I halfheartedly did some spontaneous drawing and after a while got into it and drew a set of shackles and a ring. When I dialogued with these bizarre items I learned that (surprise!) I was sure motherhood would tie me down, especially in my career, and that the ring was a ring my mother had given me that she had been given by her mother and her mother by her mother. I couldn't believe how much I wanted to pass that ring on to my daughter.

It was very clear to me how I had been changed by this passage or, more accurately, the acknowledging of a possible passage. I had let the cat out of the bag. I saw the gift as being a chance to be honest with myself and my partner and to make a conscious choice and perhaps to stop the bickering that had been arising between us for the last year or so.

"What do I want the next part of my life to look like?" at first seemed way too big of a question to consider right then, so I went out to dinner instead. But as I was eating, it occurred to me that the question didn't need to be so far-reaching; "what the next part of my life would look like" could mean "What would my life look like as I made a decision?" I decided I wanted it to look brave, informed, and creative. I went back to my room and did a spontaneous visualization in which I envisioned myself moving through the next few days and weeks with a tolerance for the ambiguity I was feeling, with tolerance for Sharon's shock (we both had agreed we didn't want children), and with an ability to listen to my wisdom. I blessed myself with oil and fell asleep.

The next day I decided to make the change real by carrying around a sack of flour for twenty-four hours. What would it feel like in my body to have to account for this thing? I also tried to walk and think like a mother.

For Long Retreats

Marking a significant passage lends itself to the luxury of a long retreat. Being able to take breaks between questions, to mix other practices in to strengthen your listening, and to enhance the transformational ability of this work is precious. It is also lovely to have enough time to sink into this gradually.

For Mini-Retreats

It is very challenging to try to mark a significant passage on a mini-retreat. However, it is an excellent practice to use mini-retreats to register the many small but important shifts that inhabit your life. Too often, you experience change, and nothing is done to acknowledge it, learn from it, or let it go. Your child starting kindergarten, a small promotion at work, moving across town, a change in a friendship, and the death of a pet all can be addressed within this container. Taking yourself lightly through each of the questions or working with just one is a way to tailor the practice.

For Retreats in the World

You may find yourself wanting to do something in public as part of your passage ceremony. Attending church, scattering ashes, walking on the beach, and meditating by the Vietnam War Memorial are all examples. If you do any of this work out in the world, you need to be extra aware of protecting yourself psychically and physically, because you are especially vulnerable when you are in the betwixt-and-between world *and* contemplating change.

See Where Will You Retreat?: Create Emotional Containment.

For Retreats with Others

Involving others in the creation of your passage can greatly enliven and make real to you the changes you are experiencing. There are countless ways to do this. One is to work with the questions on your own and then come together for a rite of passage that others participate in. It could be anything from climbing a nearby peak together to attending a singles night to participating in a sweat lodge or even taking turns supporting one another in doing a vision quest.

For larger groups, try sitting together in a circle taking turns telling the group about your passage. The woman talking starts a necklace of beads and other objects. When she is done, she passes it to her right. That woman adds a bead to it, taking a few minutes to describe what she has observed about you as you've gone through this change or to offer an affirmation if she doesn't know you. The necklace is passed to each woman until it returns to the woman who started it. Then you start another, until everyone has a necklace to mark her passage.

Grieving

There are some griefs so loud
They could bring down the sky,
And there are griefs so still
None knows how deep they lie,
Endured, never expended.
There are old griefs so proud
They never speak a word;
They never can be mended.
And these nourish the will
And keep it iron-hard.

May Sarton, "On Grief,"
Selected Poems of May Sarton

There are moments on almost every retreat, and there are even entire retreats, that must be given over to grieving. To letting go. To tasting that heart-bending pain of "No, it can't be" at the same time that your body begins to accept that "Yes, it is so." The romantic myth of retreating seems to provide no room for hair tearing, groaning, or tears from the belly. Yet if you read the writings of Mechthild of Magdeburg, some of the psalms, or contemporary accounts of retreats from women like Doris Grumbach and Alix Kates Shulman, you realize that much grieving has taken place on retreat. As Doris Grumbach puts it in *50 Days of Solitude,*

> Searching for the self when I was entirely alone was hazardous. What if I found not so much a great emptiness as a space full of unpleasant contents, a compound of long-hidden truths, closeted, buried, forgotten. When I went looking, I was playing a desperate game of hide-and-seek, fearful of what I might find, most afraid that I would find nothing.

Even if you ignore your grief, it won't go away. All the little daily losses as well as the big ones stay buried in your psyche, biding their time. Even the grief that May Sarton names in her poem, the grief that can never be mended, benefits from being brought into the light. "Grieving is not in response only to those who in my life who have died. Grief involves every person, object, or incident from which I have walked away with a sense of being incomplete," writes Elaine Childs-Gowell in *Good Grief Rituals*. In the world of the psyche, there is no time. A friend's hurtful remark from months ago, if it was never brought into the open, looms as large now as if it just happened. The psyche nurses the wound that hasn't been acknowledged and grieved.

On retreat you stop. All the dross of life that keeps old grief at bay is left behind. There is nothing between you and your truth. This can be terrifying. You can feel trapped, lost, a tidal wave of grief crashing over you. But if you can ride your sorrow like a boat in a storm, you will come out the other side freer and possibly more open, trusting, aware, and energetic.

If you are actively grieving, you could set up a retreat to explore the issue. When grieving and healing the legacy of childhood abuse, Saral took a three-month retreat, working with a therapist once a week. Or you might find yourself overtaken and surprised by grief in the middle of a retreat. If this happens, consider it a moment of grace, a juncture. If at this time you can't quite open to the grief, no matter. Many times I have squelched such feelings and missed such opportunities. There will be another such moment down the retreat road. As long as you and I can remember to practice self-kindness, the way remains open.

Prepare

Music that helps you feel your grief and a scent that evokes feeling. They do not need to be specific to your life. For example, the soundtrack to the film *The Mission* makes me weep no matter where I am.

Comforting things like a mohair blanket, a photograph of a happy time, a bag of chocolate malt balls.

A check-in person.

A physical way to express anger—bread dough to pound; a tennis racket, a ball, and a wall; loud music to stomp around to.

A place where you feel safe crying and screaming.

Sage, incense, or other dried herbs and a container to burn the incense in.

Matches.

A feather or fan to spread the smoke (optional).

A symbol of what you are letting go.

See Courage: Support on Retreat.

Emotional Container

Yes, I'm pushing the Tupperware again. Doing grief work can be frightening. The more serious the issues you are working with and the more fragile you feel, the more important it is to create a container, a beginning and end to your grieving experience.

One way is to set a timer for a short period of time, say twenty minutes to an hour. Work with your grief only until the timer goes off, then immediately indulge in a soothing, self-nurturing treat like a foot soak in warm water and peppermint oil, or stroll to a creek, or massage your temples and neck while curled up for a nap under an eiderdown comforter.

Arrange to have a check-in person on call so that if you need an outside reassurance, he or she can be reached quickly, by phone or in person. *Give yourself permission* to call if you feel the need. Or retreat with another person close by. Sometimes simply knowing you have firm plans to meet someone you love after your retreat, someone who is healing and grounding, creates the container you need. A pet on retreat can also be a comforting anchor. On more than one lonely descent into the darker regions of my self, I literally clung to my dog for reassurance.

Touching Grief

Gather a selection of music and a scent that evoke feeling for you. What constitutes good music to grieve by is highly subjective, and it is sometimes difficult to find the music that moves you in this way. Locate a music store that lets you listen before buying. Visit a library with music selections. Raid a friend's music collection.

These music selections were chosen because many people experience them as opening the heart and awakening emotion. However, they might not do that for you. Listen *before* your retreat.

- Brahms: Piano Concerto no. 2, Allegro non troppo, first movement; Symphony no. 3 in F Major, opus 90, first movement

- Bach: "Come Sweet Death"; Prelude in B Minor

- Vaughn Williams: Fantasia on "Greensleeves"; Pastoral Symphony; Symphony no. 5

- Marcello: Oboe Concerto in C Minor, Adagio

- Bruckner: Symphony no. 8, second movement, Scherzo only

- Holst: The Planets, Uranus and Saturn

- Mahler: Symphony no. 10, third movement; Symphony no. 5, Adagietto

- Beethoven: Symphony no. 3 ("Eroica"), second movement; Symphony no. 7, second movement

- Albinoni: Adagio for Strings and Organs

- Sibelius: "Swan of Tuonela"

- Erik Satie: "Three Gymnopedies"

- Debussy: Afternoon of a Faun; La Mer, first movement

- Rachmaninoff: Symphonic Dances, opus 45, first movement

- Puccini: "I Crisantemi," string quartet

- Michael Hoppe: "The Yearning"; "The Dreamer"; "The Poet"

- Tim Wheater: "Heartland"; "Green Dreams"; "Timeless"; "Eclipse"

- Michael Nyman: *The Piano* soundtrack

- Ennio Morricone: *The Mission* soundtrack

- Peter Gabriel: *The Last Temptation of Christ* soundtrack

See Resources for more.

Choose a scent quickly, either by letting an idea pop into your head, by exploring your bathroom and spice cabinet, or by visiting a health food store with a range of essential oils and lotions.

A few evocative smells:

- Cinnamon

- A particular brand of laundry detergent, shampoo, soap, aftershave, or perfume

- A loved one's piece of clothing

- Fresh-cut grass (you can find a lotion at the Gap that smells like this)

- Chocolate

- Sachets

- Rose, lavender, lilac, freesia (flowers or essential oils)

- Bread or cookies baking (use premixed cookie or bread dough, and put it in the oven at the beginning of this exercise)

- New hardcover books

- Old leather

- Beeswax candles burning

Make a comfortable nest for yourself, a place in which you feel protected and physically held, perhaps surrounded by pillows and flannel blankets or outside in the sun in a sheltered spot. Go to extra trouble to be sure you have what you need close by: water, tissues, your cat, a warm shawl.

See Good Ways to Listen: I Am Enough.

Close your eyes and breathe deeply. On an inhale, repeat, "I open to all my feelings," and on an exhale, "I am safe." Repeat until you feel calm and ready.

Put your music on. Listening to it on headphones is especially effective. Repeat your retreat intention to yourself, even if it has nothing to do with grieving.

Surrender to the music. Feelings, images, bodily sensations, ideas will begin to drift past you. Avoid analyzing, controlling, or interpreting. Instead, let the music take you with it. Sink into the flow. Follow whatever emerges. If there is an image of a door, open it. If you see a flower, smell it. If you are having an associative flow of ideas, go with them instead of blocking them by thinking, "This is a waste of time" or "I should get up and write these down." The music is your guide, your energy. You are along for the ride. You don't have to do anything.

Whenever it feels right, take a whiff of your chosen scent. You may do so if you start to think too much or if you get pulled out of your reverie by a noise or if you want to go deeper into your feelings and memories.

Imagine that you are spinning a waking dream. The sole purpose is for you to feel. There is nothing to fear. You are perfectly safe.

See Resources for a list of uplifting music.

When your music comes to a conclusion, you might want to replay it, play another piece that is uplifting, or do something soothing. You might also wish to write about what you experienced. Here are some journal questions to reflect on:

- How do I feel in this moment? Do I feel different than I did before I started?

- How did this experience relate to my intention question?

- What surprised me?

- What new insights did I glean?

Getting Current

Getting current with your grief may mean dealing with your feelings in a more verbal, linear way. You may want to do this before or after you do Touching Grief. This practice is especially useful when grieving the world's predicament—the famines, wars, and starving children we read about—and when we feel powerless to do something about it and then disassociate from our grief. Feeling our grief may be the first step in unfreezing and working toward change. Arn Chorn, an eighteen-year-old Cambodian refugee and survivor of the Khmer Rouge, told a general meeting of Amnesty International in 1988, "I am not ashamed to cry. All of us need not be ashamed to cry. In fact, maybe the first thing we have to do is cry. Our tears may even be the power necessary to change violence into love—change human madness to human kindness. The tears may be the water of new life." Sometimes part of a retreat needs to be about grieving for the suffering of others.

Get your journal and a timer. Set the timer for five minutes, or fill five pages. If you wish, you might put some evocative music on in the background. Whatever happens, keep your hand moving across the page until the timer goes off or your pages are full. Write anything, but keep writing. A question to get you rolling:

- What do I need to grieve for?

If you get stuck, keep your hand moving while considering:

- What don't I want to grieve for?

When your time is up or your pages are filled, stretch your body. Breathe and scan how your body feels, especially areas like your jaw, shoulders, hands, and belly. What feels tense? What feels open or loose?

Come back to your journal and dialogue with the part (or parts) of your body that are tense or light, or that you are simply more aware of. Start the dialogue by writing across the top of a sheet of paper:

- _____(Body part), what can you tell me about my grief?

Breathe into that body part and wait for it to speak. You might want to write the response with your nondominant hand, or you might want to stand, sway, or rock while you write. See what comes out. No need to force it, no need to judge it.

Take a short break.

Come back, set the timer for another ten minutes, and write with the statement

- The way I now feel about my grieving is . . .

If you get stuck or feel you are staying on the surface, write about

- I am still avoiding _____ because . . .

Anger and rage often need to be cleared before you can grieve. Read over everything you have written. Does anything on your lists give a hit of anger? Choose one. Now is the time to let go of (perhaps only some of) your anger. Choose something physical that will allow you to experience your anger. Get as physical with this as your surroundings and body allow. You want to open your chest as much as possible. Try wrapping a towel around a broom or tennis racket and pounding the bed while yelling what you are angry about. You may feel you are trapped in a bad 1970s encounter group. You can put on bell-bottoms, but do it anyway. Connect the physical with the verbal. You can pound bread dough, run hard while shouting (obviously not a good choice for a crowded park), throw old dishes or flower pots (you can buy cheap ones for just this purpose at a thrift store or yard sale). I once did this practice standing on a riverbank throwing clay into the water. Each plop of clay was another oppressive event, person, or belief that I was holding on to: Doug rejecting me in tenth grade; bad investments; cellulite; cold sores; not getting into graduate school; not being a brilliant literary prodigy. Ten years later I still remember how good that release felt.

When you are ready for some gentle self-soothing, perhaps after a break, ask yourself one final question:

- What am I willing to grieve?

Read over your list again and choose *only* those events that you are honestly ready to grieve, even if only partially. If there are issues you enjoy brooding over or that scare you too much to face, leave them alone.

Stand where you have some room.

In a loud voice, say, "I am grieving for. . . ." Name what you are willing to grieve for.

In a louder voice, say, "I am grieving for. . . ."

Take in a very deep breath, and as you exhale say, louder still, "I am grieving for. . . ."

Throw your arms out and yell, "I am grieving for. . . ."

Drop down to a small voice and say, "I am grieving for. . . ."

End by whispering and perhaps rocking or hugging yourself, saying, "I am grieving for. . . ."

Be still and feel.

Repeat this as many times as you have the energy for. Don't push yourself to do more than you feel able, and don't push past the point where you can deeply feel. You can always come back to this later in your retreat or on another retreat. You do not need to go through the entire exercise to do this last part.

End with some sweet self-nurturing.

Ceremony for Letting Go

When a concrete loss has happened and has been mourned, a time comes when a ritual letting go can be of help. A death, a divorce, an abortion, a miscarriage, an injury, the loss of money or possessions, the loss of innocence or trust, the end of friendship or group—there are many times in each of our lives when we need to let go.

See Opening Ceremony: A Sample Ceremony.

Name one person or event or thing you wish to let go of. Be sure you are ready to let go, and be sure you have done your grieving. Doing this ceremony doesn't mean you won't grieve again, but it does signify a desire to move on.

You will need something aromatic to burn: sage, incense, or other dried herbs; matches; a container to burn the incense; and a piece of a paper. You will also need a feather or fan to spread the smoke (or you can use your hand). If you are doing this inside, open a window or disengage the smoke alarm. You will also need to find or make a symbol of what you are releasing. A piece of jewelry, photo, or handkerchief from your deceased loved one, a dollar bill or a sketch of your failed business, and a baby bootie to symbolize the child you decided not to have are examples. Finding or making this symbol can take time and can open new levels of grieving. If necessary, take the time.

Center yourself. Take time to relax your body. Ask for protection from your Divinity. Visualize yourself surrounded by healing light or held by loving arms.

Visualize the person or thing you are letting go of. Use all your senses—sight, smell, taste, touch, and hearing. If you have good memories, replay them. If it is something or someone you never got to experience, use your imagination.

When your visualization is complete, write a prayer or litany of gratitude for this person or event. What are you thankful for in having known this person, in having had this experience, or in having experienced this loss?

Light your incense or herbs and blow on them three times. As you do, say aloud, "I release you." Stay with the feelings that come up. Let them out verbally if you can, through song or simple sounds.

Fan or blow your smoke in the direction of the east. As you do, remember what it was like in the beginning, remember the hope, the promise. Spend a moment remembering. Then say three times, "I release you."

Fan or blow your smoke in the direction of the south. As you do, recall the childlike, emotional qualities of this experience or relationship. Spend a moment remembering. Then say three times, " I release you."

Fan or blow your smoke in the direction of the west. As you do, recall what was strong and wild about this part of your life. Spend a moment remembering. Then say three times, "I release you."

Fan or blow your smoke in the direction of the north. As you do, think about how this loss brought vision into your life, what you have learned. Spend a moment with this. Then say three times, "I release you."

Fan or blow your smoke in the direction of the center, toward the sky and the earth. Tear up and burn your paper of gratitude in the same container as your incense or sage. As you do, fan the smoke toward the sky or out an open window. Bless what you are letting go of.

Say a final good-bye in whatever way comes to you.

Sit with how you are feeling until you feel done. If you do not feel you have been able to release at least some of your grief, take a break and do something physical or rest. Then repeat the ritual.

Unplanned Grief

*See also
Uncomfortable
Beginnings,
Middles, and
In-Betweens.*

If you are in the middle of a retreat that wasn't supposed to have anything to do with grieving, and you suddenly find yourself awash in sadness, loneliness, and regrets, don't panic. This is a very common reaction and actually is a very good sign. It means that the retreat process is working at your very core and that the energy in your body and psyche is opening up. Scan the ideas below, but get out of the verbal, controlling mode as quickly as you can.

- Imagine that you are on a surfboard, riding waves of grief. Tell yourself, "I am safe. I can stop this whenever I want. I am loved. I trust this process."

- Hold on to something—a blanket or pillow, the sides of a chair.

- Breathe deeply and slowly.

- Make noise. "Aum (*om*)," "Ahh," chanting a phrase like "All will be well," or just making sounds—what one friend calls spirit songs.

- If you feel that you aren't moving as deeply into your grief as you wish, do one of the activities under Touching Grief. Don't stop to prepare— put on some music, pound a drum, grab a scent, or stomp around the room.

- If you are feeling overwhelmed or panicked, say to yourself,

    I feel sad. I am not my sadness.

    I feel lonely. I am not my loneliness.

    I feel angry. I am not my anger.

- After you've gone as far as you need to or can, always do something kind for yourself. *Never* chastise yourself for not doing a good enough or deep enough job. *Always* praise and be kind to yourself.

See Good Ways to Listen: Soothe.

Stories

Diana went on a three-hour retreat Thanksgiving morning.

> I decided to go into the bog for three hours and concentrate (I felt a very strong need to do this) on "Was I doing the right thing?" with respect to resigning from work next August.

> I chose the bog because it's like the womb of Mother Earth. When it starts getting cold in the winter, the bog stays green and steams with heat from within for a long time before finally freezing. To me, nature has all the wisdom we need.

> Not knowing what the weather would be, I needed a shelter. I thought of a teepee and asked my husband, Herb, to help. We went out one day, and I chose my spot: a depression on the edge of the woods just before the expanse of cattails started. All the poles I needed were lying around there. We started standing them up, and after the third pole the teepee

was standing on its own. Herb had to tie the poles together at the top, but otherwise I did as much of the work as I could on my own. It was a fine teepee. I called it the medi-teepee, as in meditation teepee. Herb called it the spirit teepee.

I came back the next day and cut a bundle of cattail reeds to use for flooring. I brought twelve apple-sized stones to use for my fire ring. I wrapped my teepee with sheets and spread the floor. Then I did my ceremony of sanctifying the area and calling on the forces that be. I placed a flag in each direction (red, yellow, white, and black), calling on the strength of each power. I scattered birdseed in thanksgiving. I went inside and settled in. I wrote in my journal, "I waited. My first prayer was a grieving over the loss of my spirit soul in my life. To use my brain organ as I do at work, so fully and so hard, I close down and shut out my feelings and my heart so that I can concentrate on inventing and accomplishing things that have nothing do with who I am. I miss her—I hope it's not too late." I cried very hard. It felt good. I was happy to discover this ache within, because I can now hold it and comfort it!

Rhonda is a mother, an artist, and a teacher. She was in the process of helping her father to die. This is a story of several mini-retreats she did before and after he died.

When my dad was dying and I was spending a lot of time with him in the hospital, I would retreat to walk the beach. Usually I focus my time by looking for brightly colored shells, beautiful pieces of the ocean. But on these retreats, I found it impossible to pick up pretty shells. I was sad, I was angry, I was very lost and confused.

I started looking for small pieces of wood, driftwood, instead. I searched for wood that was aged, worn, had traveled and lived, and grown someplace else. I gathered wood, each new piece more beautiful than the last. I felt I was holding many small stories, many lives, in my hands. Doing this got my mind off my dad's pain and connected me to something larger.

After my dad died, I retreated into myself for a long period of time. I didn't want to talk to anyone. The solace of the retreat space in my home was both comfort and pain, as I had to be more present to my grieving, instead of downing a cocktail or two. I kept doing small retreats, inching along in my grief. I ironed, I read, I gardened. I needed to feel the earth, to aid in growth, to see things come alive. Being in silence most of the day was also important. Then, one day, I took up the wood again. I painted a large flat piece of wood black. In an hour, I arranged all the small, beautiful pieces of wood together, overlapping each piece so they meshed, so they became one. For days, I returned to my work table and glued a few pieces down. I loved working on this. I couldn't wait to continue attaching all the pieces together.

As I worked, I thought of the beach, the individual stories of Dad's life and of those I love. This sculpture was his life, it was his story. It was a dedication to him. I was thanking him for being my dad and all that we learned, loved, and shared together. Every time I see it now, I think of Dad.

For Long Retreats

A long retreat often includes a descent into grief. It doesn't mean that your life is a mess or that there is something wrong with you. It is part of the archetype. The gift of having more time allows you to circle back to this material a few times, thereby moving to deeper levels. Be aware that on a longer retreat, especially on one in which you plan on dealing with troubling issues, you must have a check-in person available.

For Mini-Retreats

Don't let having a limited amount of time stop you. Mini-retreats can be very useful in dealing with grief. Remember Holly Hunter's character in *Network News?* Each day she took the phone off the hook (her opening ceremony) and sobbed for a minute or two—sobbed for all the horror and sorrow she witnessed as a news producer. Then she put the phone back on the hook and went back to business. It illustrates that when we make room for grief, we remain engaged with humanity and can be more human ourselves. The more often you take small time-outs for grief, the less garbage will come bubbling up at inconvenient times.

See Retreat Plans: A One-Day Grieving Retreat.

For Retreats in the World

Grieving on retreats in the world is not advised, although traveling to see your childhood home, hiking in the mountains, or attending a concert or church can be an excellent prelude to doing one of these practices.

For Retreats with Others

Use the power of others to help yourself heal. Be sure you have created a sacred space where you will not be disturbed. Sit in a deep listening circle

See Retreating with Others: Deep Listening Circle.

around the subject of grieving, letting go, or loss, or call a circle to witness what each woman discovered while doing any of the above practices. Once everyone has had a chance to speak, any woman who wishes to be helped comes forward and lies in the middle of the circle on a blanket and pillow (placed there ahead of time). Someone puts on soft, healing music. The women gather around the woman lying down. Each woman lays one of her hands on the woman seeking healing. Her third eye (the area between the eyebrows), the top of her head, her heart, her solar plexus (the soft area below the breastbone), her hands, belly, knees, and feet should all be gently pressed on at some point during this ritual. The women doing the healing then place their free hands on their own bodies, each on a place where she feels her healing power lies. The woman receiving the healing relaxes and imagines healing energy streaming from each of the women's hands. The women touching her visualize their healing energy streaming into her body, connecting with her healing light and the light everyone else is sending, and then streaming back into their bodies until one throbbing circuit can be felt. Humming, singing, or toning may spontaneously happen. Slowly, everyone moves in a clockwise direction around the woman lying down, shifting positions. The woman at her head moves her hand to her solar plexus. The woman at her solar plexus moves to her hands or belly. Everyone shifts, slowly. Continue moving around until every part of her body has been gently touched and each woman is back where she started. End with three long *oms*, breathing from your belly.

Slowly, silently, switch positions and do the next woman.

Here is a variation from a grieving ceremony my women's group did for one of our members. The woman who wishes to be healed collects small stones before the ritual. She asks the stones for their permission to participate. After the stones are gathered, she holds them and thinks about what she wants drawn out of her, what she wants to let go of or be healed of. An hour or so before the ceremony, she heats the stones in the oven at 250 degrees. During the ceremony the warm (not hot!) stones are placed on the woman's eyes, mouth, solar plexus, and belly, and she holds one in each hand. The other women place their hands over or on other parts of her body. The rest of the ceremony is the same.

Reviving Your Spiritual Direction

*"I have kept my little rule and maintained my little fasts and
said my little prayers faithfully," the disciple said to the holy one.
"Now what can I do to be enlightened?" And the holy one stood
up and stretched her arms to heaven. "Why not," she said, spreading
her fingers wide, "why not be completely turned into fire?"*

Joan Chittister, *In a High Spiritual Season*

Seeking spiritual renewal has many degrees. You may be lost in a dark night of the soul, a lonely, dead, gray place. You may have temporarily fallen away from an adored spiritual path because of illness, pressing commitments, or boredom. You may be considering questions of the spirit for the first time. You may be experiencing a crisis of faith. Whatever your reason, the loving-kindness of taking yourself on retreat invites your yearning for grace to be fulfilled.

How have you come to feel lost in this area of your life? Perhaps the overwhelming misogyny of the major religions has soured you in your quest. Perhaps a painful experience associated with your spirituality has blocked you from reaching out. Peg Thompson in *Finding Your Own Spiritual Path* lists common obstacles to spiritual renewal: fear of being wounded or abandoned by the Divine; fear of intimacy with the Divine, fear of being truly known; defiance against a harsh religious past; bitterness and despair over prayers that were not answered in the past or over asking for help in the past and being admonished to pray instead of being helped; shame because having a spiritual life seems weak, nonintellectual, uncool; confusion because we don't know how to pray, meditate, or actively seek the Divine; perplexity because organized religion doesn't speak to you and your attempts to find an alternative path have been tepid or disappointing.

Whatever your reasons, taking the time that a retreat requires may bring the reconnection to spirit that you seek. The act of retreating sends a signal to yourself that you are worthy of a spiritual life. If you beat yourself up and push yourself unmercifully, then you practice self-hatred, and you effectively block a relationship with the Divine. The practice of honoring the self that happens on retreat may spontaneously reawaken your connection to the sacred.

And a more direct inquiry into your spiritual life may need to be undertaken. What is missing for you? Where did you get lost? What are you yearning for? What obstacles are you erecting? How have you been wounded? What do you believe?

Prepare

Your journal and a pen.

Drawing materials or clay.

Meditative music.

Imagining the Divine

In *The History of God* Karen Armstrong writes,

> I wish I would have learned this thirty years ago, when I was starting out in the religious life. It would have saved me a great deal of anxiety to hear—from eminent monotheists in all three faiths—that instead of waiting for God to descend from on high, I should deliberately create a sense of God for myself. . . . They would have warned me not to expect to experience God as an objective fact that could be discovered by the ordinary process of rational thought. They would have told me that in an important sense God was a product of the creative imagination, like the poetry and music that I found so inspiring.

When I read the words "create a sense of God for myself," I felt I was on fire. How could I do that for myself? In the past, when friends or family spoke about their relationship with the Divine, I was always fascinated but puzzled. I didn't know whom I was going to have that relationship with. And I didn't know how to pray or whom to pray to. I needed a place to start. I needed images and names for the Divine, *names that I could relate to*. Perhaps the same is true for you. Perhaps this practice will help you build a bridge toward what is ultimately unnameable, yet not unknowable.

Copy the words below that resonate, intrigue, and puzzle you into your journal. If you see words that you feel you should copy but you don't feel comfortable or drawn to them, don't.

God	Illumination
Goddess	Mary
Blessed Virgin	Messiah
Atman	Muhammad
Adonai	Mother
Holy Spirit	Father
Buddha	Redeemer
Jesus Christ	Shekinah
Creator	Sophia
Deepest Self	Spirit
Authentic Self	Vishnu
Divine	Wisdom
Eve	Yahweh
El	Compassionate One
Eternal Light	Loving Guide
Lord	Breath of Life
Queen of Heaven	Spirit of Life
Gaia	Universe
Great Mother	Universal Mind
Great Spirit	Spirit of the Universe
Higher Power	Spirit of Nature
Holy Ghost	All-Powerful, Guiding, Creative Intelligence
Jehovah	
Kali	Great Reality Down Deep Within Us

The Mighty Purpose and
Rhythm That Underlies All

Mother of All Living

Father of All Living

Divine Feminine

Divine Matrix

Healer

A God Who Looks Like Me

The Still Presence

Presence of Infinite Love

The Source

White Buffalo Calf Woman

Krishna

Inanna

Ishtar

Astarte

Womb Mother

Cerridwen

Lilith

See Good Ways to Listen and Contemplations.

Choose one or more of your selected words. Using spontaneous painting, clay, or collage, create an image inspired by your chosen words. Let your intuitive heart guide you. What does this mean? It means that the process of making the image—of how it feels, of what thoughts and feelings occur to you—is what is valuable, not the finished image. This is not art making, this is ceremonial discovery. You might like to keep a journal or tape recorder close by to record impressions while shaping your image.

See Courage for how to dialogue.

When you are through, sit in silence with your image for a few moments. Dialogue with it. Let your image speak through you. Recall Karen Armstrong's words, "God [is] a product of the creative imagination." Contemplating this evokes a feeling of prayer, but instead of a prayer of petition, this is prayer of connection. "We can think of prayer as any practice that fosters or expresses our relationship with the sacred as we understand it. . . . When we pray, we *actively seek a relationship to the divine,*" is the way Peg Thompson defines it (italics mine). If we think of prayer as entering into a dynamic, intimate relationship with the awesome energy of the universe, we stop seeing ourselves as unworthy or inert and begin to imagine communicating with, co-creating with, the Divine. Which is not to suggest this is a neat process, a "create-your-own-God" package. A relationship with the Divine is above all a relationship with *mysterium tremendum,* with an overwhelming mystery. We may create an image or a sense, but never a definition. There is intimacy but never comprehension. The Divine is not "an objective fact that could be discovered by the ordinary process of rational thought." Cultivating this relationship requires and creates faith—faith in your own worthiness to be in such an intimate relationship, faith that the process of co-creating your life with Spirit is truly occurring, and faith that although you can neither see it nor taste it, the mystery is loving you back.

Gratitude, worship, devotion, being held, and being known can all be experienced as prayer. Somewhere between what Jesuit retreat leader Anthony de Mello described as lovingly gazing at the blank that is God and the form of prayer I learned in a Baptist Sunday school I attended briefly as a child lies a shimmering range of ways to be in relationship with the sacred. I kept thinking of all the ways I am in relationship with people, places, and animals in my life and how these relationships are sometimes a form of prayer. Prayer became alive to me as a way to care for my daughter, my garden, my body. I could communicate with my renewed image of the Divine through these acts as well as through dancing, writing, and talking. And I was worthy of accepting communication back.

Now that you have an image of the one you seek a relationship with, what do you want to say? Try avoiding words, and use your body to establish connection. Using gestures or dance, express with your body your doubts, your desires, your gratitude for this new or renewed relationship. Or you may love words, as poet Kathleen Norris does, and through the psalms, other poetry, or your own writing you can declare your feelings toward the Divine. You may want to repeat one of the sacred names you chose over and over while breathing deeply. You may sit in silence, using your image as an icon to softly focus on. Experiment with establishing a living relationship that fits you, a style and rhythm that fan your desire. Don't force yourself. Avoid beating yourself up if nothing comes alive for you during this exercise. Just leave it be for a while. Similarly, don't avoid a path that appeals to you because it feels too new or too different from what you believe. Trust that what you are drawn to today is right for you and that the response of your heart will tell you if you are worshiping in a way that is true.

Define and Undefine Your Spiritual Life

Sometimes you lose your connection to the Divine because you don't know what you need from this connection or what role a spiritual path plays in your life. Why practice a spiritual discipline? Why be a spiritually oriented person? Why nurture your spirit? What does *spiritual* mean?

See Introduction for one definition.

Sometimes you lose your connection to the Divine because you are trying to control it, because *you* insist on defining what your relationship with the Divine will be. Perhaps it is only a relationship about self-improvement, thinking optimistic thoughts, or creating your own reality. Or perhaps it is primarily a punitive relationship, one of judgment and moral direction.

Read the list in Contemplations: Ways to Work with Questions and Other Material for ideas on how to work with this question. Center yourself before encountering the questions below. Ask for help, even if you don't know whom you are asking.

- What am I yearning for in my relationship to the Divine? What is missing in this relationship? What is already present and good?

Be willing to sit with the discomfort of not knowing what you yearn for. Be willing to be greedy and childish in your desires. Be willing to acknowledge ideas that are foreign or threatening to your idea of who you are and what you believe. Practice trust.

- What limits do I put on my relationship with the Divine? What am I not willing to accept or be open to when exploring my spiritual path?

Same approach—center yourself, ask for help, and then contemplate the question however you choose, taking all the time you need. Listen to the mere whisperings of your imagination. Honor them.

- What does being spiritual mean? What does having a spiritual practice mean?

Same procedure. Take a break if you need one. Finally, take the sentence stem below and complete it fifty times.

- I believe . . .

What emerges from doing this practice? What did you learn? Are you surprised? Reassured? Threatened? Challenged?

Randi discovered in answer to the first question that the central limit she put on her relationship was "fear of getting close to Spirit." Jackie found she needed to "surrender to the mystery of life and stop controlling everything." Mona defined being spiritual as "living the golden rule, even toward someone who cuts in front of me in line at the store or plays rap music on the subway." Another woman found that writing down what she believed took her entire retreat, because "it is so easy to mouth spiritual ideas and so hard to make them a true part of your life. I didn't want to write down anything I wasn't willing to live. After I made my list, I asked myself, 'How am I living these beliefs?' That led me to make a list of ways I would like to."

Can you do the same? Reading over what you wrote in each section, are there one or two actions that, if you did them on this retreat, could reinvigorate your spiritual life? What emerges may be simple and basic, like being kind to yourself and others, or puzzling and hard to know how to do, as with Jackie and her idea of surrendering to mystery. "I had no idea how to do this—there wasn't a clear first step. So I tried asking my Higher Power what I should do and kept trying to just be still and wait, over and over, throughout my retreat." What do you need to do?

Become an Empty Vessel

One morning when I was trying to pray, requesting help with this chapter, a voice asked, "How can I fill you up when you are so full already?" The image of an empty bowl came to mind. I was shocked into stillness. In that moment I stepped back and saw my spiritual practices as mainly telling and thanking, not listening and being. A feeling of being hollow arose—as if there were an empty space starting at my throat and expanding into my torso. An empty hourglass vessel. I named myself "Hollow Listening Woman."

See Good Ways to Listen: Being.

I decided this was an excellent practice for me to continue—to spend a few moments each morning sitting silently, focusing my mind on the feeling of being hollow: empty, open, clear. I think of this as prayer, but instead of asking or complaining or even giving thanks, I keep my heart and mind focused on being empty.

When I can stick with it, when I can resist the need to beg or cajole, when I can calm my frantic thoughts with this spacious image of my body as an empty vessel, sometimes I am graced by a feeling of something pouring into me. Sometimes this is an idea or image, but mostly it is a feeling of depth and peacefulness, as if I'm sinking into something infinitely vast. Yet if I hope for something to come, nothing does. If I feel like I am waiting, it doesn't feel right. I have to focus on being empty and that alone.

Spiritual renewal may come through emptiness, by becoming a vessel that the Divine can pour herself into. Let an image of emptiness occur to you. Meditate on it. Become a hollow listening woman.

Discipline

Discipline has a bad reputation. Images of nuns with rulers and fasting until you faint come to mind. Yet loving discipline is a cornerstone of meaning and renewal. You don't beat yourself into prayer, meditation, or helping others; you acknowledge your resistance, give it a hug, and keep going.

Pick any spiritual practice that you know, think you know, or have always wanted to experience. Praying the rosary, meditating on the Buddhist loving-kindness prayer, reading from the Koran, meditating on your inhale: the choices are endless. Keep it simple—let it be something you can do on retreat, without preparation or fuss. Choose a practice that revolves around silence and that can be done in ten to thirty minutes. Do this practice regularly on your retreat. No thinking, no wavering, no changing your mind. If you are on a very short retreat, then do a shorter practice (say five minutes) every half hour or hour of your retreat. Don't skip this because you assume you don't know how to do a practice correctly.

See Resources for books about varied spiritual practices.

But what if you don't have any idea what spiritual discipline to practice? What if nothing comes to mind? Then either choose a practice from one of the books listed in Resources, or sit in silence for twenty minutes and watch your breath. No mantra, no special instructions. Yes, volumes have been written and thousands of opinions are held on how to sit in silence. You don't have to do any of them. Just sit. Decide before your first session where you will sit and how. Spend a few moments becoming comfortable, making sure your lower back is supported. Sit up if you are physically able, because if you lie down you may fall asleep. Return at regular intervals to the same place, the same position, and sit in silence. Use a timer; do not watch your watch. Allow yourself no variations. Observe what you obsess about. Observe the silence that falls over you. No conclusions need to be drawn. Nothing needs to happen except to sit in silence.

If you tried sitting in the past and hated it, then walk in silence in nature. If nature is not available, you might need to wear headphones with very simple instrumental music to block out distractions. The same precepts: Do nothing but walk. Do not talk to anyone. Observe your reactions, resistance, repetitive thoughts. No conclusions, no striving, just walking in silence.

After doing any form of sustained discipline, you will feel yourself opening. You may not have learned anything intellectually. You may not see angels or have tea with Gandhi. You may not shave your head and take up a begging bowl. But you will *feel:* a deepening, a quickening, an enlivening, a relief. When you do, express gratitude to the sacred as you know it.

(If you read this before your retreat and a discipline comes to mind that involves a special setting or other people, say attending the hours of the liturgical day within a religious community, then by all means pursue your idea.)

Addressed to the Heart

One of the ways we dull our spiritual senses is by forgeting to observe the riches that are being offered to us each moment. We forget to marvel at the fingernail on the tip of each finger, the sunlight pouring through white muslin curtains, that eating peaches and cream creates energy to fuel the brain that is reading these thoughts. Mystics seem to be the only ones who are able to walk around in awe of the indescribable wonder of life. "Look around you, enjoy every flowering bush, every tall tree, and know that the spirit of God has made them lovely for you," St. Clare of Assisi declared.

It is time to be a mystic.

Spend part of a retreat, or all of a mini-retreat, being alert to what is being offered to you. Imagine that life is one giant gift, wrapped in reverence, being offered to you by your Divinity. Sit down. It need not be anyplace special. Take a few deep breaths, and then simply receive what is being offered. These are good questions to start with:

See Good Ways to Listen: Divine Landscape: Nature as Mirror.

- What is being offered to me by all that is holy?
- What gifts of spirit or grace, what messages from the Divine, are addressed to me?

Use all your senses to answer these questions. Look around. What is being offered for your eyes to feast upon? Listen. What is being offered for your ears to resound with? What is being offered for your taste buds to savor? What is being offered for your nose to inhale into you? What is being offered for you to embrace? What is being whispered into your heart?

You may spend five minutes or an hour on this practice. It is mysterious and can be profoundly moving. You can do it while walking, in your office, on the bus, at home, anywhere. On a long retreat, use this practice to punctuate your retreat. Set an alarm to gently remind you every three or four hours, sit down wherever you are, and open to what is being offered.

Unfold into gratitude without answers.

Melting

See Grieving: Emotional Container for creating a safe place.

Using spontaneous writing or painting, make a list or draw images of everything you dislike about yourself, everything you cannot forgive yourself for,

---

everything that you may torture yourself about. You are taking an inventory of your brittle, hard, ancient hurts and defects. Be fierce.

When your list feels complete, put it next to an image of the Divine. This may be an image you have made or an image you found or already love. It may be a tree or a rock. It may be a shrine of images.

Center yourself in whatever way you choose. Close your eyes. Imagine your image of the Divine as you know it coming toward you. Whatever comes to you is fine. Spend a few moments feeling this presence. See your Divinity enveloping you in a hug. Open yourself to how this feels, this love and acceptance. Be aware of feeling inadequate, unworthy, or unclean. Imagine your Sacred Being bathing you in holy water. Take time to imagine where you are, what the water feels like, smells like, even tastes like. Linger. Trust whatever details occur to you.

As you are bathed, allow your mistakes, your wounds, your shortcomings to fall away. However you feel or visualize this happening is perfect. You may see darkness streaming out of your body. You may imagine symbols for different items on your list and see these symbols being dissolved or transformed by the water. You may hear yourself listing the things you hate about yourself and hear a voice responding with "And that, too, is accepted." Your vision may expand beyond this bath. Follow your imagination. Open to the love that is available. Stay out of your mind, out of what you believe or don't believe. Focus on being held, bathed, and accepted.

Soma Source

See Contemplations.

Feeling in our bodies our relationship to the Divine, beyond words and theory, is often where women find spiritual renewal. We have been taught for thousands of years that our bodies are unclean, that we were not made in the image of the Divine, and that we must split spirituality from matter. Of course, in doing so, the feminine has been exiled, and a barren trap of self-hatred and separation from the Divine has been erected around us.

By reuniting our bodies with our spirits, we can move out of the often deadening *rational* place of trying to have a relationship to the Divine. We can then move into a holy, visceral knowing that we are Divine, that we are part of the whole. A body-based relationship to spiritual renewal can also get us past our fears of being intimate with the Divine by helping us honor our bodies and acknowledge the Divine similarities between our bodies and the earth and between our regenerative powers and the regenerative power of life. In the end, the spiritual life is not one of intellect. It is knowing in the body that we are all one.

Here are several quotes to inspire your imagination to move closer to your Divinity. There are some instructions for movement and ritual, but please take them only as starting places. Move into a nonrational state where directions are meaningless.

Maya Angelou stated in *The Feminine Face of God*,

> One says, "I am Thine" to that force of energy that has created us. It's only when you can give over the concern about everything else—whether the bills are paid or the phone is ringing—and join that moment, join that other body, that you can have total completeness in sex. So it is the same as the development of true spirituality. You must admit to yourself that you are part of everything, and then there is total enjoyment.

Sit quietly and contemplate Maya's words, especially *give over concern, join,* and *part of everything*. Find a physical position that communicates that you feel physically closed, shut away from what Maya is describing. Stay with that posture for a while. Intensify it if you wish. When you are ready, find a position that communicates the opposite, that you are opening to "I am Thine," to joining, to giving over concern, to merging with something larger than yourself. Move back and forth between closed and open. You may feel like changing the movements as you go along. You may feel like staying closed longer than open. You may find yourself enlarging or lingering over the transition between being closed and being open. See if you can sense which position you are more familiar with and which you yearn for more. Allow "that force of energy" to speak to you and through you, and allow the words to be embodied in you.

> The Mother has one law: "Create; make as I do . . . transform one substance into another . . . transmute blood into milk, clay into vessel, feeling into movement, wind into song; egg into child, fiber into cloth, stone into crystal, memory into image, body into worship."

So proclaims artist and former nun Meinrad Craighead. Take one or two phrases of this passage, and create something using your body. How does this statement inspire you to manifest your spirit into being? Yes, that may sound vague and esoteric. I'm asking you to make a leap into imagination. Forget making sense. Move your body, sink your hands into clay, lift your voice—spirit and matter coming together.

I too can bring my breath down to dwell in a deeper place where my blood-soul restores to my body what society has drained and dredged away. . . .

There is no defense against an open heart and a supple body in dialogue with wildness. Internal strength is an absorption of the external landscape. We are informed by beauty, raw and sensual. Through an erotics of place our sensitivity becomes our sensibility. . . . Steam rising. Water boiling. Geysers surging. Mud pots gurgling. Herds breathing. Hooves stampeding. Wings flocking by. Sky darkening. Clouds gathering. Rain falling. Rivers raging. Lakes rising. Lightning striking. Trees burning. Thunder clapping. Smoke clearing. Eyes staring. Wolves howling into the Yellowstone.

This passage is from *An Unspoken Hunger* by Terry Tempest Williams. Find an inspiring place outside or in nature to read it. How can you actively absorb into your body inner strength from the landscape around you? How can you be "a supple body in dialogue with wildness"? Don't think you have to be in the wilderness—wildness is all around. You can meditate on a bowl of rocks while sitting in the bathtub. Where did these rocks come from? In the eons of their existence, where have they been? The water that surrounds you, where did it originate? Can you feel the clouds gathering, the rain falling? You can do this in a backyard, in a park, on a rooftop gazing at clouds. The untamed is always all around you. Locate it. Be in dialogue with its beauty through your body.

Stories

Barbara is a therapist and movement teacher. She also leads women's retreats.

It is the first morning of my retreat, and I rise with the sun to practice my own version of flow-yoga by the pool. I can move only slowly. Like a lava flow creeping across the land, I am thick and hot, but powerful in my slowness—definite and intentional, guided by gravity. My body says, "Stay low . . . deep in your pelvis. Get seated there. Be in the exquisite moment and be satisfied with every minute breath and movement. Take your time and surrender. Take all the time you need."

Yesterday afternoon, as I dozed in and out of consciousness on the lanai, I heard the geckos chirping and through the slits of my eyes saw the glazed and fractured light shimmering on the ocean . . . in the clouds . . . through the leaves of the trees. I began to dissemble . . . to come apart. At some molecular level I spread out, admitting these other living beings into and between the fragments of me. Dissolving into a quivering tapestry of light, sounds, and color . . . one fabric. My witness self was still there to notice this phenomenon and to have a moment of alarm. Whoops! I'm not supposed to do this. I've got to keep it together. Then, in quick succession, a flicker of joy, then humor and recognition. Oh yes! This . . . !

Later, doing movement by the pool, I partly reclaim this state as I open my eyes and trace the outline of the horizon, a tumble of bright bougainvillea, graceful silk tree, clouds and sea, ploughed fields, fluttering palms, stone wall, water. A voice (my voice) says, "The mother and the father are one."

I notice that I am silently weeping. My friend R's simple song comes to my throat.

> Give thanks to Mother Gaia.
> Give thanks to the Father Sun.
> Give thanks to the plants in the garden where
> The Mother and the Father are One.

More tears. I am being reminded to integrate the masculine and the feminine. To respect the Male Divinity as well as the Goddess. Six months before, on the same land, I experienced a deep and spontaneous sharing with a friend. It was as if a veil were pulled aside and I suddenly realized how alienated I had been from the Father God. My hellfire and brimstone Christian fundamentalist upbringing had turned me off to the image of God as a punishing and critical father. In my twenties I turned to the Great Mother Goddess for comfort and healing. Now I am being guided to the next step. It is time to turn to the male side of the Divine (of my own psyche as well) to clear away the false images and find my own true relationship between the two sides.

As if to acknowledge my surrender to the task, I plunge into the pool headfirst. I am naked except for my gold ring with a triangular blue topaz, the ring I gave myself as a symbol of the sacred trinity—Father, Mother, and Divine Child or Christ Being.

Kneeling in the grass, with the hot sun on my face, I pray to be shown a way to be in a true partnership of the masculine and feminine. Opening my eyes, I see two bright red dragonflies beginning their mating dance, swooping joyfully in tandem. I speak aloud, "See, just like that! We can be like that and dance and fly together!"

The answer to my prayer hasn't come as a detailed blueprint or a list of "to-do's." But I trust somehow if I can hold this image of the dragonflies in my heart, the process will unfold.

For Long Retreats

See Retreat Plans: A Three-Day Spiritual Renewal Retreat for ideas.

For Mini-Retreats

Defining and Undefining Your Spiritual Life, Discipline, Melting, and Soma Source all make good mini-retreats in themselves. Combine Defining with Melting, Defining with Discipline, or Discipline with Soma Source.

For Retreats in the World

Do an opening ceremony in your own way and space, then attend a religious service that you have always wanted to try, or return to a religious place you are trying to understand. Do not require yourself to interact with others, to be greeted, or to wear a name tag. For now, take what you wish without judgment of yourself or others. Then visit a place in nature or go back to your retreat space, and do Defining and Undefining Your Spiritual Life.

For Retreats with Others

See Retreating with Others: Deep Listening Circle.

Try doing Defining and Undefining Your Spiritual Life on your own and then coming together in a deep listening circle to share what you found. Or do Soma Source in a circle together.

Stuck in the Airport of Life

Only she who listens can speak.

Dag Hammarskjöld

When I asked my friend Vivian why she would go on retreat, she mentioned several reasons, but one in particular stood out. "There are so many hats to wear and demands placed on women, we are thrust from this to that. I get overwhelmed. I always wish I could take time to make a transition, to get it clear in my head, to get used to the idea. Then maybe I wouldn't feel like I was stuck waiting at the airport of life. You watch everyone else go by and get on their flights. You know you want to go somewhere, you're just not sure where."

In interview after interview, I heard women telling me stories of how they had gone away to be by themselves when they simply had no idea what to do next, when they had no energy, when they thought they had no options. Whether you are stuck on a creative project, calcified in a relationship, or drowning in a general life morass, creating a retreat that includes motion, breaking out, risk, acceptance of the past, and self-celebration *may* revitalize your life.

Of course, there are many degrees of being stuck. For some of us and at certain times of our lives, a retreat will offer some energy or solace, but it may only be the beginning of a long process of change and grieving. If you are fearful that one retreat won't unstick you, go on retreat anyway. Not to start because it won't all be resolved in a few hours or days is to lose hope.

Prepare

Timer.

Your journal and a pen.

A few medium-heavy objects that, if possible, are symbolic of your stuckness. Rocks will work, too.

Body mud, green clay from a health food store, or oatmeal, water, and honey.

Drawing materials.

Rattle, drum, or other percussive instrument.

Dance music and a way to play it.

Why Are You Stuck?

There are different kinds of stuckness. Some require lots of self-kindness. Some require forgiveness. Some require moving into greater stuckness and, in fact, becoming a total sloth. Some require change and risk. Sometimes being stuck is based on depression or illness that must be recognized if it is to be healed and learned from. Here are some exercises that will help you figure out why you are stuck.

- Choose three words to describe your situation. *Disinterested, tired, blah* were mine on a recent day. Or try *trapped, scared, worried.* What about *overwhelmed, ugly, fat?*

See What Will You Do?: Ways to Choose What to Do.

Write one of the three words you just came up with in the middle of a piece of paper. Do a cluster with it. Keep your hand moving until you have filled the paper. If you get stuck, start a new offshoot (but not a new cluster—don't get a new sheet of paper) with one of your other two words.

- Grab your journal and write for three minutes or until you fill three pages with completions of the following sentence. Keep your hand moving for the entire time, even if you are sure it will kill you. You can always nap afterward.

    I first started to feel stuck when . . .

- Choose one of the words below or as many as you wish to complete the statement

    To open up my flow of health, energy, and well-being, right now I need to . . .

    Crack open my heart

    Move my body

    Have someone shake me

    Have someone hug me

    Run toward something or someone

    Run away from something or someone

    Sob

    Hide

    Curl up

    Cuddle

    Be tender with myself

    Accept my past choices

    Make a plan

    Tear up my plans

    Talk to someone who hurt me

    Write an enraged letter to someone who hurt me

    Thank someone for loving or caring for me

    Do everything completely differently for a while

    Be out of my life for a while

    Ask forgiveness from myself and others

    Get outside help

    Surrender

    Do nothing

    Eat and watch TV

    Get sick

Get well

Sleep

Sing

Dance

Be in nature

- Read what you wrote. What words and themes of action emerge? You may find the same thing written several times, in slightly different words. It is time to *do* something, right now, on this retreat. Let the words you choose get you moving—driving to a lake, putting on music to dance, making an appointment with a therapist. What could you do, right now, that would engender hope, spark creative energy, lift the corner off a depression? What small baby step, just one, could you take right now?

Accepting Your Stuckness

Sometimes change cannot occur because you have not fully accepted where you are now. Locate a few heavy objects that, if possible, are symbolic of what you feel is clutching you around the throat, what is weighing you down, what is lodging in your heart or hanging over you. The item(s) must be light enough that you can comfortably place them on and around your body but heavy enough to feel their weight. (If you are disabled or injured, ask someone to help you set up, then leave you alone for ten or fifteen minutes.) One woman used an antique oak music box that her ex-husband had given her, placing it on her chest. Another used files from her tax audit, making an outline around her. Miranda used copies of her heavy thesis laid over her body. A writer friend used her old manual typewriter and dozens of copies of her out-of-print book. If you can't think of or don't have on hand the right items, gather a few medium-sized stones and write on each what burden it represents. Or use workout weights, cans of food, or bottles of water, and mentally name what each represents to you.

See Good Ways to Listen and Opening Ceremony for ways to create.

Lie down with your items close by. Take a few moments to get comfortable and to center yourself. Place the weight on and/or around you. No self-flagellation; you should feel the weight but, of course, it *should not* hurt. Close your eyes. Take a few deep breaths. Start by reviewing what you wrote about being stuck. Then move into feeling the weight on you. Breathe into the sensation of being pinned down, surrounded, or burdened. Or perhaps you feel reassured? Perhaps it feels familiar in a sad but safe way? Breathe into the feeling. Follow it. Stay with it until the moment feels complete, unless you become uncomfortable. Then by all means, shift around or remove the weight, but then close your eyes and stay with the feelings.

Nothing else to do. Just feel and accept.

Where Have I Been and Why Did I Need to Go There?

I want to fly from point A to point E, skipping the essential learning and suffering in between. I want to forget that I cannot reach E without passing through B, C, and D. And when being at E doesn't seem so hot, it can be truly challenging to value the intermittent stops. When I get stuck, it helps me to go over past choices (notice I do not say *mistakes*) and remember why I made the decisions I made and what benefits, often unforeseen and sometimes slim, resulted. I can sometimes break free from my calcified position by refusing to beat myself up for past choices, by refusing to rewrite the past or to edit out the positive, or by refusing to pretend I had more information at the time than I actually did.

Divide a piece of paper into four columns. In the first, write down every choice in the past that you regret or that you question or that you wish you could have forgone. List missed opportunities, mistakes, injustices. Some of my (big) regrets: not writing in a disciplined way for eight years, buying our house at the worst financial time since the 1920s, not enjoying Lily as a baby more, not enjoying being young and without responsibility more. These regrets have kept me stuck more times than I care to admit.

In the second column, list what benefits have come from each choice and/or why you in that moment chose what you chose. Sometimes you have to search for benefits or even ask others for help in remembering that time in your life. For example, when I searched for the benefits of not being disciplined in my early writing career, I found a big one was my life falling apart. Squandering my time and early efforts was part of the spiral downward (a horrible two-year period) that led me on a very fruitful search for self-kindness and spiritual meaning, a search that continues today. If I hadn't made that (and other) mistakes, I would not be writing this book today.

The third column is what you imagine you could have done if you had chosen differently. I fantasized that if I could have written *exactly* the right scripts and met exactly the right people and said exactly the right hip, cool things, I would be set for life.

In the fourth column, imagine how your life would be different if you had made that choice instead. I imagined I would be a better writer today. I would have written *Thelma and Louise* and would have won an Oscar. I would have lots of flowered linens lying perfectly pressed in a cupboard with lavender sachets layered between them.

When you are finished, read over the columns while asking yourself,

- Could I really have made that choice any differently knowing what I knew and being who I was at the time? Did I have the skills, experience, capital, information, or energy needed? Check to see if you are

    Disqualifying the positive

    Making yourself into a different person

    Overgeneralizing

    Rewriting the past or mind-reading

    Being overly critical

- What beliefs about myself or others have been created or reinforced through this choice? Choices that we can't accept, forgive ourselves for, or see the value of tend to reinforce childhood concepts of shame and guilt, and they may even form a few new ones. Some ruinous beliefs I came away with include that I can't be trusted to handle money, that I am lazy and bad for not being clever, and that I can't do anything right. After you have named the beliefs you can put your finger on, look over the list above and see if these beliefs fall into any of these categories of thinking.

End by taking your choices and beliefs and doing the practice in Reviving Your Spiritual Direction: Melting, starting at the third paragraph.

Imagery to Transform an Issue

This imagery exercise is from Belleruth Naparstek, a clinical social worker. You can find it in her book *Staying Well with Guided Imagery*.

Let the issue or area of your life you wish to transform appear to you as a symbol. For instance, say you want to transform your inability to get your career going. Perhaps the symbol that occurs to you is a closed door. Or you are generally feeling stuck in your life. Perhaps a symbol of a blank book comes to you. Let it come; don't refuse it, don't analyze it. Your symbol may change during your imagery. This means your unconscious is working. Trust it to do "a wise and responsible job," as Belleruth puts it. If no symbol occurs to you, use images of the actual people or things you wish to work with. Be sure you are focusing on something about you, something within your power to change. Don't analyze the visualization as you do it or the symbols as they occur to you. You can do that afterward. Finally, don't get discouraged. Repetition makes this exercise more powerful. Eventually, "this imagery takes off."

Allow your body to be comfortable and fully supported. Arrange your head, neck, and spine so that they are as straight as possible.

Spend a few minutes becoming quiet and relaxed. Taking deep, cleansing breaths, inhale down deep into your belly. Exhale out any tension you find. . . . Send your breath to any areas of your body that are tense or sore. Exhale any tension or soreness out of your body, so more and more you feel loose and warm and soft and receptive. Stay with your breathing for a few minutes while focusing on letting go. . . .

When you are relaxed, imagine yourself in a place that you love and feel utterly safe in. This can be a real or imaginary place. Spend a few minutes letting this place become real to you. Take this magic place in with your eyes. Notice details of color and shape. Take a deep breath and taste the air on your tongue. Feel the texture of what you are sitting or lying on. Listen to the sounds of the place. Smell its rich fragrances.

And as you become more attuned to the beauty of this place, let yourself feel thankful and happy to be here. You might feel a kind of tingling . . . a pleasing, energizing feeling in the air all around you. Perhaps a sense that something wonderful is just about to happen envelops you.

And as you look in front of you, you begin to discern a kind of transparent screen forming there. It becomes more and more opaque and solid as you look at it.

And as you watch the screen, you gradually become aware that a form is beginning to appear on it. As you watch, it becomes more and more defined, until the three-dimensional image of a symbol is quite clear. You can see that this is the symbol of whatever it is you want to work with or change. As you watch, it becomes more defined and crisp and clear. You might notice that you watch it with an alert but peaceful detachment, calm and curious. You may even want the image to turn, slowly and steadily, so you can see it from every angle.

And note anything you wish about your symbol, the colors it might be, the sounds associated with it. There might be a fragrance or smell to it. Or it might have a quality of hardness or softness. . . . It could be heavy or light . . . big or small . . . bitter or sweet or sour. . . . Just take a few moments to let yourself be curious and observe your symbol in a state of friendly, detached interest, with all of your senses . . . (pause for a few moments).

And now, if you are willing and want to, see if this image on the screen is willing to shift or change in any way. See if it wishes to move in any direction. No need to push or pull it. Just let it transform, if it wants to and if you want to. If it doesn't, that's all right, too. In fact, it's good to know that it isn't time for change. But if it does, and it might, just watch the shift occur. Observe the transformation, however subtle or bold, with all of your senses. . . .

Understand that this transformation need not be complete. It need not be exciting. It need not even make any sense. Just seeing the shift with all of your senses, for however long it takes, that is all that matters (pause for a few moments).

And now, understanding that you can come back and work further with the screen and your images whenever you wish, taking your time, you can begin to let the image fade. Again you notice the screen, and gently that fades too.

You are coming back into your special place . . . relaxing there for a few moments . . . scanning your body . . . noticing if it feels any different, lighter or expanded . . . noticing if your sense of smell or taste or touch is more acute . . . breathing deeply as you slowly come back to your surroundings. Knowing in a deep place that something powerful has happened . . . and you are better for this. . . .

And so you are. . . .

Take a few minutes to write or draw notes about your experience.

Creating Energy

Sometimes being stuck is about entropy. Ruts. Sameness. You need to shake things up to start the process of change.

- Devote all or part of a retreat to doing things differently. At home, sit in different chairs in odd places. Look out windows you never do. View your furniture from strange angles. Sleep in a different place. Eat wild foods at surprising times. Eat off different dishes. Don't eat at all; drink all your food. Dig out old music or tune in to a radio station you have never heard before, and really listen. Read books you would never read. Out in the world, start a conversation with someone you would never dare speak to. Go someplace you have never been in your town. Abandon every daily ritual, every familiar signpost, even if only by a few degrees. At the end of this, do spontaneous writing or painting with the statement

See Feeding the Artist: Be Outrageous.

What is emerging in my life right now is . . .

- Cover your entire body with body mud, which you can find at the drugstore. Or make a paste out of oatmeal, a little honey, and water. Or buy a big jar of green Egyptian mud at the health food store. Don't be stingy; lather it on. Then lie down someplace comfortable to let it dry. Outside in the warm sun is ideal, but on a towel under a heat lamp in your bathroom or on a sheet draped over your couch with a space heater nearby will work, too. Don't do anything while you wait for your mud to dry. Remain still. Focus on the feeling of tightening. Of drying. Wait until it feels like a dry, scaly skin. Then stand and walk very slowly and carefully to a full-length mirror (you might want to spread out a sheet or large towel under you). Stand still for a moment, looking at yourself, your covering of mud. Imagine that a beam of energy is entering your body through your head. Feel it filling you up with a burning desire to move. But remain still. Feel this energy coiling inside, heating you up. You want to move but you hold yourself back, gathering the energy into a steady blaze. When you feel you will go crazy if you don't move, take another deep breath and hold still for another long moment. Savor this moment of wanting to have energy, of wanting to be energy, and of not allowing yourself to move. Then, burst free. With sound (a roar, a gasp, a warrior song), move your body and break free. Don't think—move! Leap, bend, twist, shake, throw your arms wide. Feel the mud cracking. Watch the mud cracking. Use every muscle you can find: pinkie, jaw, big toe, breasts, belly, scalp.

Take a warm bath or shower. Watch the mud washing away. Close your eyes and imagine the healing power of the water mixing with the beam of energy to provide you with the perfect mix of self-love and self-motivation. Feel that this perfect blend is entering your body, enlivening your flesh, available to you from now on.

See Resources.

- Shamans throughout the ages have known that sound can heal. Find some truly inspiring music to dance to. It must be music that demands that you move. It should be at least twenty minutes long.

You will need a rattle or other percussive instrument, such as a drum or tambourine. You will also need privacy and clothes that inspire you or at least allow you to move.

Take the three words from the first practice in Why Are You Stuck?, and choose three words that describe how you would like to feel instead.

Repeat your stuck words over and over again, without music, without rattling. Embody those words: how do they make you want to move or not move? Keep repeating them over and over, a hypnotic chant of stuckness. When your *body* feels it has been stuck long enough (do not hurry this stage), pick up your rattle or drum and disperse the energy the words have created by shaking them away. Shake your rattle and your body at, under, around, and over these words, this energy block. But keep chanting the stuck words while you do so, until you feel the energy shift. When you feel the shift, switch to your new words, your words of change and hope. Move your body in a way that embodies those words. Put on your music and dance your way into seeing and feeling the possibility and promise of these words. Feel their energy stream into your body. Place their power in your body by linking the words with movement and sound. Keep moving until you feel finished.

Stories

This is Cynthia's story.

I was diagnosed as having prolactin-secreting tumors on my pituitary gland. These tumors had produced a dangerously elevated prolaction level of 190 (normal is 29 or less). A side effect of this condition was suppressed periods. I had not had a period in over three years.

I found a doctor willing to treat me with a medication instead of with surgery. This drug would reputedly shrink my tumors and reduce my prolactin levels.

Unfortunately, I experienced severe side effects, including nausea, dizziness, and constipation. I felt miserable much of the time. Plus, my business was extremely demanding. I was suffering not only physically, but also mentally and spiritually. I knew I needed to get away. But where, and how?

I thought of Mexico. I had begun to plan a trip when, magically, my friend called to say she was leading a women's retreat in Baja. It would be a long weekend with a small group of women at an isolated private home along the coast. I said yes immediately.

The journey was a passage to another world. We arrived late at night with the stars blazing overhead. We slept in a two-story thatched palappa open to the cool, clear night air. It was exhilarating.

The retreat was largely unstructured. We ate fresh, organic food from the garden, plus homemade tortillas and goat cheese. There was no phone, no fax, no e-mail. Occasionally we joined for meditation, visualization, and movement exercises. All was relaxed and unhurried.

On the second day, I wandered by myself to the pristine beach, which stretched for forty miles with not a soul in sight. Instinctively, I lay down on the sand. I stayed there for what seemed like a long time. I felt I was sending a message to Mother Earth: *Take me, heal me.*

There was nothing to say, or be, but myself. My body relaxed and surrendered completely. When I finally got up, covered with sand, I walked back to the house as in a dream. My friend saw me and asked, "Where have you been?" I silently answered, "To the center of the earth."

My period started the next day. I could hardly believe it and told no one. But inside I knew I was embracing a return to the feminine, divine principle within me—a homecoming long overdue.

For Long Retreats

Long retreats lend themselves to working through a stuck place. Combine the practices here with some of the exercises in the books listed in Resources, and try working with other people to increase your motivation.

For Mini-Retreats

Baby steps are a very, very important part of change. It cannot be overstated that taking many small steps will lead to great change. Many people find it much easier to keep their eyes on the task immediately at hand and away from the big picture. Take one practice and devote a mini-retreat to it. Perhaps do this once a week. Keep a journal to note any changes in your behavior or attitude or in how others perceive you.

For Retreats in the World

Risk can be an important part of getting unstuck. In addition to the practices here, you might want to take a retreat in the world to try something new or scary. You might try eating out alone, camping alone, attending a workshop to learn more about a possible career change, doing anything out among others that feels risky. Doing it within the container of the retreat frees you from having to interact with others—the point is to stay as self-contained as possible—and helps·you feel safer. Be sure to reflect on what you learned and felt as part of your closing ceremony.

For Retreats with Others

See Retreating with Others: Affirmation Circle and Deep Listening Circle.

Working on stuckness with others can be very powerful. Often when you are very stuck, you need someone else's energy to help you get motivated. Gather a few friends alongside you, and devote a day or weekend to recharging one another. Start with an affirmation circle, and end each day with one as well. Use the circle to witness one another's responses to the first practice, Why Are You Stuck, or simply have each woman talk for ten minutes about her barriers. Be clear before this retreat begins that *no advice* is to be offered except when asked for and still only within the confines of a deep listening circle.

Completion

Returning Home

*"I don't want to be heading home. I'm not ready." The sun had slipped
below the horizon. The white, leading edges of the predicted storm,
wispy trails of clouds I call mare's tails, had turned magenta and or-
ange. The day was done. My old life was not. It was somewhere at the
base of that beautiful sunset. Same house, same people, same patterns
waiting for me to rejoin them. But I was not the same, I had no intention of simply slipping back into the old routines. . . . This second half
of the trip had to be about preparing and rebuilding.*

Ann Linnea, *Deep Water Passage*

What will it be like when I go home? If you've been gone for several days or a
week or more, you may feel fear and dread at this question. Will I still love
my partner? Will I hate my house? Will I despise being a mom? Will I refuse
to go to work on Monday morning? Will I decide to radically alter my life?
How can everything seem the same when I feel so different? How will I make
time for me, for more retreats, for what I like to do, now that I have tapped
into this hunger? Will I lose everything I learned, gained, and found on retreat, especially my sense of self, my center?

Paired with these questions might be an incredible hunger, an ache, to see and
touch the people or place you love. I often find myself on the drive or flight
home from a long retreat literally straining forward in my seat, I'm so eager to
get home. These two reactions, dread and eagerness, can mix together to form a
perplexing ambiguity. You can end up feeling like you are waiting for a thun-
derstorm to break on a still, humid August afternoon in an Indiana cornfield. If
you've been retreating for only a few minutes or hours, the feeling about going
home may be "So soon?" You may feel sudden, immense tiredness, irritability,
or an attitude of "Why bother? What did ten minutes accomplish?"

The unadorned fact is that returning to your everyday life is always a little
rough. It is always a letdown—a bigger letdown the longer you were gone or
the richer your experience. Either you didn't have enough time or you fear
losing what you found. It may seem that everything from the weather to your

---

boss to your six-year-old is in league to rip every shred of peace and self-knowledge you just gained away from you. "I like to come home to a clean house and the kids asleep, then start the next day as normal as possible. If I come home to chaos, I want to kill myself. The whole experience gets diminished," recounts Diane, a business owner and mother of two. Frankie said a few days after her retreat, "I already need to go again." You may see your renewed peacefulness draining away at an alarming rate. If you have a particularly bad reentry, you may use it as a reason not to retreat again.

The fruits of your retreat, unprotected, cannot withstand the onslaught of profane space and ordinary life. Preparing to return home and performing a closing ceremony offer some protection and will help make your return easier and keep the spirit of your retreat alive longer. On mini-retreats, this preparation, no matter how brief, will strengthen your resolve to retreat again and, over time, will forge a conduit of peace and perspective running from your retreats into your daily life.

Prepare

Read this chapter before or during your retreat.

Preparing for Reentry

What will make it easier for you to return to your ordinary life after your retreat? What situations, distractions, problems, habits, or people is it good to avoid for a while? What will rob you of your restored good nature faster than anything? For Diana after a night away, it is a dirty house. For Loni after an hour alone at the park, it is getting stuck in traffic. For Jackie, after visiting her best friend in a seaside town, it is coming home to an empty house. Before and/or on your retreat, spend a few moments considering how you can make your return home more pleasant and self-nurturing. What will make it easier? Asking your partner to take the kids out for pizza so that you can return to an empty house? Scheduling a massage or other treat for the day after you return? Making dinner plans with friends you love and feel safe with? Avoiding high-traffic routes or rush hour?

Consider:

- In the past, what has depressed me when I returned from a vacation or time away?

- What has been my best reentry from a retreat or vacation?

- From this retreat, what is the best reentry I can imagine?

One coming-home-from-a-long-retreat strategy that works for me is giving myself mini-retreats over the next couple of days. Examples are a massage, a yoga class, a walk alone, and a hot bath. Taking even more retreat time is, of course, very difficult to do because I feel I have already been selfish to my family and taken too much time off from work. But if I can allow myself a little more pleasure, to truly take it in and enjoy it, I have something to look forward to, and it helps prevent the Puritan backlash syndrome (see below).

If you live alone or if your children have recently moved out, you may need to reenter by connecting with a friend or partner. Take care of yourself. Don't wait to make plans until after you return; call or write a friend before you leave or, if you didn't have time before, then call during your retreat.

If you are doing a mini-retreat or a retreat in the world and you feel every time you return the benefits of your retreat are wiped out within two minutes, set aside a bit of your retreat time for a leisurely reentry. If you have an hour and your retreat is going to be in the park, come back fifteen minutes early and putter around your home or office without engaging with others. You might have to hide in your bedroom or behind a closed door, and be sure not to answer the phone. Ease back into life.

Backlash Remedy

After you have given yourself a retreat lasting longer than a few hours, you may sometimes experience the backlash effect, also called the Puritan backlash syndrome. This is a feeling of guilt that presents itself as goody-goody or overcaretaking behavior. You may decide to stay up all night writing every person you have neglected to keep in touch with. You may start a strict new diet, composed primarily of soy cheese and wheat grass juice. You may be drawn to wear a hair shirt and carry a small leather whip.

This is behavior to be wary of.

Sometimes on retreat you get a brilliant idea, some new project you want to do so badly you can't wait to get started. You don't want to waste the inspiration. *The new behavior or project you are starting feels powerfully self-affirming.* This is good. It doesn't involve hair shirts. But the opposite reaction, feeling guilty that you've had a good time, that you have done something for yourself, can throw you into wanting to make up for having been gone. You restrict, push, and even punish yourself, often by doing really nice but rather over-the-top things for others (making every item for a giant school bake sale). Then, like a pendulum, you swing (more like careen) in the other direction (for example, eating every item you just baked). If you find yourself in this self-punishing or overdoing-for-others mode, immediately give yourself a treat. Ask yourself, "What do I really, really want right now?" *Whatever* the answer (okay, sex with Sean Connery might not be possible right this minute), give it to yourself. No substitutes. If you want a banana split, don't have a low-fat banana muffin. If you want a massage, don't go for a run. If you need to be alone again, sit down with your partner and your kids and tell them you are struggling. Remind them it has nothing to do with them. Tell whomever you share your life with that by keeping the good stuff of retreat fresh, you will be a more pleasant person to live with.

Coming Home to Your Relations

It is almost always threatening to an intimate partnership to consciously take time away from each other. Even in the most egalitarian of relationships, a ripple is registered on both of your unconscious minds. You have gone somewhere where he or she can never follow. What happens on your retreat is a secret. It cannot be told. It is beyond words. Yes, this is true even when it doesn't seem like very much happened or when you were gone for only an hour. Great care must be taken to reenter the relationship after a retreat, especially an extended retreat. You will need to communicate in a way that brings the retreat into your relationship and reassures both of you of your connection, without diminishing the privacy and sacredness of your experience.

"What did you do all that time? Did you miss me? Do you still love me? Why do you need so much time alone?" These are the questions (said and unsaid) that might greet you at home. These questions are not paranoid attempts to control your every move but rather are signs of your partner's fears. Be prepared to reassure your partner in a way that he or she can hear. Ask yourself, "What is my partner's greatest fear in our relationship? How does my leaving exacerbate that fear?" We fear being abandoned, sold at a garage sale like last year's Thigh Master or ginzu gadget. We fear our lover's discovering that being away is better than being with us. We fear change. Even though we may consciously want the best for our lover, the infant in us wants everything to stay the same.

Prepare your homecoming. If you've been gone for a weekend or longer, meet outside your home. This is an especially good idea if you have kids or work together. Take a few moments outside your shared habitat to connect before you are sucked back into the whirlwind. Start by thanking your partner not only for managing the practical while you were gone but for supporting you in deepening your inner life. Ask what he or she has been doing in life and has been feeling about your being gone. When the time comes to talk about your experience, have a metaphor handy to convey the spirit of your time apart. "It was liking hitting a home run with all the bases loaded." "I felt as powerful as that day we hiked Mount Shasta." "It was like church when the meditation time makes you feel really calm." Remember to mention missing your partner. Mention any anxiety, loneliness, or fears you had. The ones at home like to know it wasn't all cake and roses.

You may feel like warning the one you love that you may be irritable for a while. Reassure him or her that it isn't because you don't want to be there but that making the transition from sacred time to profane time is jolting. Strive to keep the communication lines open. Some couples and families with older children find that using a shared journal or notes to communicate allows things to be said that would otherwise be forgotten. Whatever you do, don't avoid talking about your experience. If you come in the door, even after a retreat of a few hours, and your partner asks, "What was it like?" and you say, "Oh, nothing much; we can talk about it later," and then later never comes, you are going to find that the next time you want to retreat, you will meet resistance or hurt.

If you have retreated to contemplate a troubled relationship, you must be extra gentle with yourself as you return. If you've come to a painful decision, take it slow. Get some sage outside advice before proceeding. If you didn't come to any earth-shattering conclusions and are exasperated or disappointed by that, read over Being, in Good Ways to Listen. Hold the tension of not being sure for a while longer. If you have ideas for change that you need to share with your partner, consider carefully when and where to do so. Pick a time when you are both rested and will not be interrupted. One of the quickest roads to disaster is to come home from a retreat bursting with hopeful ideas for big changes and to dump them on your partner. Resist doing that!

See Transforming Fear of Coming Home, below, and also Courage: Softening Fear.

If your partner knows you have gone away for this reason, you owe it to him or her to set aside time to discuss what you learned or decided.

Children, parents, and friends tend to be a little less threatened and less curious about your retreat, although young children need special reassurance. Making time to be alone with each child soon after you return is always smart. Prepare for a temper tantrum or general whininess for an hour or day after your return if you have younger children. They express their dismay at being left by saving their intense feelings for you. It is a sign that they love you and feel bonded to you, so frame it as a positive sign, breathe, and remind yourself it won't last.

What if you have taken a retreat without telling anyone that it was one? What if you believe the idea would be too weird or threatening to your family or friends? Or what if you've simply been using your lunch hour or the time when the children are at school, without any fanfare? In this case, trust yourself to let others in on your experience when you are ready. Be clear why you are keeping this to yourself. Ask yourself, "What do I fear happening if I share this experience with _____?" Sometimes our beliefs about how another person will react are fabricated to protect ourselves from true intimacy and vulnerability. Other times our reluctance to talk about our experience is excellent advice from our authentic self to protect us from insensitive or shallow reactions. Investigate instead of blindly reacting.

One of the saddest things that can happen upon returning from a retreat is that when you tell someone what you've been doing, he or she derides or minimizes your experience or criticizes you for going. In spite of yourself, you can feel doubt, guilt, and shame as well as anger and resentment. You could explain to this person how precious this time was for you, *or* you could explain how utterly stupid, asinine, off base, unasked for, and a waste of air those comments are. However, if you are married to this person or if he is your boss, you might need to keep your choice comments to yourself. Get away from this person as soon as possible, take a few deep breaths, and recall a centered feeling or image from your retreat. If you have a talisman or a snapshot of the heart, grab on to that. If the encounter continues to rankle you, arrange another retreat, even for ten minutes, ASAP. Do not let parsimonious, narrow, uninformed monkey minds ruin your faith in your own way, your own power, and your own wisdom. Remember Audre Lorde's words, "We have been raised to fear the yes within ourselves . . . our deepest cravings. And the fear of our deepest cravings keeps them suspect, keeps us docile and loyal and obedient, and leads us to settle for or accept many facets of our own oppression." Not us, no way.

See Closing Ceremony.

Transforming Fear of Coming Home

If you find yourself putting off returning home, not planning a closing ceremony, or feeling angry, resentful, and irritable or clumsy and out of your body as your retreat draws to a close, or if you find you're spending much of your retreat obsessing on returning, you must put a little conscious attention into working with your fears *now*.

Finish this sentence:

- What I fear happening when I return home is . . .

Make a list, either in writing or in your head. Sit with what you discover. Literally sit still and get as close to your fear as you can. Perhaps ask your fear:

- What do you want?
- What are you hiding?
- What gifts do you bring?

This fear of returning home should not be minimized. Sometimes exploring and facing your fear becomes the focus of your retreat. You may realize on retreat that what your retreat is truly about is prying yourself out of your life so that you cannot return to business as usual.

If you start to feel you cannot return to some aspect of your life (a relationship, job, home), don't panic. Assure yourself that you won't do anything or change anything before you are completely ready. Calm your body by inhaling deeply and repeating to yourself, "I am strong." As you exhale slowly, say to yourself, "I am calm." Do the trust list in Courting Yourself: Suggestions for Wooing. Dialogue with your fear. If a question or decision emerges (having a baby as a single mother, leaving my marriage, quitting my job, moving to Australia) that you wish to resolve now, explore the practice One Who Chooses. If you are on a mini-retreat or a retreat in the world and must be somewhere soon, spend the time you do have becoming calm and gaining perspective instead of forcing a decision or biting your nails in a panic. Make a firm date to do another retreat as soon as possible. Don't put it off! Be sure to end your retreat with a firm closing ceremony. This will allow you to leave your questions, agitation, or fear on the retreat instead of dragging it home to pollute your life.

See Courage: Softening Fear.

"All will be revealed" is a comforting mantra, as are "One day at a time" and "All will be well, and all will be well, and all manner of things will be well." Prayer, meditation, breathing into your anxiety and pain, and spontaneous writing and drawing about the proposed change are excellent ways to remain present and avoid complications that arise from burying feelings. Once you go home, seek out someone wise to talk to about your conflict. Whatever you do, don't beat yourself up, and don't buy into the idea that if you had just stayed busy, if you had just avoided this retreat, you would be better off.

Emerging

The first few minutes, hours, or days after a retreat often have an altered quality to them. Patricia Hart Clifford in *Sitting Still,* her account of a one-week Christian Zen meditation retreat, writes,

> After the retreat, I was in the flow. The air smelled fresher, foliage looked greener, food tasted better. There was a synchronicity to the events of my existence that I had never experienced before. Everything seemed to be in the right place at the right time. I was filled with tremendous joy.

I remember walking into the tiny rail town of Moosenee in Quebec after three weeks on a wilderness retreat. I felt like a visitor from Mars. Everything, from the twenty-four-dollar cheese pizza to Inuit teenage girls dressed in Guess jeans, was a source of astonishment. Everything seemed bigger, louder, faster than before. I felt like I was moving underwater. The reaction is less intense after mini-retreats, when I tend to feel a little slow, solid, centered. It is a wonderful feeling, and I wish it lasted longer.

Observe how you emerge. That's all. No need for preparation, no need to change or share what you feel. Be in it. Don't cling to it. It will dissipate. Enjoy it while it is here; such is the gift of being present.

Closing Ceremony

The eyes of my eyes are opened

e. e. cummings

Ending your retreat with conscious care is as important as beginning it. No matter how small the amount of time you've spent retreating or how slight your shift in perspective feels, you have been between worlds. There is a tendency to want to stay in the retreat space, to live within the archetype, especially after an intense retreat. But you can't. You must summon yourself back. Remember the women emerging from the menstruation hut to a feast—they didn't drift back into their lives, they were hailed, acknowledged. Consciously stepping back into ordinary space and time brings self-acknowledgment. It helps you retain the energy and integrity of your retreat, your faith in the retreat archetype, and it delivers the riches you have found into your daily life.

Prepare

You will need all or some of the items you used in your opening ceremony.

A talisman to remind you of your retreat.

An offering of thanksgiving.

A closing reading (could be the same one you opened with).

A Few Guidelines

- Scan the guidelines in Opening Ceremony, or recall what worked for you when you opened your retreat.

- Review your retreat. Ask yourself, "What had heart and meaning for me on this retreat? What do I wish to bring home?"

- Find or make a talisman that symbolizes what you wish to bring home—the feeling, belief, or memory you will wish to recall. This talisman will remind one or more of your senses that, indeed, you did take a moment for yourself, you do have faith in your inner knowing. Marcie said, "I count on my senses to help me not talk myself out of it." Once home, it is incredibly easy to begin to doubt your experience. But if you can use your senses for the "immediate apprehension of the mystery," as Mircea Eliade wrote, then you will be less inclined to dismiss your reality. Bernice, a dentist, wears "a purple knit beret on retreat. If I'm facing a hard day, or feeling ugly, or stressed, I wear my beret." Candace, a therapist and retreat leader, plays the same sonata she listened to on her first retreat when she needs to touch the peace of that retreat. I always bring home a piece of rock, shell, sea glass, or other small object. I collect these in a bowl where I can see and touch them often. Over time, I have forgotten which pieces are from which retreat, but I am inspired by the glowing whole.

  Scents and colors make effective talismans, too. Amie has wrestled with anorexia on and off for years. She anointed herself with sandalwood oil during a week-long guided yoga retreat. "Since then, when I am in battle with myself and starving myself, I reach for the sandalwood. The smell touches something in my body, and I just melt into that place I was in on retreat; I actually feel more self-accepting." Randi has a permanent shrine at home. She brings back an object from each retreat to place on her shrine. "That collection comforts me. And when I want to retreat but I can't, I look at my collection of talismans and think, 'I did it once, I can do it again.'"

- Repeat your metaphorical action from your opening ceremony, perhaps by reversing it. If that isn't possible or appropriate, find an action that symbolizes completion, containment, and rest to you. Lola Rae Long, retreat coordinator at the Ojai Foundation, suggests that retreatants say, "I am ready to step back into my life" as they step over a line drawn in the earth or through a gateway or as they emerge from a bath, a lake, or the ocean. Lucinda Eileen, a ritualist and Unitarian youth leader, stresses how important finishing is. "Say something like 'I have done this and this is why _____ (fill in the blank). I honor this space. It is accomplished.'" The power of speaking aloud your own truth, as *you* see it and believe it, should not be underestimated.

- Make an offering of gratitude and thanksgiving for your retreat. Make this offering to the Divine and/or to your family, partner, friend, retreat coordinator, sponsor, therapist, and to the place you have been re-treating. Allow a spontaneous expression of your gratitude to flow forth. On a retreat at the Ojai Foundation, I left a small crystal and to-bacco prayer ties in the crook of an old oak that had sheltered me the day before as I wept. On a shared retreat in a tiny canyon, my women's group passed around a lump of clay. Each of us shaped it a bit and pressed flowers, leaves, and odd natural items into it. It looked like nothing recognizable, but it shone with its own sacredness. We left it to decompose under the root of a pine tree. If you wish and have time, you could make an offering to leave behind.

- Repeat your reading from your opening ceremony, or choose another passage.

- End with energy. Sing along to a gospel song, take a brisk walk in the wind, *om* (Aum) three times while stretching your arms over your head, take a shower and use rosemary bath gel or oil, or simply wash your face, brush your teeth, and study yourself in the mirror for a moment. What will leave you feeling energized, ready to sail into your life? Do you dare grab the energy and bring it home?

See Resources.

For Experienced Retreatants

You may find yourself using the same talisman over and over again. You may also find yourself not needing a talisman for each retreat and preferring what my friend, writer Randi Ragan, calls a "snapshot of the heart," an emotional or physical sensation to carry with you. It could be a healing image of a blooming lotus you received in meditation, the comforting heaviness of a rock you sat on in the sun, how your couch supported you as you sat and prayed, or an ex-panded second of heavenly connectedness that washed over you. To make a snapshot of the heart, step back during such a moment or sensation and, using each of your senses, record it as if you were a camera. Tell yourself, "I will remember how light my body feels, the smell of this pine tree, the taste of this tuna fish sandwich, the prickle of the pine needles under my neck." As you etch it into your senses, touch your thumb and forefinger together and hold for a minute or two. Whenever you need to recall your snapshot, press your digits together and recall what each of your senses recorded.

A Sample Ceremony

Here is one way to leave retreat space.

- Read aloud what you read in your opening ceremony. Spend a moment seeing if any new feelings or insights arise from this reading.

- Restate your intention. Think about how you have explored it, answered it, lived with it. Perhaps record an expression of where you have roamed—a list of what you've learned, a mandala of your emotions and impressions, a spoken litany of where you've been.

- Decide on a talisman. Hold it, wear it, hear it, or smell it. Close your eyes. Visualize or sense the Divine: Jesus Christ, the Goddess, Mary, Buddha, Krishna, God, or a brilliant fountain of light. Ask the Divine to consecrate your talisman, to make it alive with the power of your retreat. See your talisman being blessed and infused with unconditional love from the Divine. You don't have to do anything to receive this gift except accept it. Energize your talisman by chanting a vibrant *om*.

- How do you wish your retreat to grow into your life? Articulate a very simple statement of how you wish your retreat to manifest and remain in your daily life. "I seek daily perspective." "I will be present with my kids for a few moments each day." "I will take twenty minutes for myself each day to simply be." "I wish for this peace of mind I feel now to grow in my heart." This is not about change but about planting the seed of your retreat. Close your eyes. See your wish written in glowing script across your heart. See your Divinity blessing your wish in whatever way feels appropriate.

- Close, clean, pack up your retreat container. If you need to dismantle your shrine or clean up the bathroom, do so lovingly and consciously, thanking the space for containing you. If you are at home, consciously release the space so that it can return to ordinary living space (this is especially important if you live with others). Pack with care any retreat supplies you will use again, and store them someplace safe yet convenient.

- With your talisman in hand, step over the threshold of your retreat space—whether that is your bedroom door, front door, car, yurt, sacred circle, or tent. As you do, say out loud something like "My intention on this retreat was to _____. I honor my self for locating a piece of my truth. It is true. So be it."

- Ground the energy of your retreat in your body by drinking a cup of hot tea, walking around the block or down the mountain, eating something wholesome, touching the earth, or hugging a loved one.

Stories

This is Patricia Hart Clifford's account of the last meditation period of a week-long Christian Zen retreat.

When the gong rang for the last time, we made deep bows, touching our heads to the floor in a gesture of gratitude. Then we stood and at the sound of the little bell bowed to each other and to the cross on the shrine. Everyone filed out to go to the chapel for the closing mass. I stood rooted to my spot. Sunlight streamed over me through the windows, lighting up the shades of blue in the carpet and the shapes of rocks in the sand. . . . At lunch, the dining room filled with a riotous explosion of gleeful voices, although any conversation at all seemed superfluous. . . . We made our good-byes swiftly. Then I was outside bidding farewell to the Iceland poppies, their parchment petals gleaming in the midday sunlight. I drove out of the gates not anticipating or rehearsing what was ahead. My one thought was, "I can't believe I almost didn't do this."

Sandy did a one-day retreat in her home.

My retreat was about meeting my authentic self. I had married myself in a ceremony several years before, and I decided to repledge my vows as part of my closing ceremony. I played the "Long and Winding Road," which I had played the time before, and several more songs, including Holly Near's "Sing to Me the Dream." I thanked my authentic self for coming. I put my ring on. I had written vows to myself—these were wiser than the ones a few years ago, and I read those. Then I played

"Hymns to the Silence" by Van Morrison. I thanked the qualities of play, forgiveness, and freedom for being with me, as well as Buddha and the others I had called in my opening invocation. Then I blew out my candle.

A closing ceremony leaves you wanting to invite yourself back again and again. Will you? Can you? Must you?

Living Your Retreat Every Day

*You have a solemn obligation to take care of yourself
because you never know when the world will need you.*

Rabbi Hillel

You have been changed. Now comes the task of living with and integrating that change.

But you may say, "I don't feel changed. My retreats have all been too short or too shallow or not spiritual enough to matter."

I repeat, you have been changed. You have entered into a relationship with yourself through intentional sacred solitude. You have paused. Something has shifted.

You may turn your retreat talisman over in your hand during a demented day at work and a slowness, a calmness blankets you, and a new way to look at the problem at hand occurs to you. Or a cherished habit drops away, seemingly without effort (I pretty much stopped watching TV after one long retreat). You may be compelled to take up the violin again, make a quilt, join the church choir, become a vegetarian, look up an old beau, or get up early and step outside to watch the sky for a moment. Your honest, gentle efforts and your resolution of purpose will provide nourishment for your daily activities for some time to come.

The question becomes, How do I bring this retreat into my daily life? How do I plant it and keep it alive?

Pay Attention

You must watch for the effects of your retreat, for they can easily be dismissed. You must pay attention to the small alterations and conversions that take place. How you have been changed will not declare itself as a full-page ad in the *New York Times* or as a guardian rabbit who accompanies you everywhere (but whom no one else can see). As someone I deeply respect once said, "Life is a spiral. You keep coming back to the same place, only you have taken one step up the staircase." These steps can be hard to discern, especially if you are enjoying primarily mini-retreats.

Each time you act from your deep self, each time you remember to be still and listen, each time you take a step toward something you wish to change or you forgive yourself for making a mistake, pause and take it in. Offer thanksgiving. Notice these ripples of change.

Specific ripples to watch for:

- Being more self-referenced. Asking yourself, "What do I think, feel, need, or want?" before considering what others think, feel, need, or want.

- Feeling more centered, less affected by the criticism of others, by bad news, or by minor irritations.

- Being more open and flexible. Finding that changing your plans, letting the house get messy, or being fifteen minutes late to a party somehow doesn't irritate you as much.

- Feeling less at the mercy of your inner critic, pusher, or judge. Feeling more able to tolerate, dialogue with, or love her presence. Experiencing less guilt and shame and fewer shoulds and hurry-up-you-are-not-doing-enough-fast-enough thoughts.

- Feeling lighter. Seeing a subtle shift in your daily attitude—a little more hopeful, up, or easygoing.

- Becoming able to say no when you need to without excessive guilt or excuses.

- Finding yourself able to carve out time for what you enjoy and for more retreats.

- Becoming more aware of your body and what it needs. Drinking enough water, going to the bathroom when you need to instead of holding it, eating when you are hungry, stretching and breathing when you are tense.

- Engaging in a spiritually nourishing practice more often.

- Reconnecting with your spiritual discipline. Finding renewed faith.

- Staying more current with uncomfortable feelings. Allowing yourself to feel them in private and/or express them when appropriate.

- Experiencing more energy and/or direction in your work or parenting.

- Feeling more at one with others and with nature.

- Getting less caught up in crisis, either by maintaining perspective, by refusing to engage, or through better preparation.

- Becoming more at peace with your past choices.

Nobody, even after ten years of standing on one foot on a thirty-foot-tall pillar in the middle of the desert eating nothing but locusts and drinking nothing but ant blood while reciting the Buddhist heart sutras, could fully embody this list. I have compiled it *only* to help you notice what you might otherwise dismiss. If it makes you feel inferior or goal-oriented about retreating, tear it out, burn it, and mail me the ashes. I'll wear them in penance.

Bring Your Retreat into the World

The renowned scholar of mysticism Evelyn Underhill wrote, "The spiritual life of individuals has to be extended both vertically to God and horizontally to other souls; and the more it grows in both directions, the less merely individual and therefore the more truly personal it will be." Writer Patricia Hart Clifford believes:

> At some point for all, spiritual insight must turn into action if it is not to become hollow. On a retreat, silence functions as a cocoon in which attention can develop. Silence protects the spirit from external assaults so that the wings of freedom can grow. But while silence can nurture the budding soul, the real test comes in the flight. No breakthrough on retreat is as important as the resulting actions in the world.

What if you were asked by your God, a child, or a stranger on the street, "How will you bring your retreat home?" Without making it a should, a goal, or a have-to, how will your experience, or your experiences over time with mini-retreats, take root and grow?

The possibilities are as varied as the women reading this. Perhaps working with your critical voice spirals into being a daily example of a woman who practices self-loving kindness in front of her children. Or discussing "What is enough?" with your retreat group becomes a desire to live a simpler life, consuming fewer unnecessary goods and less energy. Perhaps a weekend retreat in your home grows into helping one homeless woman and child get off the streets. Grieving a rape that happened to you ten years ago heals into offering your services at a rape crisis center.

Let it become. We are often too trapped by cynicism, denial, and survival to make a difference yet are exhausted by our own harsh standards of what a good woman should do. Somewhere between these two unhappy extremes lies an oasis where service feeds balance and meaning rather than a false sense of perfection or martyrdom. Let the process grow "vertically to God and horizontally to other souls." Keep listening to your inner voice to determine when and what you should do.

Daily Practice

Your retreat springs from and is guided by your inner knowing. But how do you maintain some kind of communication with that inner knowing between retreats? Without this communication, it will be much harder to hear the call to retreat when it comes again. You need simple, daily ways to stay in touch with your authentic self.

My favorites are:

- A daily check-in using the questions from What Will You Do?: Check-In. Writer and therapist Gunilla Norris does this by figuratively attaching a thought she wants to integrate into her life to a clothespin. It might be "Listen" or "Remember the world" or "It's okay to rest." She dangles the clothespin from a string in a doorway. Each time she walks through that doorway, the clothespin nudges her. She stops, breathes, and remembers. "Having it be at the level that I had to actually bump into it seemed to help," she says on her audio tape *Being Home*. I like to use sachets instead of clothespins, and instead of repeating a word, I ask myself a check-in question. "What am I feeling?" and "How can I slow down?" are my current favorites. Another way that I teach in my workshops is to stick gold stars throughout your life. Paste them inside the bathroom medicine cabinet, on the bottom of the refrigerator door, inside your closet, on the rearview mirror and visor in your car, anywhere slightly out of the way or on the edge of your peripheral vision. Place them out in the world, too, on the way into the dry cleaner's, on a bathroom stall at work, on your child's stroller. Each time you see one of these stars, physically pause, breathe, and repeat an affirmation like "I can choose to make time for my inner life" or a check-in question like "Is this how I choose to spend my time?" Or write your favorite check-in questions and affirmations on index cards and hide them in your purse, wallet, files, books, coat pockets, junk drawer, freezer, and spice jars, and wrapped up with the hidden emergency chocolate. Or set your watch or kitchen timer to go off a few times a day. When it does, ask yourself, "What do I need to do to nurture myself today?," and then do it for yourself as soon as you are able.

- I stay centered by writing about anything for three pages in my journal first thing every morning.

- Sitting meditation is one of the most ancient ways to become and re-main awake. While there are as many ways to meditate as there are ways to smile, my favorite is to sit, early in the morning before anyone else is awake, on a cushion with my spine erect. I set a timer for twenty minutes and close my eyes. I breathe and focus either on a word (*peace, om, God, Goddess, Divine Source, Jesus*) or on my breath. When my attention wanders, as it will countless times, I bring it back to my focus.

- Yoga has been another practice for me, even if that means three half–sun salutations or half a yoga video. Another regular practice for me, often as part of my opening ceremony, is walking. Although I have never practiced formal walking meditation, when I walk I try to put my focus on the outside world, on the sensation of the breeze on my skin, on the sun and shade on the mountains, on the sound of the wind in the trees, instead of on my little worried mind.

- Sometimes I end the day by doing a spontaneous painting on how I feel about today, what I learned, or what I wish to let go of. I do this in bed, not with paints but with colored water pencils (to protect the sheets).

- Creating and tending a shrine has waxed and waned as a spiritual prac-tice in my life. Thomas Moore in *The Re-Enchantment of Everyday Life* writes, "Above all, a shrine gives presence to a felt but not always visible sentiment or realization. Significant intuitions and emotions about finding a place for the holy urge themselves toward some kind of ex-pression, and a shrine comes into being." My friend Diane has a shrine in her bedroom built around a plaster cast of her body when she was pregnant. On it are feathers, pictures, a bell. Anna's shrine has a chime, photos of herself and her godchildren, incense, all sorts of little boxes, angels, a Buddha. Each woman sees her shrine every day and perhaps lights a candle on it or adds flowers to it, bringing the sacred into her consciousness.

I almost always resist doing any of these practices. I always enjoy them once I start and stick with them longer than I thought I would. To get started I say, "I'll draw (or meditate, walk, whatever) for five minutes. If I don't feel like continuing after that, I give myself full-hearted permission to stop without feeling guilty."

A Retreat Practice

It is impossible to retain the luster of a retreat forever. Preparation and a closing ceremony offer some protection from the onslaught of life—but only some. There is no magic pair of boots with which you can stride through the shit of life without becoming dirty. You will lose some of what you found, whether that is energy, creative inspiration, perspective, or self-love. You will "work your hind legs off" again or find yourself "half a bubble off plumb." Such is life. You die a thousand tiny psychic deaths. And a few big ones, too. But you can also be reborn a thousand times. Like the resurrection stories found in most cultures, you can find your self again. Historically, that has been through commitment to a spiritual practice. One aspect of this spiritual practice can be a regular commitment to retreat.

Your commitment might look any number of ways, the constant being your commitment to listen and honor your own rhythms. "If one sets aside time for a business appointment, a trip to the hairdresser, a social engagement, or a shopping expedition, that time is accepted as inviolable. But if one says: I cannot come because that is my hour to be alone, one is considered rude, egotistical, or strange," Anne Morrow Lindbergh wrote in *Gift from the Sea*. She made time once a year, even with five children and her own notoriety, for three weeks at the beach. Regularly scheduled retreats are immensely reassuring to the parts of your psyche that believe you will give in to what Lindbergh describes, that you will once again place the incessant demands of life or what others think over your need to reconnect.

Through any retreat you do, you prove to yourself that you value yourself. Now if you can convince yourself that you will *continue* to listen and value yourself, you've found the secret door. This trusting commitment will lessen the disappointment, fear, irritability, and clumsy awfulness that can arise as you watch your retreat become buried under an avalanche of making dinner, meeting deadlines, balancing checkbooks, and nursing sick babies. By committing to returning, you will not have to close yourself off from others because you fear giving up what you have reclaimed. You can embrace giving because you know you will go home to your self, again and again, whenever you must.

Pat retreats once a year with old friends over a long weekend. She feels she has maintained her marriage through retreating four times a year with her husband. Randi celebrates her birthday on a yearly retreat. Mary retreats with the women at her church once a year, as does Carol. It is the promise to yourself that seals the deal. "For quite a while, I had planned on retreating alone for one month to mark my fortieth birthday. Then my husband's eighteen-year-old niece came to stay with us. She was severely depressed and learning disabled, and neither of us knew her very well. It was really tempting to say, 'I won't take my retreat.' Instead, we enlisted support from friends, family, and community so she didn't feel abandoned, so my husband didn't feel abandoned, and so I could still go." Make a commitment to yourself for a day once a month, a weekend once a year, two hours every Saturday.

Ask yourself:

- Do I truly long for and need more retreats?

- What would my ideal retreat practice look like?

- What would be too much? What would feel like a burden, another should? What commitment feels right and doable (start small) yet does not feel like I'm shortchanging myself?

Keep It Simple

Of course, all of these practices will get consumed by overcommitment, by illness, by forgetfulness, by the need to tune out for a while, by any number of life snafus. But the combination of commitment to retreating and daily mindfulness will form such a strong channel among your authentic self, your instinctual rhythms, and your conscious mind that you won't stay gone for long.

Retreating with Others

Women who create such ritual retreats together,
listening thoughtfully to each other's voices, have the
transformative potential to change the world.

Virginia Beane Rutter, *Woman Changing Woman*

Sharing a retreat, especially a self-created retreat, is an intimate process, for it is in sharing silence and solitude that we can encounter true intimacy. Even if you are simply near each other for safety's sake, you are setting off into the unknown together. You are acknowledging in the presence of another that you have needs and yearnings. It is important that you feel completely comfortable with the person you retreat with. It will kill your retreat if you feel restrained, polite, or unable to pursue certain activities or even thoughts because of who is accompanying you. Look for someone you feel at ease with and can be vulnerable around, someone who has respect for silence and the interior world. "No retreat is better than one you don't want or can't manage," advises therapist and group leader Marcie Telandar. Choose carefully, and be certain you have plenty of privacy and free time.

That is, of course, if you wish to be alone. If you yearn to retreat but are more drawn to the idea of being with people than being alone, you may wish to attend an organized group retreat.

If you wish to set up a retreat with others, first decide with whom you might like to retreat. If you have a close friend who is open to the process, you will create a different kind of retreat than if no one comes readily to mind and you decide to approach three women in your book club or temple. If you have an

See Resources: Books Listing Retreat Centers, Leaders, and Adventures for help finding such a retreat.

ongoing women's group with whom you would like to retreat, your retreat is going to be different than retreating with a group that has no shared history.

What if you can't think of anyone to retreat with? You can retreat alone at a retreat center and use a retreat coordinator as your support. You can attend an organized retreat with the hopes of meeting one or two like-minded people to continue a retreat practice with in the future. You can join an ongoing class, church, study, hiking, art, or meditation group and perhaps meet someone there who is interested in doing a retreat in the future.

After you have chosen someone to ask but before you do, decide what your intent for organizing a shared retreat is. It may be to reconnect with a friend, to deepen the connections with an ongoing group, to learn from other women, to have support for and reflection on your own process, to jump-start yourself into new behavior or out of a rut, to be able to afford a cabin or hotel, to feel safe in nature, or to do certain kinds of work (like working with dreams) for which you want another person. Deciding why you want to retreat with others does *not* mean you are the group leader. This will be a leaderless retreat or, rather, an all-leader group. Each person is responsible for herself. Instead of controlling or leading, you initiate a direction, then each woman takes an equal amount of responsibility getting things ready for herself and her role in the group. Keep it simple, surrender to the inevitable changes and snags that happen when other people join together, and powerful things can happen.

If you want to lead a retreat, be clear that you will not have the same experience as the other participants. It will be hard work, and you will invite projections from others. It can be hard on friendships. Tread lightly, and investigate your reasons for wanting to lead. Do you want to be the expert, the spiritual guru? Or do you believe it won't happen if you don't do it?

Give a few minutes' thought to how you see people supporting one another on this retreat. Some examples of shared retreats:

See Deep Listening Circle later in this chapter.

- Driving to the country and renting a cottage with a friend. Coming together for dinner each evening and for a deep listening circle. You should feel comfortable when being silent together or when passing in the hall, and there should be room around the cabin to hike and be alone.

- Four women from the same church retreat together to learn from one another. One woman loves poetry and bring selections to work with. One woman is well versed in reading tarot cards. Another has led a dream circle. One woman is experienced in voice work and singing. Each woman plans a *short, simple* segment of the retreat on the theme of self-knowledge, leaving long in-between times for solitude and self-directed work.

- Three friends from a twelve-step program retreat together to offer support for starting new projects and goals. They use deep listening circles, brainstorming, and barn raising to overcome entropy and fear about getting a job, getting out of a relationship, and starting a novel. They spend about half their time working on their intentions alone.

- Two old friends meet to renew their friendship and themselves. They spend some time together playing, some time apart working on the states of their beings, and a little time in circle catching up on the state of their friendship, on what needs clarification, and on gratitude.

See Retreat Plans: A One-Day Retreat with a Friend.

Approach the people you would like to retreat with, and propose your basic idea. Do so when you have a few quiet moments to talk. Start with the general idea. "I want to retreat, and I want some company and support. This will not be a group retreat per se because a lot of the time we will be alone, working on our own. But we will come together at previously agreed-upon times for previously agreed-upon activities. We might choose to support one another after we've returned home." Then describe your idea: "On this retreat, I hope we could rent a cabin in the state forest, support one another in feeling safe in nature, have a morning dream circle and an evening 'state of our individual retreats' circle." Be sure to say you are not the leader and that your idea is only a starting place. You might want to have this book on hand to refer to or for the others to flip through. Offer two or three possible dates. Although you will most likely need to meet again, making time to do your retreat will almost always be your biggest obstacle, so address that issue right away.

Once everyone has agreed to retreat together and you have set the date, decide the following things:

- *Shared intention.* If you haven't already, form your individual intentions (you could do this at your planning session). Then complete this sentence: "What would support me in exploring this intention is. . . ." Read this aloud and fashion an intention that supports all. Remember to frame it as a question. For example, three friends retreated together. Their separate intentions were:

    I intend to ask myself, How can I rest and hear myself think? What would support me in exploring this intention is help overcoming my critic and slowing down.

    I intend to ask myself, What is missing in my life? What would support me in exploring this intention is someone to bounce off what I come up with.

I intend to ask myself, How can I better foster creativity in my life? What would support me in exploring this intention is doing projects with others to get my creative juices going and talking about my fears and blocks.

Looking at what was important to each, they came up with this intention:

On this retreat we intend to support each other by listening, meditating, painting, writing, and affirming one another.

It is important to remember that the majority of your retreat is done alone. It is very easy to get into doing everything together, but that may not allow you to hear you own wisdom and may require more proficiency in group process. Leave about 50 percent or more of your time for solitude.

- *Structure.* Avoid a precise schedule, as it may create tension and conflict. Instead, flip through the book and make a list of the practices you want to do together. Add additional ideas. Scratch off anything that doesn't fit your intention. If necessary, use the deep listening circle to further prune the list. Then, only if necessary, decide what you will do when. For example, if you want to visit a nearby beach, what time? Or if you will do a dream circle, roughly what time will you meet? Make your mantra "Simple is best."

- *Where?* Avoid retreating at a participant's house. While convenient, it usually leaves the woman whose house it is feeling like a hostess, running and fetching. If this is the only location available, discuss ways to minimize the burden on her. The place you choose should fit everyone. No one should feel unsafe or stressed about money, nor should it be difficult to get to, involving much travel. Nothing brings out the worst, and the best, in people faster than traveling. Keep it to a minimum and plan exactly what arrangements you do make. If you are planning a retreat in the world where traveling is necessary, discuss how to minimize stress and how to maintain retreat space. Good places to retreat: rented cabins or vacation homes, especially in a state or national park; private land where you can pitch tents; retreat centers; a friend of a friend's house, shack, or cabin; a mobile home.

- *For what amount of time will you retreat?* Does anyone need to be back at a precise time?

- *Who will bring what?* Look over the activities you will do and put together a list of supplies. Keep in mind expense. Use what is easily available, and precisely share material costs.

- *Where will you meet, when, and how will you get there?* Leave a window of arrival time so latecomers won't irk others.

- *What you will eat, who will bring what, who will cook?* Potluck meals are good, as are precooked food and, if possible, having dinner delivered and making very simple meals for breakfast and lunch. Be aware that preparing food together invites conversation. Do you want this to be a social time? Do you want to bring wine? Sweets? Meat? Do you want it to be a time of silence?

- *Chores.* Who will do what? Plan your retreat at a place where chores can be kept to a minimum, and where no one will be worrying about damage to an expensive couch or wondering who will wash the sheets.

- *Interruptions.* How will you prevent interruptions from the outside world? What will you do if they happen? If you will be completely away from civilization, how will you be reached in an emergency?

- *How will you open and close your retreat?* You may wish to create your own ceremonies before, after, or around the shared one. Many shared retreats begin by sitting in circle with each person talking about her intention, hopes, and fears for the retreat and her hopes for group work. I remember just such a moment at the beginning of a wilderness trip I co-led. Each of the twelve women spoke about her reasons for coming and what she hoped to get out of the week. There was a palpable energy generated. Later, a local Anshiabe woman who had come to lead the sweat lodge said to me, "God was in the room. When you feel that pressure and stillness pressing down, God is there."

Each woman might bring or plan one element of the opening ceremony. One group of five women declared their theme as renewal and their intention as "On this retreat we intend to support each other by letting go of control, risking being silly, and listening to each other." They decided beforehand to dance their opening ceremony. Someone brought music and a boom box. Someone else brought rattles and feather boas. Another woman brought ostrich feathers to balance on their palms while they danced. It evolved into an hour and a half of dancing, singing, and crying, ending with each woman shouting out her intention and then all dancing in a circle around their retreat space.

Give thought to your closing ceremony, too. Be aware that the tendency is to skip this part or minimize it. Be sure to allow enough time. Don't hurry this part.

- *Ground rules.* How will you avoid and deal with chatter, nervousness, the need to goof off and blow off energy, emotional crises, differences of opinion, and hurt feelings?

Decide on a way to maintain concentration and silence. The most common problem with women retreating together is the desire to make one another comfortable and, in so doing, chatter, lose their own centers, or, fall out of calmness. This comes up especially when women are being silent together, holding the tension of a spiritual moment, or in ritual. Doing what ritualist Lucinda Eileen calls "turning the circle" helps maintain the retreat container. Examples of this are each woman pressing her fingertip into her neck and feeling her heartbeat, taking three deep breaths together and letting out a big "Ah" with each exhale (good for nervous energy), or focusing her attention back on a focal point, perhaps a tree, shrine, or flower arrangement. By consciously holding the energy, each woman's experience will deepen. Together, choose a way to help this happen. (One way is to bring a bell or chime. When someone feels the energy is scattered, she hits the chime and calls for everyone to center.)

Decide on times when you can blow off energy and be silly together. Not every moment on retreat must be solemn. Great laughter and silliness are indispensable. But decide how you will channel that energy so that it doesn't become a way to avoid transcendent moments or intense feelings and so that no one steps on someone else's concentration. Set aside time for group play. Work with clay, do Getting Juicy, get physical, or tell jokes and bawdy stories. Don't try to stay in ritual or serious space together for too long; an hour is a long time to maintain focus.

Call a deep listening circle when you need support for crisis or if you feel you are not being heard. An unplanned benefit of a shared retreat can be to learn how to speak from your heart to someone who has hurt you and to speak up when you feel misunderstood or unclear about something. Sometimes the logistics of a retreat can create just such a moment. Bring it into a circle and see what comes of it.

If you find yourself in conflict or feeling off base, use What Will You Do?: Check-In as a group. Anyone in the group can call for a check-in when she feels it is needed. Everyone uses the same question, perhaps "I feel, I need, I want" or "I am feeling" or "I need to be supported by. . . ." Sit in circle. Each person centers and checks in with herself. Then share what you found in circle. Keep going around until a direction or resolution has been reached. You can also use this check-in to open a deep listening circle and to encourage self-responsibility.

Reading over this list can make a group retreat sound pretty overwhelming. It need not be. Keep stripping your plans to the bare minimum. Retreat with only one or two people. Spend most of your retreat exploring at your own pace.

Deep Listening Circle

"Deep listening is miraculous for both listener and speaker. When someone receives us with open-hearted, non-judging, intensely interested listening, our spirits expand," writes Sue Patton Thoele, author of *A Woman's Book of Courage*. To be listened to in such a way on retreat provides a very strong container for your emotions, allowing you to push yourself to new heights and depths, to be more courageous and steadfast. When you articulate what is happening in your inner life and you see that others care enough to listen, your journey becomes more real and precious. To hear what others are dealing with helps you feel less alone and less sorry for yourself.

The purpose of sitting in circle is to be heard without judgment, advice, or intervention. The simple tool of sitting in circle can profoundly enhance your retreat and even change your life. These guidelines are based on the work of Christina Baldwin and Ann Linnea of Peer Spirit.

You can use circle for just about any situation. Christina Baldwin, in her amazing book *Calling the Circle* (revised edition, Bantam, 1998), gives examples of business, community, family, and spiritual circles. On retreat, the focus most often will be on what is happening for each person on the retreat. You might also focus on your intentions or dreams, on discussing a particular practice you all did, or on a topic you set before the retreat. A circle, Baldwin reminds us, is consecrated space that contains our stories and provides a "place" for telling them. In consecrated space, there are basic guidelines which help us know what to do.

The basic guidelines are:

- Arrange your seating in a circle.

- Everyone places something in the center that designates the Divine to her. This creates sacred space and sets a context for relying on Spirit to guide you. "Each person places ultimate reliance in the center and takes their place at the rim. . . . Attention is always held within the perimeter of the circle. Attention focuses at the edge when people are talking and focuses at the center when there is silence or the need to remember guidance," writes Christina Baldwin in *Calling the Circle*.

- Open the circle with a simple ceremony. Reading a quote, singing a song, sipping water from a shared cup, or meditating in silence for a few minutes centers each woman and helps her to speak from her heart.

- Decide on your subject or restate what it is. "What is this circle about? What do we want to accomplish by sitting together?" Often on this kind of retreat your subject will be what has been happening for you in your solitary work. Use a talking piece, something you hold in your hand to remind you to speak from your heart and to remind everyone else not to interrupt.

- Take turns speaking about the subject at hand. Say what you think and feel about what is happening for you in this moment. Use "I" statements. Speak through any tears or laughter that arises. Avoid talking just to hear yourself talk; concentrate on what you are saying. Using a timer is often a good idea, as it ensures everyone equal time and limits the resentments that can arise when someone talks longer than others.

- While someone is speaking, everyone else listens from the heart. This means listening without thinking about what you are going to say next, not passing judgment in your mind, and making *no interruptions*. No comments at any time unless they are specifically asked for. And even then, comments are offered only after the woman speaking is finished. Cross-talk, chatter, and advice ruin the spirit of circle.

- Close the circle with a simple ceremony. In my ongoing women's group, someone reads a paragraph about a woman's life from Judy Chicago's book *The Dinner Party*. Dennie LaTourelle, leader of the Aluna Community in Santa Barbara, ends her circles with each person appreciating someone else in the circle. A prayer round, in which each person prays aloud for herself, others, and the planet, is another venerable way to end.

Guidelines to remember and agree to before you begin:

- What is said in circle never leaves the circle. Confidentiality allows people to speak their minds knowing that they will not be gossiped about later.

- The circle is a practice in discernment, not judgment. No one's view is right or wrong; it is simply different. You can listen and speak without having to be in agreement.

- Each person takes responsibility for asking the circle for the support she needs.

- Leadership rotates. Every woman helps the circle, and the retreat, by assuming small increments of leadership. Take turns calling the circle together, opening the circle, facilitating it, minding the timer, and closing the circle.

- Each person takes responsibility for agreeing or not agreeing to participate in specific requests. One person can say, "I don't support this action, but the group may proceed if it chooses." Each woman has the space to not agree or participate in everything. This creates trust in the group and in yourself.

- No interruption.

- When troubled, frustrated, or fearful, someone in the circle may call for silence, a song, a time-out, or holding hands and breathing together to reestablish the focus on the center and to remind participants of the need for spiritual guidance.

- No violent language or threats of violence. If you address conflict, everyone must agree to remain respectful.

- Ask before touching. Everyone has a different personal history regarding touch and may have had painful experiences of intrusion. Sometimes, among women, it is assumed that hugs and back pats are automatically okay. Ask one another first.

The deep listening circle may be used in a number of ways on retreat. Here are several.

Dream Circle

Convene a circle first thing in the morning. One woman tells her dream. A fragment or dream from another time is fine, too. After she is finished, each woman in the circle relates what she felt and saw when listening to the dream, using the sentence "If it were *my* dream. . . ." This is *not* interpretation but each individual's reaction to the dream images and emotions. So you would not say (even to your closest friend whom you know better than yourself), "When you talked about the overflowing toilet, I thought of your marriage." Instead, "If it were my dream, the overflowing toilet would feel like a blockage. When you told the dream, I immediately thought of everything I feel guilty about, everything that feels undone. I also worried about how I was going to get the shit out of the carpet." Stay with *your* feelings. Use "I" statements. After everyone has had a turn, the woman whose dream it is has her turn. "If it were my dream. . . ." Then she expresses any "Aha!" experiences she has had listening to everyone else's reactions. Some discussion usually follows. Then on to the next woman's dream. This is not a quick process, but doing it every morning of a retreat, especially a long retreat, can be very enriching.

Affirmation Circle

There are a number of ways to affirm one another using the circle.

- End a circle by appreciating each person for something she said or did during the circle or recently on the retreat. Examples are "I appreciate you for being so honest about your struggle to love your stepson" and "I appreciate how well you listened to me in this circle."

- With larger groups (of at least ten), have half the group sit comfortably, eyes closed, breathing deeply. The women sitting concentrate on opening and receiving. The other half stand behind the seated circle, each person placing her hands on the shoulders of a woman sitting. Each of the standing women thinks of two affirmations she would like to say to the women sitting, affirmations that would support them in the work they are doing on retreat. Examples are "I choose to have the energy to find work I love," "I choose to find time for myself in my life," and "I choose to accept this divorce and still love myself." Notice the affirmations are stated as "I" statements. This gives them a powerful immediacy, as if the women sitting were hearing their own voices speaking positively to them.

  Each of the women standing leans down and whispers one affirmation into a woman's ear. Then the standing women move to the right and whisper an affirmation in the next woman's ear. Everyone keeps going until the women standing arrive back at the women they started with. Go around the circle again, whispering a new affirmation. When finished, silently switch positions and repeat the process. The standing women sit, listening and receiving. It helps to play music softly in the background.

- Have each woman write down three to five affirmations she wants to hear, each on a separate piece of paper. One woman passes one of her affirmations to the right. The woman on the right looks her in the eye, slowly says her name, and repeats her affirmation aloud to her. For example, if I am sitting in circle with Randi and Maggie, I hand Randi one of my affirmations and she says to me, "Jennifer, you are a capable and loving mother." Then Maggie does the same. Then Randi and Maggie repeat in unison, "Jennifer, you are a capable and loving mother." Then the woman who has been affirmed has a chance, if necessary, to be her critical voice and say all the nasty things she has thought while being affirmed. Then the women in the circle respond with another round of the same affirmations.

Then it is Randi's turn. Keep going around the circle until each woman has heard all her affirmations echoed back at her and has had a chance to whine as her critical voice.

- Share a boasting session. Each woman stands up and boasts about herself. Boast, brag, gloat, swagger, proclaim everything that is wonderful about you in the most glowing terms imaginable; crow, show off, relish yourself. In this circle, interruption is permitted in the form of egging a woman on to new heights of bragging. This is a very difficult exercise for most women to do.

Soliloquy Circle

The soliloquy circle is the format my women's group uses. We select a topic, then discuss it within a deep listening circle. We each get three to five minutes to speak. After one woman is finished, questions are allowed, and then it is the next woman's turn. After this initial round, we follow with shorter rounds, adding ideas that have occurred to us or responding to what others have said but, again, without interruption. The act of articulating your thoughts about a subject and being heard as you do so brings clarity, insight, and self-compassion. Hearing other women's thoughts, sometimes very different from your own, engenders an expanded worldview and, with it, tolerance. The goal is never group therapy or a group bitch session but a clarification of values and ideas from a personal point of view.

On a shared retreat, each woman can bring one to five topics, written on small pieces of paper. Put them in a cup or a hat, and draw one to plunge into. You could also brainstorm topics that relate to your retreat theme or intentions.

Here are some of our favorite topics, which would work well on a retreat:

Creativity	Looks
Death	Feminism
Heroes and Sheroes	Women's and Men's Roles

Sex	Love
Random Acts of Kindness	Grace
Ten Years from Now	What Is Enough?
Friendship	Inspiration
Purpose	Surrender
Suffering	Power
Shame	Adventure
What Is God?	Peace
Adventure	Gratitude
If I Had Five Other Lives to Lead	Faith
	Healing
Truth	Balance
Trust	Self-Care
Integrity	Forgiveness
Courage	

Retreating Together in the World

When you are going to share a retreat in the world, get together before you start and plan a way to help one another hold and protect retreat space. Sometimes just being together will make you feel set apart from the everyday world, but small gestures like wearing the same pin, being silent together (or almost silent), whispering a centering word to one another from time to time (*peace, breathe,* and *at-one-ment* are examples), and imagining before your retreat that you are all surrounded by a cone of brilliantly hued light will help.

Afterward

Part of the magic of a shared retreat is supporting one another through the integration of your retreat into daily life. It could be as simple as when my dear friend Barbra and I retreated together one day and, at a family dinner that evening, we kept winking at each other. It could be exchanging a weekly postcard or a phone call of encouragement. It could be deciding to meditate or pray together at the same time each morning for one week.

If you want to give more elaborate attention to supporting one another as you carry your retreats into daily life, you might try the contract and buddy system we used on a week-long retreat I co-led. Each woman committed to two things she wanted to accomplish for herself. Then she committed also to one Act of Beauty, as Brooke Medicine Eagle calls the commitments she asks people to make "not for myself alone, but that all people may live." She says, "Acts of Beauty . . . extend our personal wholeness into the world by giving the gift we came to Earth to offer. . . . We are in this world not only to lift ourselves and grow but also to share our gifts and talents with others."

After deciding upon a worthy, concrete goal to be completed by a certain date, each woman also declares what she is willing to give up if she doesn't meet her goals. Partnerships are formed to support each woman through calling and writing to check her progress and to offer encouragement. For example, you might commit to finishing thirty pages of a novel within three months, and if you don't, you will give away half of your book collection to charity. You might commit to giving free haircuts at the homeless shelter once a month for one year or you will halt yoga classes with your favorite teacher for six months. You might commit to reading one book about marketing and making five cold calls within one month or you will attend a Toastmasters meeting and give a speech. Notice that the commitments are concrete, adequate time (but not too much!) is given, and the stakes are commensurate.

SAMPLE CONTRACT

I, _____(YOUR NAME), love and honor myself enough to bring

the gifts of this retreat into my life. I pledge to do so through the act of

_____ by _____ (DATE). By

signing my name below, I agree to this contract with my whole being.

I freely offer to give _____ away as evidence of my

commitment to this action and to myself.

_____

Sign and date

After support is no longer needed, be willing to let the group end. Often a shared retreat is so much fun and so spiritually nourishing that you will want to hang on and keep the group going. Do you have a purpose in doing so? Does everyone have time and the same level of commitment? It isn't fair to form an ongoing group out of what was presented as a one-time experience, and trying to prolong the experience often doesn't work. The last thing retreat leader David Knudsen said to our group after a three-week intense retreat and wilderness trip was, "What you are looking for isn't here at Northwaters. It is inside you." Like Dorothy in *The Wizard of Oz,* just click your heels three times and go home.

Retreat Plans

I remembered once seeing a tea party some little girls had set up outside, mismatched china, decorations of a plucked pansy blossom and a seashell and a shiny penny and a small circle of red berries and a fern, pressed wetly into the wooden table, the damp outline a beautiful bonus. They didn't consult the Martha Stewart guide for entertainment and gulp a martini before their guests arrived. They pulled ideas from their hearts and minds about the things that gave them pleasure, and they laid out an offering with loving intent. It was a small Garden of Eden, the occupants making something out of what they saw was theirs. Out of what they truly saw.

Elizabeth Berg, *The Pull of the Moon*

What exactly will your retreat look like? What will you do when?

From the outside, it might not look like much. You take a shower and dress slowly, with care, in comfortable clothes. Perhaps you create a small shrine with a candle and pictures of you at different times in your life. You walk by a creek and dip your foot in, sitting awhile. Then you walk home and sip tea while reading poetry. After closing the curtains and dancing for a long while, you collapse on the floor, weeping, then become very still, and then write in your journal. You make an exquisite salad and eat it with your full attention. Later, soaking in a bath, you do a guided meditation. Putting candles all around your bed, you read a spiritually inspiring passage aloud before going to sleep. You dream. You wake to write your dreams down and work with them a bit. You greet the morning with joy. And so on.

Traditional retreats rely on a schedule that revolves around meditation or prayer, for example, the services marking the hours at a Benedictine monastery or a sitting schedule at a Zen meditation retreat. This way of approaching time has a venerable history, and it works. But there is an important question to consider with regard to women and time. We rarely feel we have enough. Most women in the world live a life of "unspeakable toil," as Kathleen Norris wrote in *The*

Cloister Walk. When reading an article about a Los Angeles woman who commuted four hours each day and needed her toddler to poke her in the ribs on the way home to keep her awake, I began to wonder if women on retreat need schedules. Or is the primary gift of a woman's retreat the feeling of time spreading around you, becoming yours for the taking?

That said, there are times when you want a little structure, and at those times a schedule or plan is in order. Here, then, are eleven plans ranging from a few minutes to three days. Each is formulated on the assumption that you have scanned the first section of the book and have decided what your intention is, where and how long you will retreat, and the other logistics. All of the following retreat plans can be expanded, shortened, or rearranged. They are templates representing a balance among inner work, self-trust, self-listening, and fun. Space doesn't allow constructing a retreat plan for every reason or season, so use these plans to give you an idea of what flow works well, and then construct your own. I imagine that you will be starting a retreat in the morning and ending in the late afternoon or evening, but you could, of course, start at any time and simply adjust where you eat and rest.

A One-Day Well-Being Retreat

This retreat would work well for intentions having to do with needing rest or feeling overwhelmed, ill, or out of balance.

Prepare

> Your journal and a pen.
>
> Basic art materials.
>
> Dance and meditation music.
>
> A drum or rattle.
>
> Soothing treats like fluffy slippers, a new pen, a bouquet of freesias and lilies, a minty face mask.

Your opening ceremony might include a massage, a warm bath, or even a nap. (You could start your ceremony, nap, and then finish it upon awakening.)

Do Gathering the Whole (page 147). You might spend anywhere from a half hour to two hours here.

Deliberately, worshipfully, drink water or tea. Focus on the sensations.

Practice a form of check-in from What Will You Do?: Check-In (page 75). Your question could be "What do I need to be healthy?" Alter or add to this retreat plan if new information appears.

Using Spontaneous Painting or Writing from Good Ways to Listen (page 126), explore the words *well-being, health,* and *balance.*

Experiment with Good Ways to Listen: Soothe (page 124). Celebrate yourself with luxury.

Go outside and attend to nature, even if that means watching clouds for two minutes. If you can, plant your bare feet in or lie down on the earth.

Write a trust list from Courting Yourself (page 175).

What could you do right now that would be frivolous, marvelous, and astounding? What pops into your head? Is it self-affirming? Trust yourself and do it. If nothing occurs to you, fine.

Check in with yourself. The question could be "What do I need?" If you are hungry, eat something you desire with your complete attention. Do not read or watch TV while eating.

Investigate The State of Being (page 165).

Take time for your body, for something physical yet relaxing—a walk in nature, some yoga asanas, stretching to music, or dancing to trance music.　*See Resources.*

Check in with yourself.

Do a Being practice from Good Ways to Listen (page 113).

One final check-in. The question could be "What do I still need to do on this retreat?"

Do Getting Juicy (page 161).

End with a closing ceremony that includes showering yourself with gratitude for taking time for yourself, writing notes on any insights you gained, and studying your calendar. Make a self-promise to do one kind, self-nurturing thing for yourself every day for the next week. Keep it simple and realistic, but by all means consider changing your schedule to include more time for yourself. Write down what you will do on your calendar. Do something in this ceremony to make these appointments with yourself feel as important and real as your other commitments.

A Lunch Hour Retreat (Half Hour to an Hour)

You can also use this mini-retreat at the end of the day to make a transition between work and home, or use it before an important meeting or date.

Prepare

A personal stereo and music that brings you into quiet, interior space.

Begin your opening ceremony with a declaration to the effect that "I am now leaving my work. I have done all that I could for now. *I am enough*" (page 115).

Get away from your workplace and co-workers. Go for a walk to a nearby park, stop by that deserted band shell no one ever visits, climb the stairs to the roof, visit a burbling fountain, walk into a dusty library where every sound is muffled, or find a private, quiet restaurant corner. While you walk, play your music on your headphones.

Once you feel you are in retreat space (the movement and music will get you there; you need both), take ten very deep, slow breaths while rolling your shoulder blades down and toward each other.

Check in with yourself. Ask yourself, "What do I need to do to nurture myself right now?" Can you act, now or later, on what you discover?

Do Addressed to the Heart (page 231) right where you are, walking or sitting for five minutes. See, feel, hear, taste what is being offered to nourish you. See if gratitude comes knocking at your heart.

Imagine the Divine as you know it standing in front of you. You can do this with your eyes open while walking, or find a comfortable place to sit for a few minutes. (If closing your eyes seems weird, put on sunglasses.) Your Divinity showers you with a golden substance made of pure peace and spiritual protection. You somehow know that, once you are anointed with this magic substance, everything nasty, hurtful, stressful, and boring that might be coming your way this afternoon will bounce off your magic shield and slide right off you.

Eat lunch mindfully. Concentrate on slowing down, on tasting your food, on receiving the gifts of nourishment. If you are going to order lunch, check in and ask yourself, "What does my body need?"

End your retreat in two parts. One happens now, with a thank-you to whom-ever or whatever, followed by quick, energetic movement on your way back to work. Try swinging your arms and walking quickly, or, if you can, stretch your arms high over your head and imagine bringing in energy. Take deep breaths while silently repeating, "I am ready for the rest of my day. I am full of energy. Yes!"

The second part happens tonight, when you get home. Take a shower (prefer-ably in the dark or by candlelight), and name the crap of the day as it goes down the drain, everything that bounced off of your golden, protective shield.

A Two-Day Artist Retreat

This retreat would support intentions having to do with getting a new project going, recovering and trusting your creativity, solving a problem, or alleviating general depression. Adjust this schedule as needed to fit the availability of your art experiences.

Prepare

Your journal and a pen.

Art experiences (page 180).

See Feeding the Artist for examples.

Several large pieces of drawing paper.

A photo of you.

Magazines to cut up and other collage materials (page 189).

Music and a drum or rattle.

Books about lives of creative women.

See Resources.

Delicious food.

Arty clothes.

A place to walk.

Silence.

Day One

Touch on all your senses in your opening ceremony, especially the sense(s) you need to recharge. For example, if you are a painter, include visuals or lie with a cold eye pack over your eyes for fifteen minutes. Check your expectations. Be sure you aren't expecting the idea of a lifetime to visit you and make you richer than Oprah, because that expectation will kill your retreat faster than hoping to have supper with Jesus.

Do Getting Juicy (page 161).

Read up on creative women. Choose one or two creative women to become the patron saints of your retreat. When you feel stuck, bored, afraid, or too ordinary, invoke one of them. Pretend you are she or that you embody one of her qualities that you admire.

Following the ideas in Feeding the Artist: Immerse Yourself (page 179), choose and enjoy an art experience for one to three hours. Remember to try new things. Be willing to be briefly uncomfortable or even bored. Be sure if you go out into the world to take your emotional container along (page 63).

Practice a form of check-in from What Will You Do? (page 75). Ask yourself, "What does my creative self need?" Invoke your artist saint to help you.

Take a body break. Stretch your back, eat pâté and crackers, drink sparkling apple juice. Consciously rest and delight your flesh.

Melt into I Am Enough, in Good Ways to Listen (page 115).

Make a list of everything creative you have ever done. Nothing is too small. Enlarge your definition of creativity. If it comes to mind, write it down. You will return to this list several times. It will have *at least* one hundred items on it by the end of this retreat.

Time for more art immersion. If you've been reading, then do something visual. If you've been out in the world, do something at home. If you are afraid to venture out, make specific plans to visit a gallery show of contemporary photography or a slide show on the art of Bali.

Afterward: what does your artist saint say about what you just experienced?

Eat something wonderful, perhaps something forbidden. Linger on the tastes.

The time when we are drifting off to sleep is often the ripest for great ideas. Yet we rarely remember our insights. Take a Thomas Edison nap. Relax sitting up or propped up on pillows, holding something like a book in your hand. When you doze off, you will drop the item, and this will wake you. Do you have any ideas? These ideas could be about anything in your life. Write them down. Then, if you wish, take a normal nap.

Upon waking, ask yourself again, "What does my creative self need?" Pay attention to any dreams.

Do Calling the Muse, in Feeding the Artist (page 183).

Indulge in more art. Perhaps you want to read, view, or listen to something your artist saint created.

Drink water as an act of creativity.

Choose movement to rest your brain and balance your emotions. Getting Juicy (page 161), Good Ways to Listen: The Smell of Your Own Sweat (page 117), and Soma Source (page 232) in Renewing Your Spiritual Direction are possibilities.

Must be time for a snack or dinner. Perhaps a visit to a café to watch people and sip hot chocolate or wine? Remember to remain in retreat space! Avoid chatter of all kinds! Imagine that every word out of your mouth and into your ear is being etched in granite for all time.

Check in with yourself: "What do I need?" or "What am I feeling?"

Revel in more art, right up to bedtime and after crawling in. If you are at home, sleep someplace different than you usually do—outside in a tent, on the couch, or on the opposite side of the bed. Surround yourself with images, music, and scents if you like. Be sure to have a pen and journal close by your bed.

Before you go to sleep, write a few lines about your day's experience. Note especially what you felt. As you fall asleep, affirm to yourself several times aloud that you will remember your dreams, and ask your muse and artist saint(s) to help you.

Day Two

Begin your day, before you do anything, by reviewing your dreams. Write down anything that occurs to you, even fragments of images or a word. Dialogue with one dream character or object. If you remember nothing, work with a past dream or write across the top of a piece of paper, "What did I learn about my creative self last night?" Take a few breaths, and start writing with your non-dominant hand.

See Courage.

If you like, stay in your pajamas for a while.

Do Addressed to the Heart, in Reviving Your Spiritual Direction (page 231). Spend at least fifteen minutes observing what is being offered to you.

Have your morning coffee or tea in a different way or place than you usually do. Same with your breakfast. Cook something like pasta and eggs, or have peanut butter and bananas on your toast, or allow yourself a buttery croissant.

Add to your list of everything creative you have ever done.

Wear something that makes you feel like an artist: a scarf, a cloche hat, a long dress, lots of bright jewelry, silk pj's.

Check in with yourself, perhaps by asking, "What does my creative self want to do today?" or "What would my artist saint do today?"

Indulge in more art. If possible, find an art experience that relates to your dreams or to your calling in of your muse or to what you felt or observed when you listened for an address from the heart.

Practice the meditation I Am Enough, in Good Ways to Listen (page 115), while going for a long walk. Don't worry about burning calories. Focus instead on the rhythm of your walking and on your breath.

Sit silently for twenty minutes. See Reviving Your Spiritual Direction: Discipline for instructions (page 229). At the end of the twenty minutes, check in with yourself, perhaps asking, "What divine guidance do I need in my life?"

Wallow in more art. Be sure you are varying your experiences and trying new venues and mediums.

Ask yourself, "What and how would my artist saint eat?" or "What and how would I eat if I believed I were a very creative and talented person?" Give this to yourself when you are hungry.

Take a Thomas Edison nap and then a real one if you wish. If you don't want to nap, spend a few moments being (page 113).

Dialogue with your muse, your artist saint, or your creative self. There is no goal to this dialogue, no right way to do it. Experiment (page 81).

Do something outrageous. Even something small like wearing a different-colored lipstick or wearing clothes you don't usually wear can jiggle things into new light.

Sit quietly and ask yourself, "What art do I yearn to immerse myself in? What would I do if it weren't too _____ (expensive, daring, hard to find, weird)?" Do it now if at all possible.

Make a wish about your creativity. It could be to have new energy, to find someone to sing with, to trust yourself, to start or finish a particular project. Center yourself, close your eyes, and visualize your wish coming true. Use all your senses as you see yourself getting what you want. Allow yourself to enjoy it. Feel an expansion of energy in your heart. If you start to edit your scenario because it feels too good or too big, stop. Forget being small or modest. See yourself accomplishing, feeling, growing, solving, enjoying, blooming.

End this retreat by making a collage that expresses and gives energy to your wish(es). Place a photo of you in the middle of a large piece of paper. Surround yourself with images (drawn, cut from magazines, photos) and objects (search five-and-dime stores, bead stores, craft stores, and New Age bookstores for items) that evoke your expanding creativity and embody your wish coming true. If you get into comparing your collage with anything you have seen over the last two days, stop and do the meditation I Am Enough (page 115).

Your closing ceremony may include a thank-you to your muse, to your artist saints, or to any Divine guidance you may have received. If you are retreating at home, create a creativity shrine with your muse invocation and collage on it.

A Half-Day Trust Retreat

This retreat is specifically for women who feel they can't hear their inner selves. It is a good one to use if you don't have a clear intention, are especially nervous about retreating, or have never retreated before.

It is especially important to feel physically and emotionally safe on this retreat.

Prepare

> Mirror.
>
> Your journal and a pen.
>
> Basic art supplies, clay, or other ways to work with Contemplations.
>
> Round tray and objects that represent your different selves (you can gather these as part of your retreat or skip this part).
>
> Music that draws you inside.
>
> Silence.

Your opening ceremony might include affirmations of self-trust. Use the word *choose* in your affirmations, as in "I choose to listen and believe myself." If you haven't watched too much *Saturday Night Live* (where lampooning affirmations has been raised to an art), you could repeat them to yourself while looking in a mirror.

Do nothing for a time. This may be difficult. No matter, persist. Even five minutes is a triumph.

Read What Will You Do?: Check-In (page 75). Decide on a question to use. Perhaps "What do I know that I am not willing to see?" or "What am I feeling?" Whatever your choice, stay with the same question throughout your retreat.

Make a list of ten or more times in your life when you received internal guidance—an idea popping into your head, a voice telling you to take a different road or to call a friend, a feeling that you were "channeling" when writing or taking a test or doing a job interview—and times when your prayers were answered. Nothing is too small to note.

Do Gathering the Whole (page 147). You may want to skip or shorten the mandala portion because of time. But follow your own guidance.

Take a short body prayer break. See Good Ways to Listen: The Smell of Your Own Sweat: Movement as Prayer for ideas (page 119), or take the words *prayer of trust* and dance them into life.

Check in with yourself. See What Will I Do?: Check-In (page 75).

Build a trust list from Courting Yourself (page 175).

Have a rest and a snack. Ask your body what she needs to eat. Be mindless for half an hour.

Check in again. Where did the mindless time take you? What did you do?

Experiment with one of the offerings in Contemplations (page 132) that has to do with trust or that intrigues you.

Under One Who Chooses (page 196), do Part 1, starting with the words "Imagine a loving presence" and ending with "Nothing to do" a paragraph later.

Include in your closing ceremony an acknowledgment of any inner guidance you received, any ways you trusted yourself to change this plan, and a commitment to check in with yourself at least twice a day for the next week.

A Three-Day Spiritual Renewal Retreat

This is a good retreat for checking your expectations about your spirituality. Sometimes we go on retreat hoping to see God, lose ten pounds, and write a dozen symphonies like Hildegard of Bingen. Well, maybe not *this* time.

Prepare

Before your retreat, make a mask of your face. You need another person to help you. You also need fast-drying (*not* superfast) bandage tape (you'll find it at a pharmacy that caters to hospitals), petroleum jelly, something to hold your hair off your face, scissors, a bowl of water, and two cotton pads. Making a mask of your face can be claustrophobic, so do it in a calm place with someone you trust. Cut the bandages into approximately half-inch strips, with a few quarter-inch ones, too. Pull your hair off your face, and slather your face with petroleum jelly, especially around the hair line. Lie down. Your friend places the cotton pads over your eyes, then wets each strip of bandage before laying it on your face. She builds a support for the rest of the mask by first making a *T* of half-inch strips across your nose, chin, and forehead, and under your eyes, overlaying each strip a bit. Then she builds a circle along the edge of your face, repeating this twice to reinforce the mask's edge. She fills in the rest of your face, doing your nose and mouth last. The mask takes less than five minutes to dry. You will feel it lifting off your face as it dries. Wiggle your cheeks and mouth to help it along. Have your friend help you pop it off. The whole process takes about fifteen minutes. Let it dry for several days, then apply a coat of gesso (you can get it at any art supply store) or wood glue to smooth the surface.

Water-based paints, charms, beads, flowers, herbs, rub-on tattoos, and wood glue to decorate your mask with. See Portrait of Your Authenticity: Prepare for how to do a symbol-gathering scan (page 189).

Drawing supplies and perhaps clay.

One or two books for reflective reading. Emily Dickinson, T. S. Eliot, stories of women on spiritual quests, the Bible, the Koran, Buddhist sutras, or the Bhagavad Gita.

See Resources for more.

Music that takes you inside, music that compels you to dance, and/or a drum or rattle.

Alarm.

Day One

Allow plenty of time for your opening ceremony. You need to believe your retreat container is strong, because three days can feel like a mighty long time. You may be tempted to break your container, but if it feels very real and strong, it will help you stay in the betwixt-and-between place. You might

---

wish to include a metaphorical action that relates to your quest for spiritual renewal. For example, Shelly retreated at a Catholic retreat center, although she had left the church twenty years earlier. She did this not because she wanted to renew her faith in that particular religion but to signal a softening about her religious past. You might also want to make a poster or collage of your intention.

Read over Renewing Your Spiritual Direction: Discipline (page 229) and choose a simple practice that draws you inside yourself. You will do this practice throughout your retreat. Take ten to twenty minutes for your discipline. You can work up to longer periods if you like. After you are finished, answer in writing or painting, "After doing this practice, I feel. . . ."

Experienced Retreatants

If you are currently dedicated to a spiritual practice and are feeling stale with it, you must spend a few minutes checking in with yourself about whether you should practice this on your retreat. Center yourself and ask, "What do I really need on this retreat?" If nothing comes to you, go for a walk and ask yourself again. You may find yourself wanting to try something different for these three days. That can feel like a radical, even scary departure. It might help to affirm your faith in your current beliefs, to ask for a blessing from your Divinity, or to simply acknowledge, perhaps by writing a note to yourself, that you will return to your own path after this retreat. Imagine you are taking a spiritual vacation. Or you may find yourself sticking to your current practice, needing that recommitment to get your spiritual juices flowing again. You are the guide. You can trust yourself.

Do Stuck: Creating Energy, the second exercise (page 245). Your focus will be, of course, your spiritual life. Do this even if you don't know why or don't think you are stuck. That may be part of the reason you are on retreat.

Rest, if possible, while in bodily contact with earth, water, or a tree.

Do Defining and Undefining Your Spiritual Life from Reviving Your Spiritual Direction (page 227).

Take a luxury break. Appease your body, your senses. Be present and utterly enjoy yourself. Bask in the sun, sink into a hot bath, eat fresh raspberries with homemade whipped cream.

Do Addressed to the Heart (page 231). Note what time it is and where you do it. You will return to the same place at the same time each day of your retreat. Find a way to remind yourself.

If you can, put on some music that makes you feel hopeful and expansive, or drum for a few minutes. Or you might light a candle. Meditate on your blank mask for a few minutes. Then make a list of one hundred things you love or like or at least tolerate about yourself—things you have done, things you like to do, moments when you have demonstrated physical, mental, emotional, and spiritual attributes. Yes, one hundred. You will have to be very specific. Some items from my list:

1. My sense of humor

8. My doggedness

11. My ability to write

25. My love of books about creativity

31. My love of reading

59. My love of gardening

61. That I cleaned my friend's kitchen one night

Do Imagining the Divine (page 224). After you have created an image, communicate with your image of the Divine. Especially explore your fears, anger, or curiosity about this (perhaps) new or expanded image.

Take a mindful mindlessness break for at least half an hour but for no more than two hours. What makes it mindful is choosing ahead of time what healthful, self-nurturing, mindless activity you will do. Avoid breaking your retreat container by doing something profane (ordinary) like calling home, watching TV, or eating too much.

Spend some time in body prayer. See The Smell of Your Own Sweat (page 117) or Soma Source (page 232).

Check in with yourself using the question "What does my spiritual self need?" Do whatever occurs to you now. Do not stop yourself because it feels crazy to hug a tree, talk to plants, or anoint yourself with oil. Follow your inner prompting.

Take a short mindfulness break. Eat, drink, stretch, or walk while staying present to your senses and your reactions.

Do Addressed to the Heart (page 231) at the same place.

Repeat your spiritual discipline. Lengthen the time you do it by five to ten minutes. After you are finished, in writing or painting answer the question "How does this spiritual discipline relate to my image of the Divine?"

Read reflectively, several times, a reading selected from what you brought with you. Read aloud. Read silently. Bring the words into your body. If you have energy and wish to, work with your passage using one of the ways listed at the beginning of Contemplations (page 133).

End your day with a ceremony of gratitude. You could do another session of Addressed to the Heart (page 231). You could list what you are grateful for. You could give thanks to your Divinity, communicate with your new image of the Divine. Note and release any disappointments about what hasn't happened yet or any expectations about what might happen over the next two days.

Day Two

Greet the day with a ceremony of renewing your intention. Upon waking, first thing, do something with your intention. What feels right? It might be reading it over a few times, or it might be a bit of spontaneous ceremony or prayer. Meditate on your intention, bring it to life in some internally resonating way.

Work with your dreams in whatever way you wish. See Retreating with Others: Dream Circle (page 281).

Communicate with, come into a relationship with, pray with the image of the Divine that you created yesterday.

Do your morning ablutions as an act of veneration. Treat your body like the most precious body in the universe. Make yourself something perfect for breakfast. Or if you always eat because of your schedule, check in and see if you are even hungry yet. Avoid caffeine and sugar if possible.

Repeat your chosen spiritual discipline.

Do the second exercise in Why Are You Stuck? (page 238). It starts with "Grab your journal. . . ." Switch the statement to "I first started to feel stuck in my spiritual life when. . . ."

Note what time you did Addressed to the Heart (page 231) and repeat it.

Read Portrait of Your Authenticity (page 188). If you find yourself getting bored or stuck, stop and do some body prayer, or do Getting Juicy (page 161), or take a run. Instead of doing a life-sized portrait, make a mask of your spiritual self. Read over the questions in the practice, then substitute these questions for each age:

What was my spiritual life at this age?

What images, feelings, places, events represent my authentic spirit?

When you come to the present day, focus on these statements:

What I most value in my life right now is . . .

My authentic self looks like . . .

Before you do the Reflecting part of this practice, put on your mask and look at yourself in a mirror.

Experiment with Touching Grief (page 212), even if everything seems okay in your life.

Do something from Good Ways to Listen: Divine Landscape (page 122).

Take a mindful mindlessness break for about an hour. Nap, exercise, eat, sew, listen to music, read. If you nap, pay attention to your dreams and your feelings upon awakening. If you walk, pay attention to what shapes and beings you see in the rocks and trees or the buildings and faces of people you pass.

Repeat your spiritual discipline. When you are through, ask yourself, "What does my spiritual self need?" Record and/or act on any ideas that occur to you.

Encounter ecstatic body prayer. See Movement as Prayer (page 119).

Surrender through Melting (page 231).

Add to your list of one hundred things you love about yourself.

Is it time yet to repeat Addressed to the Heart (page 231)?

Read reflectively a passage from a spiritual book. Work with this passage however you choose. See Contemplations (page 133) and Good Ways to Listen (page 113).

End your day with a ceremony of faith. Explore the definitions of the word *faith:* (1) confident belief in the truth, value, or trustworthiness of a person, an idea, or a thing; (2) belief that does not rest on logical proof or material evidence; (3) loyalty to a person or thing; allegiance; (4) the theological virtue defined as secure belief in a Divine Being and a trusting acceptance of that Divine Being's will; (5) the body of dogma of a religion; (6) a set of principles or beliefs.

What do you have faith in? Does faith seem impossible or stupid to you? Have you lost your faith? Ruminate. Meditate on your mask. Sleep with your mask close by, so that you can see it first thing upon awakening.

Day Three

Begin your day by communicating with your image of the Divine and with your mask. What feels right? What doesn't feel right? Read over your intention. What is it still trying to tell you? What is left undone?

Once again, treat your body with sweet, loving kindness. Start your day in the best possible way. Perhaps take a long soak in the bath.

Repeat your spiritual discipline.

Name your spiritual obstacles or yearnings. Frame them as hopeful questions using, "What could my spiritual life be like if . . . ?" See One Who Chooses: Part 1 for ways to reflect on this question (page 196).

Indulge in the realm of the senses. Check out Soothe in Good Ways to Listen (page 124).

Remember to do Addressed to the Heart (page 231), same place, same time.

Read over Returning Home (page 251). Give some thought to returning home. What feelings arise? What plans need to be made?

Do a Being practice from Good Ways to Listen (page 113).

Finish your list of one hundred things you love about yourself. Make sure it has one hundred items on it.

Repeat your chosen spiritual discipline.

Work with the second quote in Soma Source (page 233). When you are finished, sit quietly and ask yourself, "What is emerging in my spiritual life?" Paint, sculpt, write the thoughts and feelings that emerge.

Listen to an uplifting piece of music while doing nothing else. If you are in nature, lie on the earth and listen to the symphony around you.

Do spontaneous writing for three pages or for three minutes on the statement "I will bring this retreat into my everyday life. . . ." Keep your hand moving. Don't edit or censor.

Spend whatever time you have left directed by and listening to your own spirit. Don't do another practice. Follow your own yearnings and promptings.

End your day and your retreat with a ceremony of hope. Make a painting of your wishes. Recite a litany of what you have confidence and trust in. Make a ceremony out of your favorite spiritual quote or passage. Honor and celebrate yourself, the Divine, and anyone or anything else for this retreat.

A One-Hour Getting Current Retreat

This is an easy retreat that you can do often. You will not have formed an intention yet, so that activity is included.

Prepare

> Your journal and a pen, and perhaps basic drawing materials.
>
> Something soothing to do, like a warm bath, a hand or foot massage, or rocking in a hammock.

Spend two or three minutes working on the first two statements found in Forming Your Intention (page 41):

- When I hear the word *retreat* right now, I see and feel . . .

- What I most yearn for in a retreat right now is . . .

Be open to surprises.

Create a brief opening ceremony inspired by your intention. Or relax by breathing deeply for several minutes and try this one: Visualize yourself in your present life but with everything just the way you want it to be—the ultimate control fantasy. The laundry is all finished and put away, the cupboard is full, letters are answered, work is caught up. End by washing your face, hands, or teeth and saying, "I am now cleansed and in sacred space."

Place your writing or drawing materials close by. Do the end of the practice Standing on Top of Your Life (page 158), starting where it says, "Get out another sheet of paper" and ending a couple paragraphs down at "symbols that is important." Meditate or dialogue with what comes up for you.

Do something soothing for yourself. If you can't think of anything, look over Good Ways to Listen: Soothe (page 124) or do one of the practices in Courting Yourself (page 172).

Remember to do some kind of closing ceremony, no matter how brief. Choose a centering word or "songline" that will help you remember the sense of peace or well-being you may have felt in this hour. Repeat this word to yourself through the coming hours and days.

A Half-Hour Jump-Starting
Your Creativity Retreat

Do this retreat before beginning work on a creative project, before going into a important meeting at work, or before spending time with a young child. You can do this as a retreat in the world, although if you work in a cubicle with no privacy, you will need to find a private space or go for a walk.

Prepare

Any materials you need for your opening and closing ceremonies.

Spend a couple of minutes working with the second intention statement from Forming Your Intention:

- What I most yearn for in a retreat right now is . . .

Your opening ceremony needs to include changing your location in space. Move your body someplace different (if you are working in your office or studio, walk outside), or if you do this retreat often, move to the same place each time. Center yourself by lying down with an eye pillow on, putting on headphones and listening to music that is very imaginary and inspiring, drinking a glass of water very slowly and with full attention, or taking a shower and doing I Am Enough in Good Ways to Listen (page 115).

After your opening ceremony, do Calling the Muse from Feeding the Artist (page 183). Focus on the section starting with "Center yourself however you choose" and ending with "Does the muse demand anything from you?" at the end of that paragraph. Take about ten minutes for this fantasy.

Do something outrageous or out of character or simply something you wouldn't usually do at this time. Say "I love you" aloud to yourself, decide to call your lover later and tantalize him or her with sexual talk, decide when you walk back to your office to give five dollars to a street person, eat chocolate for lunch, or take off all your clothes and roll around in your backyard.

Imagine in your body that you are totally, completely, oh-so-ready to be creative. Feel the creative engine revving throughout your body. Imagine your mind coming alive. Feel your muse whispering in your ear. Feel as if you are already working, already surging into it, feeling fantastic. Say over and over to yourself, aloud if possible, "Yes. I am eager. I am ready. Yes!"

End with a moving closing ceremony. Repeating the statements above ("Yes; I am eager; I am ready; yes!"), begin moving toward your work. More than moving, be aching, charging, bolting for your work. As you reach your workplace, your studio, your computer, your piano, your meeting, or your child, imagine your muse blessing you, infusing you with burning, validating light. See this light coming out of your fingertips, out of your eyes, out of your mouth. Affirm to yourself that you are back from your retreat and ready to create.

A One-Day Grieving Retreat

You don't need to be grieving something specific or tragic. This may be a good choice if you are feeling depressed, listless, or cut off from your feelings or if something final, big or small, has occurred.

Prepare

An especially safe physical and emotional container. Have a check-in person on call (page 83).

A bit of nature.

Music that puts you in touch with sadness, intensity, and depth of feeling and music that makes you want to dance.   *See Resources.*

Your journal and a pen.

Several large sheets of paper and basic drawing supplies and perhaps clay.

Drum or rattle.

Create an especially nurturing, safe physical container as part of your opening ceremony. You might also wish to create a grief shrine with pictures and symbols of what you are grieving.

Begin with Nature as Mirror (page 123).

If you don't know or need to become clearer on what you are grieving for, work with Getting Current (page 215).

Move and then relax your body. A brisk walk in nature followed by a massage given by someone who comes to you would be ideal, or do yoga followed by a hot, fragrant bath.

Immediately after, do the Touching Grief (page 212) exercise. End by listening to uplifting music, taking another bath, sipping hot chocolate, napping, or doing anything you have carefully chosen beforehand that makes you feel taken care of.

Try Standing on Top of Your Life (page 158) or Why Are You Stuck? (page 238) or Ceremony for Letting Go in Grieving (page 217).

Attend to your bodily needs with great love and care.

Under Suggestions for Wooing Yourself (page 175), do the practice that begins "Imagine love beaming from your hands."

Do as much as you wish of Imagining the Divine (page 224) or Melting (page 231).

Repeat Nature as Mirror (page 123) one last time.

Jive with Getting Juicy (page 161). Segue right into your closing ceremony.

Perhaps close with a symbolic gesture of letting go. You might burn, bury, mail (no mail bombs, please), or give away something, or do the second practice under Creating Energy (page 245), the one where you cover yourself with mud. The mud could represent your grief. Name it before you wash it off. You might wish to create a memorial: send money in a loved one's name to a beloved cause, or paste together a collage representing that time in your life that is no more.

A One-Day Birthday Retreat

This can be expanded into a weekend celebration that includes other people. Remember that when you include other people, everything takes much longer and you must be open to change.

Prepare

Pictures of yourself at different ages.

Your journal and a pen.

Music that takes you on an interior journey.

If you are going to do Portrait of Your Authenticity, see Prepare in that chapter, page 189.

Excellent self-nurturing tools and opportunities: the directions to a great hike, an extravagant lunch of fresh lobster and Swiss chocolate, a warm rock to lie on.

Create a shrine as part of your opening ceremony. The shrine will include pictures of you as a child, as a teenager, at other important times in your life, and in the present. You might also wish to carve into a candle a word or words that represent one or two wishes for the coming year. Light the candle and let it burn throughout your retreat. (But don't leave a candle unattended, especially outside.)

Love yourself with Reclaiming Your Desires (page 173).

Rollick in some first-class soothing and self-nurturing. Use Check-In (page 75) or the questions you just did to point you in the right direction.

Make a list of everything you did in the last year that you are proud of, that you liked, enjoyed, loved, relished.

Check in with yourself and take a break as directed by your check-in.

Play with Marking a Passage (page 203) or Portrait of Your Authenticity (page 188).

Do Touching Grief (page 212), even if everything seems okay in your life.

Addressed to the Heart (page 231) is calling you.

Check in with your cherished self.

Shake a leg to Movement as Prayer (page 119).

Frame your life, set your sights, name a resolution for your coming year. Use The State of Being (page 165) to tell you what you need and want. Be sure one of your resolutions is based on becoming more self-accepting.

Check in with "What do I want?" and give it to yourself.

End with a closing ceremony that affirms and energizes you and creates a commitment to your new goals. Happy Birthday!

A One-Day Retreat with a Friend

This plan is designed to help you reconnect with someone you love but haven't seen for a while or someone you need to get current with.

Prepare

Each woman gives thought on her own to how she wants to open and close the retreat. You might wish to bring photos or mementos of your friendship and build a friendship shrine. Also, each person must review the guidelines for deep listening.

Journals and pens.

Objects that represent your different selves (you can gather or make these on retreat).

See Resources. Music to meditate to and music to dance to.

Drums and rattles (optional).

When you meet in your retreat place, spend some time getting unpacked and settled. Decide where your main retreat space will be.

See Retreating with Others. Do the exercises in Intention together (page 41). Form an intention for your shared retreat. You can do this before you retreat if you like. Discuss briefly how you would like to open and close your retreat, but don't plan exactly what you will do. Instead, talk about your intent and your ideas, and decide how you will begin each deep listening circle; holding hands, breathing, or lighting a candle are simple and perfect.

Go for a walk together and chat. Agree to spend the last ten minutes of your walk in silence, to enter your retreat space in silence, and to begin your opening ceremony in silence.

Dedicate your time together with your opening ceremony. The different elements you each brought will come together if you listen to yourself and your friend.

Craft a trust list (page 175). List what you trust about your friend. Read your lists to each other.

Sit facing each other, knee to knee, and in a deep listening circle explore the following questions and topics. You can also do them as timed spontaneous writing practices and then read them to each other.

- A friend to me . . .

- Why are we friends?

- What do I get out of being friends with you?

- What do I bring to our friendship?

- What would I like to have change in our friendship?
- If you could do anything with me on retreat, what would it be?

End with a hug, stretching, or dancing together.

Take a solitude break.

Remaining in separate space, do Gathering the Whole (page 147). Come together to work on your mandalas. When finished, discuss in circle what you learned. Add to each other's mandalas.

Take a break together. Walk, eat, laugh, relax. Down time. But remain conscious of cutting off feelings or deep discussion out of fear of intimacy. Note this and bring it up in the next circle. Do a check-in somewhere in the break.

When you are ready, come together for another circle. The topics this time are:

- What was the most meaningful spiritual experience you ever had?
- What is your belief about the Divine?
- What is your greatest sorrow?
- What is your greatest joy?
- What do you see as your greatest contribution to life?
- What are you most afraid of?

End this circle by doing the first practice under Suggestions for Wooing Yourself (page 173).

Time for more solitude. A nap or exercise might fit here. Notice how much more you appreciate your friendship when you have a moment to step away from it.

Listen to yourself. See Good Ways to Listen (page 113).

Come together. Contemplate something from Contemplations together (page 132).

Reading it to each other, do Melting (page 231).

Take a rest and fun break together. Segue into Getting Juicy (page 161). Play off each other's energy. Be silly together.

Sit in a final deep listening circle around the questions

- Is there anything I need you to know that I haven't told you yet?
- I am afraid to tell you . . .

As part of your closing ceremony, express thankfulness to each other for venturing into such scary, intimate places. Make a covenant of what you are each willing to do to keep your friendship blazing bright. Find or make a token to remember your covenant. Commit to a firm date to retreat together again.

A Two-Minute Retreat

This can be done wherever you are.

Prepare

If you can get outside easily, do so.

Take five deep, cleansing breaths. Drop your jaw. Breathe into your belly. Run your fingers through your hair. Pull slightly on the roots of your hair. Scrunch your shoulders into your ears, tense, and release. Repeat three times.

For your opening ceremony, enclose yourself in a cone of protective white light (page 64). (You can do this with your eyes open, in a meeting, or on the subway; it just takes suspension of disbelief and a little practice.)

If you can do so without attracting unwanted attention, reach your arms over your head, stretch, and imagine you are bringing this brilliant, healing light into your body through your outstretched hands. If you can't do that, imagine it entering you through the crown of your head.

Allow this light to penetrate to wherever you feel tired, anxious, sad, or worried. Let it bathe that area for a moment.

Smile (even if you don't feel like it) and say silently to yourself, "This is the present moment. There is goodness in this present moment. I trust myself to find it."

For your closing ceremony, thank the cone of light and then imagine it condensing into the palm of your hand so that your palm glows with warmth and power. Place your hand over your heart, or clasp your hands together.

Final Notes

*People say that what we're all seeking in life is a meaning for life. I
don't think that's what we're really seeking. I think that what we're
seeking is an experience of being alive, so that our life experience on the
purely physical plane will have resonances within our innermost being
and reality, so that we actually feel the rapture of being alive.*

Joseph Campbell, interview with Bill Moyer, *The Power of Myth*

I see a phenomenon happening in the world of spiritual guidance. The eternal truths are emerging, over and over again, in different yet equally urgent forms. Maybe God is desperately trying to send each of us the same information, packaged in a way that we can grasp (and be grasped by). Each book, video, and teacher seem to be saying similar things. Gunilla Norris does this in *Sharing Silence:*

> Politicians and visionaries will not return us to the sacredness of life.
> That will be done by ordinary men and women, who gather neighbors
> and friends together and say, "Remember to breathe. Remember to feel.
> Remember to care. Remember life." Let us do this together for our-
> selves, our children, and our children's children.

Slow down. Be present. Breathe deeply. Act from your heart. Be in touch with your feelings. Be kind to yourself. Think how your action will affect the next seven generations. This is the way we are trying to live. A retreat is simply another way to do this.

Cynthia Gale, a ceremonial artist, believes, "Ideally, we would all live lives so balanced we wouldn't need retreats. Most people I know retreat to reconnect with themselves, so ideally that disconnection wouldn't happen." Live the belief that yes, I am not perfect but here I am, doing the best I can. I am enough.

And my enough is connected to everyone else's enough. And so goes the precious whole, the cosmic Internet.

Creating a lively, grace-filled, flaws-and-all global community of women who are exploring how to creatively, joyfully, fully live their lives is one of the joys of my life. Be part of that community by visiting http://www.comfortqueen.com and by subscribing to my free e-zine newsletter *The Self-Care Minder.* Our cozy couch of a site features a soothing, informative mix of community, more than six hundred articles on all aspects of creating your life, free e-cards, the wonderful interactive Inner Organizer, and more.

You can also reach me at P.O. Box 10065, Bainbridge Island, WA, 98110.

May you retreat often. May your retreat deeply. May your heart be opened with grace.

I ask the Great Mystery that each of you be blessed on your journey into self-acceptance and balance.

Remember to breathe.

Namasté.

Resources

There are so many excellent books and other goodies to
enrich your sacred time. This resource list was compiled
from interviews and discussions with other women.
WARNING: It is very easy to be seduced by this kind of list.
Remember the cardinal rule: keep it simple.

Books

STORIES OF STRONG WOMEN, WOMEN ON RETREAT, WOMEN FORGING THEIR OWN LIVES

Sisters of the Earth, edited by Lorraine Anderson (New York: Vintage, 1991). A selection of
writing by women about their relationship to nature. Lots about solitude and retreat.

A Year by the Sea Thoughts of an Unfinished Woman, by Joan Anderson (New York: Broadway,
2000). A memoir of solitude and self in the tradition of Sarton and Lindbergh.

I Know Why the Caged Bird Sings, by Maya Angelou (New York: Random House, 1969).
Good for healing, courage, and spiritual renewal retreats.

The Feminine Face of God, by Sherry Ruth Anderson and Patricia Hopkins (New York: Bantam Books, 1991). Chock full of moving stories of women finding their own way to the Divine, many of them through retreats.

Through the Narrow Gate, by Karen Armstrong (New York: St. Martin's Press, 1981). A brilliant theologian's spiritual journey.

Surfacing, by Margaret Atwood (New York: Ballantine, 1987). Read when searching for self
in relationship to father and on wilderness retreats.

Plain and Simple, by Sue Bender (San Francisco: HarperSanFrancisco, 1989). Read for
courage, to become centered, and for spiritual nurturance.

The Pull of the Moon, by Elizabeth Berg (New York: Random House, 1996). For healing
burn-out, especially within marriage.

Song of the Lark, by Willa Cather (1915; New York: New American Library, 1991). A young
opera singer giving everything to her art.

Reinventing Eve, by Kim Chernin (New York: Times Books, 1987). Read during a time of descent and on spiritual retreats.

Sitting Still, by Patricia Hart Clifford (New York: Paulist Press, 1994). Excellent to read before a meditation retreat and if you are a Christian wanting to incorporate Eastern forms of meditation into your spiritual practice.

Tracks and *Desert Places,* by Robyn Davidson (New York: Viking, 1986 and 1996). Adventure, courage, and connection to wild places. Good to read when considering change and on birthdays.

Pilgrim at Tinker Creek, Holy the Firm, and *Teaching a Stone to Talk,* by Annie Dillard (New York: Harper & Row, 1974, 1977, 1982). Thick, juicy passages to *contemplate* about nature, God, and solitude.

Out of Africa, by Isak Dinesen (New York: Random House, 1938). Fortitude.

Enduring Grace, by Carol Lee Flinders (San Francisco: HarperSanFrancisco, 1993). Spiritual renewal, courage, history of retreating.

My Brilliant Career, by Miles Franklin (New York: St. Martin's Press, 1980). To inspire young women and to recapture girlhood pluck.

Long, Quiet Highway, by Natalie Goldberg (New York: Bantam Books, 1993). Read before a Zen meditation retreat or if grieving the death of a loved one or spiritual teacher.

50 Days of Solitude, by Doris Grumbach (Boston: Beacon Press, 1994). For older women and when feeling uncomfortable during a retreat.

The Fruitful Darkness, by Joan Halifax (San Francisco, HarperSanFrancisco, 1993). Nature, shamanic realms, and varied ways to retreat.

The Solitary, by Linda Hall (New York, Scribner, 1986). For young women and mothers of adolescents to read, or for teachers and those helping young women in trouble.

Migrations to Solitude, by Sue Halpern (New York: Vintage, 1993). Reflections on different forms of solitude. Elegant, thought provoking, intellectual.

Virgin Time, by Patricia Hampl (New York: Ballantine Books, 1992). For spiritual renewal.

Solar Storms, by Linda Hogan (New York: Scribner, 1995). One of my all-time favorite novels. Good for young women on retreat, mothers of teenage daughters, and the wounded child within.

A Country Year: Living the Questions, by Sue Hubbel (New York: Random House, 1986). For reading when you yearn to live in the country and to be reunited with nature and your own strength.

An Unknown Woman and *Stations of Solitude,* by Alice Koller (New York: Bantam, 1983 and 1990). These classics nurture the intellect and courage.

Woodswoman, by Anne LaBastille (New York: Dutton, 1976). Inspiration, courage, and connecting to nature.

Meeting the Madwoman, by Linda Leonard (New York: Bantam Books, 1993). Read about artist retreats, if your creativity is being sucked away in feeding others, and if you fear solitude. See especially the chapters "The Muse" and "The Recluse."

"Room 19" in *Stories,* by Doris Lessing (New York: Knopf, 1978). Read this when you can't get yourself to go on retreat.

Deep Water Passage, by Ann Linnea (New York: Little, Brown and Company, 1995). Perfectly captures the retreat archetype in the form of a great story.

Gift from the Sea, by Anne Morrow Lindbergh (New York: Random House, 1955). For beginning retreatants, mothers, and seashore retreats.

West with the Night, by Beryl Markham (Berkeley: North Point Press, 1983, first edition published by Houghton Mifflin, 1942). For courage and resolve.

Women of Courage: Inspiring Stories from the Women Who Lived Them, by Katherine Martin (Novato, CA.: New World Library, 1999). Stories in which women we admire describe life-altering moments in which they had to find strength and courage.

The Measure of My Days, by Florida Scott Maxwell (New York: Knopf, 1968). For birthdays, for courage when descending into your depths, and for help with aging.

The Cloister Walk, by Kathleen Norris (New York: Riverhead Books, 1996). For contemplation, Christians, and poets. Brilliant.

A Woman on Paper, by Anita Politzer (New York: Touchstone Books, 1988). Reading about O'Keeffe's life makes your spirit soar.

Cross Creek, by Marjorie Kinnan Rawlings (New York: Scribner's Sons, 1942). For resolve, for courage, and when considering life changes.

A Woman in the Polar Night, by Christianne Ritter (New York: Dutton, 1954). Perspective and fear of being alone.

Solo: On Her Own Adventure, edited by Susan Fox Rogers (Seattle: Seal Press, 1996). A stunning collection of essays covering every emotion you encounter on retreat. Especially good for rites of passages.

Plant Dreaming Deep, Journal of a Solitude, and *House by the Sea,* by May Sarton (New York: Norton, 1968, 1973, 1977). For older women, writers, and artists. Good when debating the question "How can I have love and have a creative life?" Read Sarton's later journals for help with aging and illness.

Drinking the Rain, by Alix Kates Shulman (New York: Farrar Straus Giroux: 1995). For feminists, writers, cooks, and women going through a divorce.

Daybook: The Journal of an Artist, by Anne Truitt (New York: Pantheon Books, 1982). For artist retreats. Also encouraging for moms to read. For older artists, see her book *Prospect*.

The Color Purple, Living by the Word, and *The Temple of My Familiar,* by Alice Walker (New York: Harcourt, Brace, Jovanovich, 1982, 1988, 1989). Food for your soul and for help grieving.

The Center of the Web: Women and Solitude, edited by Delese Wear (Albany, New York: State University of New York Press, 1993). Required reading for women in academia and women retreating to figure out how to survive in a man's world.

"Why I Live at the P.O.," in *The Collected Stories of Eudora Welty,* by Eudora Welty (New York: Harcourt, Brace, Jovanovich, 1936–1980). Read when you want to run away from home.

An Unspoken Hunger, by Terry Tempest Williams (New York: Pantheon, 1994). Read for help connecting with nature through metaphor and for her amazing prose.

Refuge, by Terry Tempest Williams (New York: Random House, 1986). Read when grieving the death of someone you love.

To the Lighthouse, Mrs. Dalloway, and *A Room of Own's Own* (New York: Harcourt, Brace, 1925, 1927, 1929), by Virginia Woolf. To nod your head in understanding, to push yourself to claim your life, and to take on artist retreats.

BOOKS SPECIFICALLY ABOUT RETREATING

Silence, Simplicity, and Solitude (New York: Belltower, 1992) and *Renewing Your Soul* (San Francisco: HarperSanFrancisco, 1995), both by David Cooper. Rabbi Cooper is the pioneer of the modern retreat movement. Good for those interested in doing a meditation or Jewish retreat.

Don't Just Do Something, Sit There, by Sylvia Boorstein (San Francisco: HarperSanFrancisco, 1996). Sylvia is the Jewish grandmother of American Buddhism. Step-by-step guide to a three-day Buddhist meditation retreat. Excellent.

A Seven-Day Journey with Thomas Merton, by Esther DeWaal (Ann Arbor, Michigan: Servant Publications, 1992). A Christian contemplative retreat on Merton's writing and photographs.

BOOKS LISTING RETREAT CENTERS, LEADERS, AND ADVENTURES

Sanctuaries, by Jack and Maria Kelly (New York: Bell Tower, 1996). The best resource for finding a retreat center for a self-led retreat. Lots of Zen and Catholic centers listed.

Vacations That Can Change Your Life, by Ellen Lederman (Naperville, Illinois: Source Books, 1996). Covers adventures, retreats, and workshops. Best overall source for all types of retreats, from self-led to wilderness adventure to educational.

Fodor's Healthy Escapes, edited by Christine Swiac (New York: Fodors Travel, 2003). A listing of spas and resorts, high end.

Yoga Vacations, by Annalisa Cunningham (Santa Fe, New Mexico John Muir Publications, 1999). Several page write-ups on international yoga retreats.

Yoga Escapes: A Yoga Journal Guide to the Best Places to Relax, Renew, and Reflect, by Jeanne Ricci (Berkeley, CA: Celestial Arts, 2003). Another great guide.

Artist's Communities: A Directory of Residencies in the United States That Offer Time and Space for Creativity, edited by Tricia Snell (New York: Allworth Press, 2000). For artist retreats.

Healing Centers & Retreats: Healthy Getaways for Every Body and Budget, by Jennifer Miller (Emeryville, CA: Avalon Travel Publishing, 1998). More budget minded than Fodor.

Websites:

Comfort Queen Retreat Database
http://www.comfortqueen.com

Retreats International
http://www.retreatsintl.org

Retreats On-line
http://www.retreatsonline.com

Yoga Retreats
http://www.yogadirectory.com

All About Retreats
www.allaboutretreats.com

BOOKS TO WORK WITH ON RETREAT

These books offer additional ways to access your authentic self on retreat. I have chosen them because they work well in a retreat setting.

The Four-Fold Way, by Angeles Arrien, Ph.D. (San Francisco: HarperSanFrancisco, 1993). For those interested in an earth-based spiritual path.

Life's Companion, by Christina Baldwin (New York: Bantam, 1990). You cannot exhaust this book's wisdom.

Calling the Circle, by Christina Baldwin (Newberg, Oregon: Swan Raven & Company, 1994; New York: Bantam, 1998, revised ed.). The best book about forming and maintaining a circle. Required reading for group retreats.

Contemporary Women Artists, by Sister Wendy Beckett (New Jersey: Universe Books, 1988). Spiritual meditations on contemporary women's art.

Fruitflesh: Seeds of Inspiration for Women Who Write, by Gayle Brandeis (San Francisco, HarperSanFrancisco, 2002). Sensual writing mediations and exercises.

The Artist's Way, Vein of Gold, The Right to Write, and *Blessings,* by Julie Cameron (New York: Jeremy Tarcher, 1992, 1996, 1999). For artist retreats.

Start Where You Are: A Guide to Compassionate Living, by Pema Chodron (Boston Shambhala, 2001). No need to wait for things to change to start creating more inner peace and wisdom.

Life, Paint and Passion, by Michell Cassou and Stewart Cubley (New York: Jeremy Tarcher, 1995). How to paint without worrying about outcome or talent.

Mandala, by Judith Cornell (Wheaton, Illinois: Quest Books, 1994). Step-by-step guide to how to create, and heal yourself, with mandalas. Accessible.

Freeing the Creative Spirit, by Adriana Diaz (San Francisco: HarperSanFrancisco, 1992). Excellent for artist retreats. Ms. Diaz's self-portrait exercise inspired the chapter "Portrait of Your Authenticity."

The Intimacy and Solitude Handbook, by Stephanie Dowrick (New York: Norton, 1993). For developing strong boundaries and discovering the balance between your need for solitude and your need for intimacy. Exercises well suited for mini-retreats.

Circle of Stones and *I Sit Listening to the Wind,* by Judith Duerk (San Diego: Lura Media, 1989 and 1993). Reading these books creates a strong retreat container. Excellent to use in opening and closing ceremonies.

20-Minute Retreats: Revive Your Spirit in Just Minutes a Day With Simple Self-Led Practices, by Rachel Harris (New York: Owl Books, 2000). Wonderful simple varied meditations.

Women Who Run with the Wolves, by Clarissa Pinkola Estés (New York: Ballantine, 1992). Any retreat will be deepened by reading a bit of this profound book. See especially the chapter "Homing: Returning to Oneself." Try doing active imagination with the fairy tales collected here. My quotes from Ms. Estés can be found on pages 281, 284, and 294 in the first edition of her book.

Finding What You Didn't Lose, by John Fox (New York: Jeremy Tarcher, 1995). If you want to write poetry to express your life but don't know how to start, this is an excellent choice.

The Zen of Seeing, by Frederick Frank (New York: Vintage, 1973). For meditation and artist retreats.

Jubilee Time, by Maria Harris (New York: Bantam Books, 1995). One of the best books for helping women celebrate growing older.

The Way of All Women, by Helen Luke (New York: Doubleday, 1995). For healing, learning about balance, and spiritual nourishment.

Meditation Secrets for Women Discovering Your Passion, Pleasure, and Inner Peace, by Camille Maurine and Lorin Roche (San Francisco: HarperSanFrancisco, 2001). An encyclopedia of feminine and body centered ways to meditate. If you've always thought meditation meant sitting still or following a guru, you need this book.

Uncursing the Dark, by Betty DeShong Meador (Wilmette, Illinois: Chiron Publications, 1992). Read this for a complete telling of the Thesmophoria. Excellent for doing active imagination with—imagine yourself there.

Writing for Your Life, by Deena Metzger (San Francisco, HarperSanFrancisco: 1992). Brilliant. Excellent for artist retreats, rites of passages, and spiritual renewal. See especially pages 78–83.

The Heroine's Journey, by Maureen Murdock (Boston: Shambhala, 1990). Excellent for an overview of women's journey. See especially pages 89–90.

Staying Well with Guided Imagery, by Belleruth Naparstek (New York: Warner, 1994). Fantastic for healing anything from depression to allergies and for helping yourself to grieve. See also her amazing audios listed under Audios.

Soul Sisters: The Five Sacred Qualities of a Woman's Soul, by Pythia Peay (New York: Jeremy Tarcher, 2002). A fascinating workbook designed to help you develop your spiritual life by learning from the heroines of a vast array of spiritual traditions.

A God Who Looks Like Me, by Patricia Lynn Reilly (New York: Ballantine, 1995). Excellent for spiritual recovery from harsh religions. Also excellent for group retreats.

Earth Prayers, edited by Elizabeth Roberts and Elias Amidon (San Francisco: HarperSanFrancisco, 1991). One of my most treasured books. Excellent for opening and closing ceremonies and to help you pray and meditate.

Cries of the Spirit and *Claiming the Spirit Within,* edited by Marilyn Sewall (Boston: Beacon Press, 1996). Poetry.

Where People Fly and Water Runs Uphill, by Jeremy Taylor (New York: Warner Books, 1992). One of the best books for understanding and working with your dreams.

Song of the Seed, by Macrina Wiederkehr (San Francisco: HarperSanFrancisco, 1995). Guidelines to do a daily mini-retreat for spiritual renewal. Christian.

A Big New Free Happy Unusual Life: Self-Expression and Spiritual Practice for Those Who Have Time for Neither, by Nina Wise (New York: Broadway Books, 2002). Brief exercises to nurture spirituality and creativity, wonderful for easing into a day off.

Dancing in the Flames, by Marion Woodman and Elinor Dickson (Boston: Shambhala, 1996). For contemplation.

Addiction to Perfection and *The Pregnant Virgin,* by Marion Woodman (Toronto: Inner City Books, 1985 and 1982). These classics are required reading for retreats, especially retreats to heal from hurrying, doing too much, moving too fast.

Videos

Most of these videos can be rented at a large video store or found at your local library. You might need to mail-order the starred titles. Try Ladyslipper (listed below) for those. If there is more than one video by the same title, I've listed the director or year in parentheses to distinguish them.

FOR ARTIST RETREATS

World of Light: Portrait of May Sarton (also about aging)
An Angel at My Table (writer Janet Frame struggles)
Camille Claudel
Cinema Paradiso
Sylvia
Vincent and Theo
Shine
The Agony and the Ecstasy
Children of Theatre Street (documentary about Kirov Ballet School)
84 Charing Cross Road
Frida
Immortal Beloved (Beethoven)
Impromptu (author George Sand's life)
In the Shadow of the Stars (opera behind the scenes)
Isadora (story of dancer Isadora Duncan's life)
Le Belle Noiseuse (young woman as muse; French)
La Traviata
Madama Butterfly (1990)
The Magic of the Bolshoi
The Magic of the Kirov Ballet
Manon (opera)
The Moderns (Paris in the twenties)
The Most Beautiful Ballets
Much Ado About Nothing
Rembrandt
Tous Les Matins du Monde (French)
Van Gogh

For Friendship Retreats and to Explore Relationships Between Women

Strangers in Good Company (also good for aging)
Absolutely Fabulous (six three-episode tapes; hysterical British TV series)
Beaches
All About Eve (also about aging and the harsh realities of competition among women)
Antonia and Jane (jealousy among old friends)
Between Two Women (mother and daughter-in-law struggling together)
Crimes of the Heart
Entre Nous
Four Adventures of Reinette and Mirabelle
Fried Green Tomatoes
Hannah and Her Sisters
Heartaches
The Long Walk Home
Outrageous Fortune
Passion Fish
Personal Best
Promises in the Dark (five hankies)
The River (Indian)
She'll Be Wearing Pink Pajamas (British)
Steel Magnolias
The Summer House
Swing Shift
Terms of Endearment
The Turning Point
The Women
The Women of Brewster Place
The Women's Room

Strong Women for Inspiration, for Examining Their Lives, for Taking Care of Themselves, and for on Retreat

*Radiant Life: Meditations and Visions of Hildegard of Bingen
Lily Sold Out!—Lily Tomlin
Adam's Rib, Bringing Up Baby, Mary of Scotland, Morning Glory, Pat and Mike, Philadelphia Story (Hepburn as a strong, fiesty, outspoken woman)
Afterburn (also good for grieving)
Alice Doesn't Live Here Anymore (one of the first single mom movies)
Auntie Mame
Autobiography of Miss Jane Pittman (also good for grieving)
Bagdad Cafe
Ballad of Little Jo
The Bliss of Mrs. Blossom
Breakfast at Tiffany's
Coal Miner's Daughter
Cold Comfort Farm
The Color Purple

Cross Creek
Driving Miss Daisy
Educating Rita
Enchanted April (the perfect movie to watch on retreat)
Gloria
Grand Isle
The Handmaid's Tale
Heart Like a Wheel
Hester Street
The Hour of the Star (Brazilian)
I Know Why the Caged Bird Sings
I Remember Mama (strong mother)
Imitation of Life
The Inn of the Sixth Happiness (Ingrid Bergman)
Isabel's Choice (for women in business)
Jean de Florette (French)
The Joy Luck Club (also a five-hanky movie)
Julia
Juliet of the Spirits (Fellini)
A League of Their Own
Lianna
The Lonely Passion of Judith Hearne
Major Barbara
Manon of the Spring (French)
Margaret Bourke-White (biography of *Life* photographer)
Marie
Marlene
Miss Firecracker
Nine to Five
Norma Rae
One Against the Wind
Orlando
Persuasion
Piano for Mrs. Cimino (aging)
The Picture Bride (1995)
Places in the Heart
The Private Lives of Elizabeth and Essex
A Private Matter
The Rain People
The Rector's Wife
A Room with a View
Rosalie Goes Shopping
Sarafina!
The Scarlet Empress
See How She Runs
Sense and Sensibility
Shirley Valentine
Silence of the North (woman living alone in Canadian outback)
Silkwood

Sister Kenny
Solo (woman hitchhiking in New Zealand)
The Story of Qiu Ju (Chinese)
The Story of Women (French)
Summer (French)
Sylvia
The Trip to Bountiful
The Unsinkable Molly Brown
Victor/Victoria
We of Never Never (Australian)
Westward the Women
What's Love Go to Do with It (Tina Turner's life)
Widow's Peak
Wifemistress (Italian)
A Woman Called Golda (biography of Golda Meir)
A Woman Under the Influence
A Woman's Tale (aging and being a nonconformist)

PORTRAITS OF PLUCKY YOUNG GIRLS

Anne of Green Gables
Georgy Girl
Getting of Wisdom
A Girl of Limberlost
Jane Eyre (the 1944 film is the best)
Journey of Natty Gann
Little Dorrit (two-part epic)
The Little Princess (1939 and 1995)
Little Women (1933 is the best)
My Brillant Career
Nancy Drew, Detective (watch the Nancy Drew series from the thirties, not the seventies)
National Velvet
Princess Caraboo
Rambling Rose
The Secret Garden (1949 and 1993)
A Tiger Walks
A Tree Grows in Brooklyn
The Trouble with Angels
Wild Hearts Can't Be Broken

Audio Tapes

Listening to spiritual wisdom on tape on retreat is a wonderful way to feel that you have a teacher by your side. I turn to audios when I am lonely or feeling scattered. I also listen to them when I walk.

Sounds True Catalog is one of the best places for tapes. Order the catalog by calling 800–333–9185 or by writing P.O. Box 8010, Boulder, CO 80306–8010 or by visiting http://www.SoundsTrue.com

My favorite tapes to listen to on retreat are *Realizing the Power of Now: An In-Depth Retreat* with Eckhart Tolle, *Yoga For Emotional Flow* by Stephen Cope, *Yoga Trance Dance* by Shiva Rea (I like all her recordings), *Midlife and the Great Unknown* by David Whyte, *The Singing Cure* by Paul Newham, *The Visionary Artist* by Alex Grey, *The Beginner's Guide To Shamanic Journeying* by Sandra Ingerman, *Dreams* by Marion Woodman, *Lovingkindness Meditation* by Sharon Salzberg, *Your Heart's Prayer* by Oriah Mountain Dreamer, *I Want Burning* by Coleman Barks. All of Ms. Estés's tapes are unbelievably wonderful, especially *Theatre of the Imagination*.

Another incredible series of tapes and music is available at http://www.healthjourneys.com —sample Belleruth's powerful *Health Journeys Total Wellness* (Audio) or any of her other superb tapes. You might also like *Joyful Mind* by Susan Piver (Audio) 2-CD sampler of seven different kinds of meditations. Listen in on the Desktop Spa for mini-retreats.

For over 15,000 music titles, visit Ladyslipper Catalog either at http://www.ladyslipper.org or request a print catalog by phoning (919) 383–8773 or (800) 634–6044. Approximately 15,000 (and growing!) catalog of women artists and musicians. Many of the selections mentioned in this book can be purchased here.

Music

Like all music suggestions in this book, please, if possible, find a way to listen to it before purchasing, because you might hate one selection or it might affect you differently. Again, this is a very brief list.

FOR MEDITATION AND CENTERING

Conferring with the Moon—William Ackerman
Le Mystere des Voix Bulgares—The Bulgarian Female Vocal Choir (mystery)
Eight String Religion—David Darling (also good for stretching)
Adagio and *Adagio 2*—Karajan
Sounds of Peace—Nwang Khechog
The Source—Osamu Kitajima (like a waterfall)
Tear of the Moon—Coyote Oldman (Native American)
Dreamtime Returns—Steve Roach (2 volumes)
Stillpoint—Gabrielle Roth and the Mirrors (also good for slow movement)
Global Meditation—Various artists (four-volume set)
The Secret of the Roan Inish—Various artists (enchanting)
Mother of Compassion—Lisa Thiel (chants)

FOR MOVEMENT

Cross of Changes—Enigma (cross between meditation and movement)
Logoza—Angelique Kidjo (high energy, get down, African)
Mosaique—Gipsy Kings
Epiphany: The Best of Chaka Kahn, vol. 1—Chaka Kahn (power of women, rejuicing soul, and dance)
Shapeshifters—Ubaka Hill (passionate movement)
Diva—Anne Lennox
Mustt Mustt and *Night Song*—Nusrat Fateh Ali Khan with Michael Brook (trance inducing)
Healing Rhythms—Babatunde Olatunji
Rhapsody on a theme of Paganini—Rachmaninoff

Endless Wave, Totem, Initiation, and *Trance*—Gabrielle Roth and the Mirrors (perfect music for movement, trance, and emotional release)
Dawn Until Dusk—Tribal Song and Didgeridoo (didgeridoo music is good for opening hips) .
Shapeshifters—Ubaka Hill
Beggars and Saints—Jai Uttal and the Pagan Love Orchestra
Riverdance—Various artists (soundtrack of Celtic dance)
Trance Planet, Volume One—Various artists (trance dancing)
The Power of One—Hans Zimmerman

FOR CEREMONY

This is good music for opening and closing ceremonies and for groups.

Miracles of Sant'iago—Anonymous 4
The Mysts of Time—Aine Minogue
Full—Rachel Bagby
Diadema—Hildegard von Bingen and Vox
Songs of the Sacred Wheel—Earth Dance Singers (chant and songs honoring the earth; excellent for groups)
Devi—Chloe Goodchild (devotional chants from a range of traditions)
Fire Within and *A Circle Is Cast*—Libana (cross-cultural songs and chants; make "I Will Be Gentle with Myself" your theme song)
She Changes and *She Dreams* by Moving Breath (group and individual ceremony, Goddess oriented)
The Virgin's Lament, Soundings, Sto'r Amhr'an—Noirin Ni Rain (Celtic, soaring, medieval)
Isle of View—The Pretenders ("Hymn to Her" is perfect for opening ceremony, moving prayer, and dance)
Heaven—Jimmy Scott (feels like going to church)
Hymns to the Silence and *Enlightment*—Van Morrison

FOR POWER, FOR CREATING, TO SAY "I CAN MAKE IT"

Classics—Joan Armatrading ("Me, Myself and I" is a great song for courage)
Voice of Light—Anonymous 4 (power and inspiration)
Nothing but a Burning Light—Bruce Cockburn
Friends—Bette Midler (for friendship retreats)
Miles of Aisles ("Circle Game" for birthdays), *Hejira,* and *Blue* ("All I Want" for liberation of the female spirit)—Joni Mitchell
Tigerlily—Natalie Merchant (check out "Wonder")
Sky Dances, Fire in the Rain, and *Don't Hold Back*—Holly Near
Raring to Go—The Roches
Cleaning House—Saffire: The Uppity Blues Women
Bach: Works for Violin Solo—Lara St. John (sensual, good for creativity)
The Best of Nina Simone—Nina Simone
Good News in Hard Times—Sisters of Glory (glorious gospel)
Still on the Journey—Sweet Honey in the Rock (affirmation of women's power)
The Great Gospel Women—Various Artists

Permissions